my dear Sheila and
It is with great ple
you my book.
love, Ehud

YES, IT'S POSSIBLE

EHUD DISKIN

Translated by
P. David Hornik

gefen
publishing house
JERUSALEM ◆ NEW YORK
Est. 1981

COVER CONCEPT: Hagar and Lior Diskin
COVER DESIGN: Pini Hamou
TYPESETTING: Benjie Herskowitz, Etc. Studios

To contact the author with comments or questions,
please e-mail ehudd13@gmail.com.

ISBN: 978-965-229-656-6

1 3 5 7 9 8 6 4 2

Gefen Publishing House Ltd.   Gefen Books
6 Hatzvi Street   11 Edison Place
Jerusalem 94386, Israel   Springfield, NJ 07081
972-2-538-0247   516-593-1234
orders@gefenpublishing.com   orders@gefenpublishing.com

www.gefenpublishing.com

Printed in Israel   *Send for our free catalog*

Library of Congress Cataloging-in-Publication Data

Diskin, Ehud, 1944- author.
    [Hen efshar. English]
    Yes, it's possible / Ehud Diskin.
    pages cm
    Includes bibliographical references.
    ISBN 978-965-229-656-6
    1. Diskin, Ehud, 1944- 2. Israel. Tseva haganah le-Yisra'el--Officers-
-Biography. 3. Israel-Arab War, 1973--Personal narratives, Israeli. I.
Title.
    DS126.6.D5813A3 2014
    956.04'8--dc23
    [B]
                            2014036037

*Have you experienced a shell explosion that brings your
     brothers' lives to an end?*

*Have you heard the whistling of bombshells that injure
     your friend?*

*Have you witnessed a mine, which vehicles and humans
     spread,*

*Leaving amongst pieces of metal only flesh and blood in
     shreds?*

*I have seen armored vehicles go silent and my eyes filled
     with tears,*

*I have viewed the heroes of generations, who were my
     brothers through the years,*

We sealed a covenant in blood, lasting for life,

*Of sacrifice and eternal friendship through stress and
     strife.*

I continued to walk through the pathways of life,

Treasuring my friends, both the dead and alive,

Leaving somewhere within my soul and heart,

A deposit of friendship that will never depart.

Ehud Diskin, June 2008

CONTENTS

Preface
. . . .
LIFE IS NOT AN ALLEGORY

We all take part in the journey of life, a journey that begins with our first breath at birth, and ends with our final breath as we depart from this world.

As for what life itself is – despite impressive scientific developments, we understand it not one iota more today than we did when the wheel was invented. Indeed, there are many theories about the essence of life, and there are those who swear blindly that they understand its significance and meaning. To them I say, perhaps it's possible you do.

However, I see myself as a mere mortal, a part of humanity, which, while more advanced than animals, is nevertheless limited. Unlike other creatures, we feel and understand the world not only through our physical and physiological abilities – the five senses – but also primarily through our mental abilities. Yet we grasp just a fraction of what is taking place in the universe. So I have concluded that no matter how much I philosophize and delve into the real meaning of life, I can never know whether I truly understand it.

Hence, this book focuses on my life and work, my principles and aspirations.

Long ago, I defined the principles by which I would live my life. One that is perhaps most important, is to try and live by my own values and beliefs rather than those dictated by family, society, or country. I recognize, of course, the need to take into consideration various constraints, but I have always believed that one should define one's goals and stick to them. These may include a lifestyle, an accomplishment, simple pleasure, or a combination of all these.

In my adult life, after adhering to this way of thinking and putting it into practice, I have realized that there is almost nothing that can withstand the power of the human will. Nonetheless, I also came to realize that one should always look for and nurture the enjoyable and pleasurable aspects of life, and try to see the positive and good side in every situation. Think positively. Live positively. This philosophy counters the challenges and small tragedies of life that we cannot ignore, and must face one way or another.

Having been born four years before the birth of Israel, I absorbed a legacy of sacrifice for the Jewish state. There I saw the people who boldly fought the enemy, as well as those who paid the price; here one day, gone the next, only to become a memory. And with all this, the love for my country and the desire to defend and protect it stirred in me from a young age and never left me throughout my life.

I have walked through the history pages of the establishment of the state and have participated in three of its wars during its first sixty-five years. To me it was always an attractive trait to remain loyal to Israel and contribute to it as much as I could.

In recounting these and other occurrences, I have tried to focus not only on the activities themselves, but also on the people. I have always thought that people are the key to all events. In this book I share with you the events, the thoughts, and reflections that have accompanied me and continue to accompany me through my life.

ACKNOWLEDGMENTS

Thank you to my wife Miri, whose tireless work and assistance in both the Hebrew and English versions of the book made things easier and better.

Special thanks to Dr. Steven Varkony, Renne Schwartz, and Travis Marshal, who helped edit the English version of this book.

My sister Ruttie and my brother Shlomo are both blessed with excellent memories that helped me greatly in remembering missing details from Israel's early days and my childhood.

And lastly, I thank my children, who supported my writing with their love.

Chapter 1

Jerusalem of Gold, Blood, Sweat, and Tears

T he truck stuttered along the dirt road, jostling the passengers
and the baggage inside. Darkness and stillness filled the air.
Only the roar of the engine cut through the silence as it mustered the
strength to move forward, leaving everything we knew behind and
heading westward. My mother held me so I wouldn't fall through
the doorless opening of the swaying vehicle. The driver leaned
forward, clutching the large wheel in both hands as he intensely
focused his eyes, trying to slice through the darkness of the road.

That night we travelled into the unknown, wending our way
through black and threatening mountains. We were three in the
truck: The driver, his attention locked on the road, intent on cau-
tiously making our way; my mother, who focused only on reaching
our destination safely; and myself, at nearly five years old, watching intently the events unfolding around me, yet too young to fully
comprehend them.

The year was 1948. We had left a besieged Jerusalem behind
us, where barrages from the Jordanian army had torn gaping holes
in many homes, shattering roof tiles, and littering gardens with
shrapnel. We traveled west on the Burma Road,[1] winding our way
up the mountainside, passing Bab el-Wad,[2] because Arab gangs had

---

[1] A makeshift bypass road built in the Jerusalem area during the War of
Independence.

[2] A point on the Tel Aviv-Jerusalem highway where the road begins to climb toward
a gorge, also known as Sha'ar Hagai. The name means "Gate of the Valley."

1

blocked the main road to and from Jerusalem as they ambushed the city.

I was born and raised in Kerem Avraham, a Jerusalem neighborhood abutting Geula Street (today known as Malchei Yisrael Street) where the streets were named after the Twelve Minor Prophets. It was a modest neighborhood, made famous by the writer Amos Oz and the poet Zelda Schneersohn, who lived there during the British Mandate. It was there that I unknowingly absorbed a sense of duty and sacrifice for the State of Israel. I saw people boldly fight the enemy, and those who paid the price; here one day, gone the next, only to become a faint memory.

Etched in my mind is an image of the family that lived next door. I can recall the scene in detail. The family stepped into the garden to soak up the warm, embracing Jerusalem sun after being cooped up in the house for days, and in an instant, all were wiped out by a direct hit of Jordanian artillery fire. Their sense of caution had been dulled by the announcement of the first truce, on June 10, 1948, and by the deceptive silence.

This family had been among those evacuated from the isolated village of Atarot, north of Jerusalem, during a siege at the beginning of the War of Independence because they lacked basic necessities such as water, food, and ammunition. I remember the tragic incident clearly, but I have suppressed the sight of it.

Our one-story house with its red-tiled roof stood in the middle of Tzefanya Street. Surrounding the house was a garden where pine trees, olive trees, and jasmine shrubs grew along the fence. At the front of the house, an iron gate led to the main street. The back of our house bordered the Spitzer School in the impressive Yehudayoff building, which had been constructed in the early 1900s in the style of a European palace for the Yehudayoff family, who had immigrated to Israel from Uzbekistan. The Israeli Nobel Prize winner Shai Agnon described it as "the grandest of buildings, fit for the Messiah."

During the British Mandate, the building served as the temporary headquarters of the British military. All that separated our house from the British headquarters was a stone fence topped with barbed wire. As a curious four-year-old, I would climb the fence, peeking over to watch the British soldiers. They looked strange and out of place, with smiling faces and red cheeks, walking with awkward strides. I envied my sixteen-year-old sister Ruttie because the soldiers always offered her gum and talked with her politely.

On March 1, 1947, the Irgun[3] bombed the British Officers Club on King George Street in Jerusalem, killing seventeen British officers and soldiers, including several senior intelligence officers, and wounding twenty-seven others. The British military responded by imposing a curfew on the neighborhoods of Jerusalem from Geula northward. They set up additional blockades on the streets and tightened security checks for pedestrians.

My father, Shmuel, was a customs clerk; my mother, Zippora, was a teacher. They didn't play an active role in the struggle against the British, but they did hide a member of the Irgun in our home, a man named Shaul Berkovich, who was wanted by the British at the time. He soon became a close friend of the family, and he greatly admired my mother.

The restrictions the British imposed on the people – along with the friction among the Jewish paramilitary organizations, the Irgun, the Lehi,[4] and the Haganah[5] – fostered a citywide atmosphere of tension and hostility. All three groups opposed British rule, but each had a different view on how to break free of it.

---

[3] A Zionist paramilitary group that operated in Mandate Palestine between 1931 and 1948.

[4] A militant Zionist group that operated during Mandate Palestine, 1940–1948. Its avowed aim was to evict the British authorities from Palestine by force, allowing unrestricted immigration of Jews and the formation of a Jewish state.

[5] A Zionist paramilitary organization representing the majority of the Jews in Palestine from 1920 to 1948. Organized to combat the revolts of Palestinian Arabs against the Jewish settlement of Palestine, it was outlawed by the British Mandatory authorities. In 1948 it formed the core of the Israel Defense Forces.

The Irgun placed more emphasis on militant power than the Haganah, resulting in inevitable friction between these two groups. On one of our visits to my maternal grandfather, Mordechai, who lived not far from us on Straus Street, we watched a standoff between the opposing groups from the apartment window. On the road below us were two trucks, one filled with Irgun members, the other with Haganah activists. They glared at each other for several tense moments. Bystanders feared the sides would start shooting, but fortunately they did not.

I remember well the day the British army left Palestine. We watched the soldiers as they climbed onto a large army truck parked in front of our house. My neighbor, twelve-year-old Eliyahu, known as Fat Eliyahu, got a little too curious and approached the truck. One of the soldiers lost his temper and kicked him hard in the buttocks. Like a scolded dog, Fat Eliyahu dashed back to the front yard of his house, tail between his legs.

After the British left, the State of Israel was established.

Upon hearing the news, I was so excited I jumped up and down on my bed shouting, "We have a state! We have a state!"

But our celebrations did not last long. During the War of Independence, our back garden became a dangerous battlefield. The Arab Legion fired its cannons straight at us, and the shells hit parts of our house. My parents forbade me to play in the garden, which had now quite literally become a war zone. In retrospect, I don't know if it was childish curiosity, a temptation of fate, a desire to do things my own way, or a combination of all of these that made me occasionally defy my parents and step into the back garden.

I would quietly sneak out and gather large pieces of shrapnel, their tattered metal edges taking various shapes in my mind's eye. I was drawn to this garden. I watched again and again as shells hit our house, spraying wedged stones close to the roof, drilling ugly holes in its wooden cornice.

The house outlasted the Jordanians. Not only was it made of Jerusalem stone, but it also had concrete walls interwoven with strong steel beams. It seems my father had the foresight to build our house as strong as an armored bunker, capable of withstanding the shells. While the shells could not penetrate the stone walls, shrapnel still inflicted damage on the iron shutters of the windows, puncturing them with holes and cracks of various shapes. We needed sandbags behind the shutters to shield us from the shrapnel, and the metal shards would pierce the sandbags, causing avalanches of sand.

Although recalling this time of turmoil brings back violent memories of my upbringing, I can't help but remember the sense of unity my family felt every time one of our windows was cracked or our house was damaged. I loved how the whole family came together. It was us against one big enemy. We all protected one another and strategized how to survive together.

My mother, a wise Jewish matriarch and our family's greatest worrier, was strong, resourceful, and sharp-minded, as if she had lived through many generations of Jewish persecution and become accustomed to standing guard and fighting back. Her strength and efficiency overshadowed my father's more placid disposition. He tried in vain to adopt a masculine demeanor during the war, a time when men fought the enemy in life-and-death battles. But my father was not of draft age during the War of Independence, so he served in the Civil Guard instead. He supervised blackouts, ensuring that all the residential buildings were kept totally dark, and distributed drinking water from the cistern in the yard of the Spitzer School.

During that difficult time, my brother Shlomo and my sister Ruttie were going through their adolescent years, trying to find their own personal independence. They too contributed to the war effort by filling sandbags in the north of the city. And I, a small boy caught up in the incomprehensible turmoil of war, witnessed everything, and tried to understand it all.

The grownups were preoccupied with survival and everyone tried to be resourceful. For me, the challenge of survival seemed totally alien. I responded to the situation with curiosity, even fascination. I watched my brother admiringly when he disobeyed my father and spent time in the back of the house, absorbed in his stamp album. We were strictly forbidden to be there, particularly when there was shelling, because it was too close to the back garden.

While some of the events felt like a game, others were simply terrifying. I was afraid to sleep alone at night, and my parents took turns staying with me until I fell asleep. I had a recurring nightmare, which persisted for decades, of a shell striking me and turning me into an upright piece of smoldering wood, partially blackened and reddened all over.

During the second truce, in mid-July 1948, Mother decided we should get away from the bombardment for a while. I left behind my shrapnel collection, the shortage of food and water, and my family's unity. My mother and I traveled west in the darkness on the Burma Road to an unknown land, a land without shelling or hunger, a land that was not Jerusalem.

By morning we reached the city of Petach Tikva, which seemed as though it were another world entirely. The Petach Tikva sun was hotter than the Jerusalem sun and there was no morning chill. Here there was peace and quiet without the daily challenge of survival – no existential anxiety, no nervous tension.

Petach Tikva was foreign to us. We stayed a few weeks with the Graff family, but to this day I have not discovered our connection to them or why they agreed to let us stay. I had the impression we were there from a lack of choice, since it seemed we were not welcome at our relatives' homes in Tel Aviv and Petach Tikva, none of whom invited us to stay.

The Graffs had two daughters, ages thirteen and sixteen. The family owned a bakery and was considered well off. As was common in those days, the loaves of bread were delivered in a horse-drawn cart. From my childish perspective, I admired the Graffs' success and their willingness to help us. And yet, despite their friendly hospitality, we still felt like strangers imposing on another family. Perhaps they saw us as refugees. Even then, in a time of solidarity and camaraderie, social status and financial standing determined one's worth. We had neither.

The lady of the house, Penina Graff, was resolute and practical. I saw her as a strong, enterprising person. Her husband seemed like a harmless soul, preoccupied with his bakery. He wore an expression that said, "Don't disturb me while I'm working." But it was the white-haired, aging grandmother who acted as the authority figure, constantly trying to subject me to her rules. But I stood my ground, refusing to bend. Once, in protest, I took a wet toothbrush, pulled back the fibers with my thumb, and let go, spraying water in her face. She chased me around the table while I continued spraying her with water. She failed to catch me.

Father did not come with us to Petach Tikva, preferring to stay in Jerusalem to defend the city, but Shlomo and Ruttie joined us later. With my father absent, I tried to latch on to Shlomo, following him everywhere he went, but he mostly rejected and ignored me, behaving like a typical teenager. I often tried to copy him. On Yom Kippur, Shlomo and I came upon a trench in the center of Petach Tikva. Shlomo easily skipped over it, while I fell in, hitting my face. It was a nasty blow, and I had blood running down my cheeks. Not wanting to seem weak, I didn't sob or groan, even as I was treated at the first-aid clinic.

In fact, I never cried from physical pain as a child. Mother once told me that when I received vaccines at my one-year checkup, I responded only with a faint groan. The doctor said it was the first time an infant had not cried from the shots in all his thirty years of practice.

My childhood was engulfed in war and austerity and there was no room for crybabies. Crying was a sign of weakness. I even stopped myself from crying when I was smacked, and at that time parents could spank their children hard without someone filing a complaint against them. I only cried when I got emotional, and then, I would hide away where nobody could see.

We stayed with the Graff family until Mother began to feel that we were imposing and had outstayed our welcome. I don't blame the Graffs. We landed on their doorstep out of the blue, almost an entire family, not knowing when we would leave. So we moved in with my Aunt Geula, Mother's cousin who lived in Petach Tikva with her husband and children. None of our family had invited us to stay with them before, and I don't know why my aunt had a change of heart.

My happiest moment during those days of exile came when we got word that the war had finally ended. We returned home to Jerusalem, back to my beloved garden, which was no longer a war zone. It was once again a peaceful place of beauty and nature, where I could climb the trees to the roof or sit among the branches in solitude.

Life slowly returned to normal. My parents went to work in the morning and came home in the late afternoon. My siblings were still adolescents and continued to ignore me. I had the companionship of the garden, trees, plants, and insects. The stone fence in the back garden was no longer a threatening place. It served as a hiding place for the swords and other weapons my friends and I made for our pirate games.

However, sometimes when I played alone in the back garden, anxiety would overtake me – a fear that someone was lurking in the shadows, waiting for me, or that a looming figure would emerge over the wall and attack. I felt much better in the front garden or on the tiled roof at the front of the house.

My friends and I would climb onto the roof through the trees, walking along one of the strong branches while holding a higher branch for balance. Once on the roof, we would remove some of the tiles, squeeze our way inside, and then, grabbing the wooden beams beneath the tiles, climb down to walk on the flat concrete ceiling. Then we would remove more tiles at the front of the house and use them to build a post where we collected tough, woody fruit (which we called "*bobkes*") from the cypress trees. We hurled the *bobkes* at the other kids who were not part of our group. For a while we even hurled small stones, but we stopped after we accidentally hit the school nurse in the face, slightly wounding her.

I realize, looking back, that playing outdoors was a release from the restlessness I felt indoors. The only time my siblings paid any attention to me was to make fun of me. Every week they made up a new derogatory nickname for me, such as Victorio Yandullu (an announcer on Radio Ramallah) or Eel. Father also encouraged name-calling, which he had apparently learned and practiced in his childhood. When he called me a *shmendrick* (Yiddish for "dimwit"), it was a sign he was happy with me, and when he called me a scoundrel, it was a sign he really liked me. Mother, on the other hand, always gave me encouragement and positive reinforcement.

From the Shaul Tchernichovsky poem that begins, "Man is nothing but a little plot of land, / man is nothing but the image of his native landscape," and the theories of psychologists who turn to childhood to find the sources of behavior, I realize now my philosophies on life were shaped by the forces of my childhood.

Like the State of Israel itself, my life has been intertwined with bloody campaigns, beginning with the War of Independence. The war stirred in me a love for my country – and a desire to defend and protect it at a young age – that never left me. Within my own family, I had on one side the support of my mother, who believed in me and was confident I would achieve greatness. On the other side, my siblings and father teased me and tried to belittle me. So even though I always believed in myself and felt confident that I could achieve anything, I also felt the constant need to prove myself. That is one reason I went in so many directions in my life, some far from easy. I wanted to prove that I could succeed at everything I attempted.

I was a very independent child. For example, when Shlomo and Ruttie were young, Mother would dress them in at least five layers of shirts and sweaters to fight off the Jerusalem cold. But I was determined to do things my way. I would rebel and insist on wearing no more than one sweater and a coat. When I argued with Mother, she said I had to dress as she wanted and not as I wanted. As an act of defiance and rage, I would run out in the cold wearing nothing but my underwear, and Mother would chase me down the street, shouting hysterically, "You'll get pneumonia!"

Once I was playing soccer in the street with the neighborhood kids when it began to get dark. Mother suddenly appeared, armed with a sweater for me. I wanted neither to be disturbed nor to wear a sweater, so I ran away from her. She chased after me, and I hid behind a barrel of whitewash next to a construction site. Mother chased me around the barrel. I pulled a stick from the barrel and waved it to shoo her away. Unfortunately, some of the whitewash splattered on her. I don't know what it did to her, but I remember that she stopped running and went home with the sweater.

This incident sowed a bitter feeling that has never left me. I loved my mother dearly, and she did not deserve what I did to her that day. At the time I thought it was a prank, but I have felt remorse ever since. As I do for another incident that I still cannot shake.

Mother used to take me to her meetings at the Education Ministry on Yellin Street, about a mile from home. Once, after waiting for her in the corridor for an hour and a half, I decided to go home alone. My sense of direction at age five was not well developed, and I soon lost my way. I wandered around the city and arrived home a few hours later, long after Mother had worried herself sick about my safety.

I did things my own way, and I craved the attention of my parents and my siblings. I used to pester Father, and he usually punished me with severe beatings. Still, I never gave up or conceded defeat, and one day I decided to pay him back for the beatings. As he came home from work, having forgotten all about the morning's thrashing, I waited for him on the roof with a bucket of lime water. When he walked under me, I poured it on his head and scampered away.

Although Father sometimes saw me as a nuisance, he was nonetheless a good-natured man with good intentions. On winter days, when I came out of the shower, he would usually be waiting for me with my underwear, which he had warmed over the coal oven. His beatings were not out of malice but out of a firm belief that "he who spares the rod spoils the child." That he hardly paid me any attention was simply because daily life was a struggle and he needed his energy to get by. I never felt angry with him; I loved him. My belief is that when parents mean well, even if they don't always act in the best way, a child should not harbor resentment for mistakes that his mother or father made in the past.

Not only will I always remember Father warming my underwear on cold Jerusalem mornings, but also I will never forget the rare walks we took together in the city. Once I went with Father to the Tel Arza neighborhood a mile away to visit his American friend, who would receive parcels from America full of candies and other goodies. Father and I also took two longer trips together: one to his friend Sarah and her daughter Duka in Tel Aviv, the other to Tel Aviv's Nachalat Yitzchak neighborhood and the house of a friend with whose son I swapped stamps.

Father would also take me to visit his brother "Loizer" (Eliezer) in the Achva neighborhood, about fifteen minutes from our house. On the way, we passed an abandoned house opposite the Schneller Barracks that was owned by Arabs who had fled Jerusalem. To me the house looked like a palace. I would peek over the high fence into the garden to watch white swans floating in the pool – an amazing, unforgettable sight.

Visits to Uncle Loizer and his wife, Yaffa, were intense and informative. Yaffa did not live up to her name (which means "beautiful" in Hebrew). She had little mousy eyes and a wrinkled face even though she was not old. Her nose resembled a pink peanut, and her mouth reminded me of a dried plum. When Father and Uncle Loizer got together their conversations in Yiddish was always the same:

"What's up?" one brother would ask.

"Don't ask," the second brother would reply, before launching into a lengthy account of his many illnesses and problems.

Then the first brother would say, "You think you have problems? You've no idea what problems I have," and proceed to recount all *his* misfortunes. It was like a Ping-Pong game, each brother trying to outdo the other's misery.

Father also had a sister, Aunt Miriam. Her husband, Pinchas, reminded me of an antique statue with white, wrinkled skin. He would sit for hours almost immobile, never joining the conversation. Every hour he would sputter a single word: *nyet* ("No" in Russian), and then fall silent yet again.

I had a good relationship with Aunt Miriam. She always welcomed me and treated me kindly, even though there was tension between her and my mother. Mother claimed that Aunt Miriam always looked for an excuse to nag her. In general, there was no great love among our extended family. My father was angry with my mother's brother, Uncle Arieh, and found all sorts of flaws in his character. And Father didn't like my maternal grandmother, Rachel, even covering her face in one of the family photos with a sticky label.

Drama and intrigue seemed to be the norm among our relatives, which I found absurd. This is probably why I have always tried to look at the humorous side of events without neglecting their practical aspects. The ability to see the absurd and only pay attention to the humor adds spice to life and makes one happier and more optimistic.

Unlike Father, I got along on well with Grandma Rachel. She lived in the extreme religious neighborhood of Meah Shearim in Jerusalem and was ultra-Orthodox, always wearing a head covering and modest dress. Every now and then, after a fight with my parents, I would find solace in her little one-room apartment. We even slept in the same bed, head-to-toe, since that's what she wanted. I spoke to her in Yiddish, because to her Hebrew was the Holy Language to be used only in prayer. I learned the Yiddish language through our conversations.

Grandma Rachel raised my mother and Uncle Arieh alone after her husband, my Grandpa Mordechai, ran away to Germany when he was twenty-two. For a while, Grandma Rachel was an *agunah*,[6] but later Grandpa divorced her. His selfish actions left her destitute, and forced her to raise the two children by herself. Grandpa Mordechai was a sharp businessman, and in the days before the Holocaust he earned a small fortune. Later, when asked why he did not support his impoverished children, he claimed he had sent them money via his mother, but that it was she who did not pass it on to his wife and kids.

I doubt his excuse was true. It's hard to believe a successful and practical businessman like Grandpa Mordechai wouldn't have made sure the money found its way to his children. I believe he simply abandoned them because he got fed up with Orthodox life, and instead of becoming a Torah scholar immersed in Mishnah[7] and *poskim*,[8] he turned to business and finance.

In Germany, after divorcing Grandma, he married a Jewish woman named Grete who was stern and completely humorless. She looked like a pickled cucumber, always angry and critical of others. Before the end of World War II, Grandpa Mordechai fled for his life and returned to Israel with Grete. He claimed the two of them had gone through the Holocaust in a concentration camp from which they escaped to Israel via Portugal. They remained in

---

[6] In Jewish law, a woman bound in marriage by a husband who refuses to grant a divorce.

[7] The first major written redaction of the Jewish oral traditions known as the Oral Law, and the first part of the Talmud.

[8] Adjudicators of Jewish law.

Israel until the early 1950s, before returning to Germany. Grete suffered from every possible illness, yet she lived well into her nineties. Grandpa Mordechai, who was tall with a shiny bald head and plump face, was graced with good health but died of a heart attack in his early seventies.

Grandma Rachel never remarried. She would deprecate her ex-husband and angrily mutter swear words against him because of what he did. And yet she saw fit to tell me that I should ignore her bitter feelings since he was still my grandpa and deserved my respect.

Grandma's poverty made her frugal, to put it politely. When the Arab laundress would come to wash clothes in our house, Grandma would take command, ordering her to use as little soap as possible and scrub the laundry with her bare hands. Uncle Arieh was a good man, hardworking and honest. He grew up with my mother in great poverty and was just as frugal. He kept two bars of soap on his bathroom sink: a cheap, yellowish laundry soap with a strong smell of disinfectant, and ordinary bath soap. When I wanted to wash my hands with the ordinary soap, Uncle Arieh barked at me in a stern voice, "Wash your hands with the laundry soap so Babba (that's what he called Grandma Rachel) won't get annoyed." I never knew if it would really annoy Grandma Rachel or if Uncle Arieh was trying to hide his penny-pinching from me by putting the blame on Grandma. I developed a friendship with Uncle Arieh's son, Moshe, which has remained solid to this day. Moshe became an accomplished lawyer and later changed his family name from Cohen to Ben-Ari.

Uncle Arieh was a political left-winger and ardent Mapainik.[9] In contrast, our family friend Shaul Berkovich leaned to the right and was a former Irgun member. Arieh and Shaul lived nearby in the Rechavia neighborhood. They were amicable toward each other and both prayed on Saturdays and holidays at the nearby Yeshurun Synagogue. When I visited Uncle Arieh in the early

---

[9] A member or supporter of the Mapai Party, the Israeli Labor Party.

1990s and inquired after Shaul, he gave me a puzzled look and said, "Don't you know we haven't spoken to each other in thirty years?"

When I asked him why, Uncle Arieh replied, "It happened one Saturday during a break in the prayers. Shaul turned to me and said, 'How are you, peacenik'?[10] So I replied, 'Are you going to take out your gun and shoot me?' Since that day we have not spoken a word to each other." I don't think their friendship was ever that deep, but I was still sorry that this mutual political animosity had put an end to it.

While on the topic of Shaul Berkovich, I should mention his wife, Tova, who was known for her high-pitched voice. Shaul and Tova lived in the same apartment building as the president of Israel, Yitzhak Ben-Zvi, and his wife, Rachel Yanait. In those days Israel's leaders lived in ordinary apartments, not luxurious homes. Tova was a wonderful housewife but she lacked tact. On her neighborly visits to the Ben-Zvis' place she would strongly disapprove of Rachel's housekeeping. On more than one occasion she ran her finger over the president's furnishings while telling Rachel that she needed to dust her apartment.

As a child I was amazed at how much the grownups tried to fool the children, as if we could not see through their false pretenses. Aunt Chava, Grandma Rachel's sister, was notorious for this. She was a plump woman with a depressed look in her eyes and a colorful scarf on her head. At the young age of nine, I was good at repairs and working around the house. Aunt Chava was so impressed with my abilities that she asked me to paint her apartment. At first, the painting went smoothly, but as I progressed so did my aunt's thriftiness. She began adding kerosene to the paint to thin it out, and by the end of the job, the paint was so diluted that when I dabbed it on the wall, it dripped straight to the floor.

At family gatherings Aunt Chava liked to brag that she was the first to whom I would show off my report card. She would do

---

[10] A term, often derisive, for people with a dovish outlook.

this very cleverly by purposefully asking me in the presence of family members, "Ehud'ele, who's the first one you show your report card to?" And when I didn't reply – because in truth she wasn't always the first – Aunt Chava would answer for me, "That's right, Aunt Chava is always the first to see your report card!"

Aunt Chava and her husband, Avraham, owned a grocery store. Avraham had a long face and wore a somber, sad expression. He was constantly henpecked by his wife, who was known for her outbursts. Avraham found solace in perfecting his Hebrew. He would correct almost every sentence you spoke to him, and he would do so with a forced, authoritative smile as if he had caught you red-handed and felt obliged to correct you.

He once received at his grocery store a printed sign from the local bakery that asked shoppers not to handle the bread. The sign read, "Do not touch." Avraham immediately crossed it out and changed it to, "Keep hands off." But that was only his initial correction. The next day, after much deliberation and research, Avraham again changed the sign, this time it read, "Not to be touched." In the ensuing days he made a series of revisions before finally arriving at the one he was satisfied with.

I have a vivid memory of an accident I had in Avraham and Aunt Chava's yard. For some reason, I stuck my hand under the chain of a bicycle that stood there upside down, and my hand got caught between the chain and the teeth of the sprocket. I was taken to the first-aid clinic, and despite the excruciating pain I once again followed my internal no-crying rule.

Mother was a sixth-generation Israeli and came from a large family. Father was a fourth-generation Israeli on his father's side, fifth-generation on his mother's side. They were both descendants of famous rabbis and great Torah scholars from a few generations back. My grandmother's sister, Aunt Mirke, made sure that I knew our family history.

Aunt Mirke always looked solemn and sad, and she wore black as a sign of religiosity and mourning. Her husband was killed during the Arab riots in 1929 and her son Moshe was killed in the 1948 War of Independence as a soldier in Shu'alei Shimshon (Samson's Foxes), considered the IDF's first commando unit. Another son, Yankele, a yeshiva student, died of diabetes in the prime of his youth. Only her daughter, Hanna, survived her.

I occasionally visited Aunt Mirke in her one-bedroom apartment in Meah Shearim and sometimes on holidays I brought her a cake. She would take me to the living room, its walls covered with photographs of thick-bearded rabbis who all looked the same to me, and with great theatrics she would clasp her hands in the air and exclaim in Yiddish, "You don't know what kind of a family you come from." After this ceremony she would turn to one of the photographs, pat her cheeks with both hands and dramatically declare, "That's Rabbi Prag – you don't know what a great rabbi he was!" She would then turn to another photograph and again pat her cheeks and proclaim, "And Rabbi Valenshteyn, you can't imagine what a rabbi he was!" I later found out that Rabbi Prag and Rabbi Valenshteyn really were famous and outstanding rabbis of their generations, as she had always let on.

My father's family also descended from famous rabbis, such as Rabbi Yehoshua Yehuda Leib Diskin (also known as the Maharil Diskin or the Rav of Brisk), who lived from 1818 to 1898. He was the leader of the Perushim[11] in Jerusalem and a prominent rabbi and *posek*[12] of his generation.

Maharil Diskin also took upon himself a lifelong commitment to care for the orphans of Jerusalem. He began his philanthropic efforts by taking orphans into his house where, in 1880, he established the Diskin Orphanage of Jerusalem. However, as the number of orphans living under his roof accumulated, he began renting additional buildings to make room for everyone. He moved the orphanage to different places in Jerusalem, constantly trying to

---

[11] Disciples of the Vilna Gaon who settled in Palestine at the beginning of the nineteenth century and opposed the Hasidic movement.

[12] An adjudicator of Jewish law (the singular form of *poskim*).

accommodate more occupants, until he found its permanent location in the Givat Shaul neighborhood, where it still stands today.

My father's great-grandfather, Rabbi Leib Chasid, was the
first scion of the family to immigrate to Palestine from Slonim,
Belarus, in 1810, and he was among the first disciples of the Vilna
Gaon[13] to settle in Palestine. Rabbi Leib Chasid came to Palestine
with his wife and daughter Rebecca, and settled in Safed. He died
at the young age of thirty-six.

My paternal grandfather, Simcha Shlomo, was among the
builders of the Meah Shearim neighborhood. He was a sculptor and
a renowned manufacturer of *shofars*. One of his artistic creations –
a dozen bitumen stone cups bearing the names and symbols of the
twelve tribes of Israel – was presented to the emperor of Austria,
Franz Josef, during his visit to Jerusalem in 1869 as a gift from
the Jerusalem community. His works are on display at the Israel
Museum and at the Wolfson Museum of Jewish Art at the Hechal
Shlomo Jewish Heritage Center, both in Jerusalem. Pinchas Ben-
Zvi Grayevsky, who researched and documented Jewish life in
Jerusalem, wrote in his book *The Craftsman and the Metalworker
in Nineteenth-Century Jerusalem*, published in 1930, that in the
old *beit hamidrash*[14] of the Hurva Synagogue in the Old City there
was a plaque on the wall that read, "In everlasting memory in this
Sanctuary of the Lord to the soul of our treasurer, Rabbi Simcha
Shlomo…who blew the *shofar* gratis on the High Holy Days." He
died in 1909 when my father was only nine years old.

Mother and Father argued all the time about which of them
came from the better family. Their claims and accusations usually centered on the negative or annoying traits of specific family
members, despite the fact that there were admirable individuals
on both sides. They each supported their case by raising as many
grievances as they could against the other's family. Father would
always harp on the members of Mother's family who he deemed

---

[13] A prominent Jewish scholar and leader in eighteenth-century Lithuania.
[14] House of Torah study.

were "parasites" since they only learned Torah and didn't work. In response, Mother would nitpick my father's sister, Aunt Miriam, accusing her of neglecting her appearance and highlighting her failure as a teacher. Mother would reinforce her indictment with complaints about Israel Diskin, my father's cousin, who was a talented lawyer but nonetheless a very strange character. When he was offered a position in the Foreign Ministry, after the State of Israel was established, he responded with an ultimatum: The position of ambassador to South Africa or nothing. Regrettably, he ended up with nothing. He once declared that he would either marry a female millionaire or never marry at all. Here too, regrettably, he never married and remained a bachelor his whole life, without a family of his own.

Kerem Avraham was bordered to the south by the Bucharim neighborhood and to the north by Tel Arza. Although our neighborhood was close to Meah Shearim, it was completely secular in the early 1950s. Only two ultra-Orthodox families lived on Tzefanya Street. Those families had two boys about my age who grew sidelocks. My friends and I nicknamed one of the boys Stinky because he really smelled bad, and the other Stretch because he was tall. We had all-out fights with Stinky and Stretch, hurling stones at one another, and using trash can lids as shields. Unfortunately, on one occasion Stinky did not protect his head with a lid, and one of the stones hit him near his eye, causing him to bleed. His mother came running angrily toward us. My fighting friends fled in all directions. For some reason I did not want to run away, and I stayed put like a soldier who refuses to retreat. When Stinky's mother reached me, she let out her rage with a resounding slap on my cheek. After the stone incident, we declared a ceasefire with Stinky and Stretch.

Around that time I began studying at Geula School, a three-minute walk from the house. I will never forget the bearded principal with his black eyes and stern glare; for us, he was the classic archetypal villain.

During recess, the other students and I played war games. Each of the two warring groups had a cache of weapons that included wooden swords, bows, and arrows. Our best hiding place was behind the stone fence in my back garden. We pushed aside a few of the large stones and hid all our weapons in the crannies. One afternoon, a member of the other group named Shraga came to scope out our hiding place. We caught him and tied him to the olive tree in the garden. We only freed him at nightfall after giving in to his pleas.

I was a romantic and sentimental child, and when I was about eight years old, I fell in love with a pretty girl my age named Hadassah. She had black hair, beautiful brown eyes, and a suntanned face. She lived with her parents behind Aunt Chava's apartment. I would excitedly visit her and bring her gifts, carvings I made from the olive wood I collected from the sawmill in Tel Arza. It was that same sawmill that inspired me to run my own business. Once, when Mother joined me on a trip to the sawmill for scraps of wood, I said to her out of the blue, "You'll see, one day I'll own a factory like this." She was very surprised, and I, too, was surprised that I had felt the need to say it.

I made olive wood boards from branch cuttings, and on them I displayed my plastic animal collection. In those days, ice cream manufacturers made ice creams with plastic tigers, lions, rhinos, zebras, and foxes inside the wrappers, turning all children into plastic-animal collectors, not to mention avid ice cream consumers. My collection included every type of animal in different colors, and I exhibited each animal in its different colors on a separate olive wood board, which I kept on my windowsill or on my bedroom furniture. My parents and siblings avoided coming into my room because the slightest wind or movement toppled all of the animals over, instigating a fight between me and the culprit.

On Saturdays we sometimes visited the Berman family. My mother was friendly with Shoshana Berman. Her husband, Todres, was one of the owners of the Berman Bakery and a cousin of my

Grandpa Mordechai. I became friends with their son, Itzik, and we played soccer together in his neighborhood, annoying the neighbors, who complained of the noise. Itzik would come to visit us too, and we remained friends over the years.

Some Saturdays I visited the Bigers in the German Colony. I very much liked Dr. Simcha Biger, the head of the family. He was my father's age, but my father was his uncle. Dr. Biger was a unique character. He was a doctor and a major in the army, which was a high rank in the small IDF of those days, and he served at the recruiting office in Jerusalem. Since Dr. Biger was an orphan, Father had helped raise him and they were very close. My mother, too, was very close to him. The German Colony was quite far from our house, and I would go to the Bigers on my kick scooter. Sometimes, when I fought with my father, I would seek refuge at the Bigers' place and sleep over.

Later, it was Dr. Biger who taught me my bar mitzvah *haftarah*[15] reading. He had a musically inclined ear and exceptional singing skills, while I lacked experience or natural talent in those areas. Once, when I sang especially badly and off-key during a lesson at his house, he got up from the table and declared, "I can't take this any longer!" Patience was not his strong point, just as singing was not mine. But Dr. Biger calmed down from his temper tantrums, and I ultimately sang the *haftarah* properly and in the right tune.

The early 1950s were the early years of the state, and a time of austerity and rationing. When chocolate was sold for the first time, we were overjoyed and grateful to the new minister responsible for it. Every family received coupons to buy a limited number of eggs, poultry, and other products. Only the wealthy elite owned refrigerators. We did not number among them, and Father and Shlomo had to get up every morning before dawn to be the first in line to buy ice when the ice store opened. Our well-off neighbors, the Schneiders, had a refrigerator and they kindly let Mother store

---

[15] Selections from the Prophets of the Hebrew Bible that are publicly read in synagogue as part of Jewish religious practice.

our meat in it. Once, when I went with her to the Schneiders, she pointed at some dirt on the refrigerator door and told me that if we had a refrigerator, it would be spotless.

At that time the relative importance of a woman was still measured by her ability to cook. Further, our family even reached a consensus on the culinary talent of the various women in our extended family. Aunt Mirke, for example, was a culinary doyenne and her noodle *kugel*[16] became a household name. Aunt Miriam's pickled black olives were excellent, and Grandma Rachel made a superb *cholent*[17] with delicious *kishke*.[18] Mother was an expert at making cheese or jam blintzes. When she finished preparing them she would boast that one egg had been enough for twenty-eight or sometimes thirty blintzes. Her record was thirty-two blintzes from just one egg. She was intensely proud of this great accomplishment because eggs were a tough item to come by in those days of strict food rationing.

In order to save money while still eating fresh fish, Mother bought carp every Friday. They would swim happily in our bathtub until we turned them into baked fish or gefilte fish[19] patties. I loved fish but my favorite was halvah,[20] a delicacy that was hard to come by in those days. In the beginning of the 1950s, when I went with my parents to the Kibush Hashmamah (Conquering the Desert) exhibition at Binyanei Ha'uma[21] in Jerusalem, I was surprised to find that every visitor was entitled to buy a gold metal box containing two pounds of halvah. My parents, of course, saw the exhibition five times to accumulate multiple boxes. When my sister was in her twenties, she dated a man from the Chavilio family, who owned a halvah factory. I tried in vain to convince her

---

[16] A baked pudding or casserole most often made from egg noodles or potatoes.
[17] A Sabbath dish of slowly cooked meat and vegetables.
[18] Beef intestine stuffed with a seasoned filling.
[19] A dish made from a mixture of ground boned fish.
[20] A sweet confection made of sesame and honey, popular in the Middle East.
[21] The Jerusalem International Convention Center.

to marry this Chavilio fellow to satisfy my own love for halva. He would have brought stacks of halvah to our house. But she preferred Yankele Kovlaski.

Mother passed her teaching certification exams and became a teacher at the school in Moshav[22] Eshta'ol in the Jerusalem Corridor. She would smuggle home eggs and chickens from the village where she worked so that we would have something to eat. This put her at risk of getting caught by the inspectors that stopped the buses to Jerusalem to make sure no one, heaven forbid, was smuggling rationed food products. Luckily, Mother never got caught.

Mother went on to have a successful career. About two years later she was promoted to principal of the religious school in Mount Zion. She went to work early in the morning and returned home in the afternoon. I was in third grade and usually finished school at midday, but I had to wait outside the house for her to return. Although I was independent, Mother did not give me a key to the house; she did not trust anyone with it. Even Aunt Chava, who lived nearby and who repeatedly boasted that she was the first one I showed my report card to, never invited me to spend the afternoon at her house. She had apparently forgotten the favor I did for her when I painted her apartment.

To pass the time while waiting for Mother, I would casually stroll around or sometimes take off my sandals and go barefoot, counting the number of footsteps it took to walk one block. I was scared to stay in the garden alone. During this time, I formed the opinion that man was basically a lonely creature who could only rely on and trust himself. Despite Mother's love and concern for me, she was busy with her work, which used up most of her energy. Father was preoccupied with himself, the neighbors, and the neighborhood. My siblings were immersed in their own things. So I basically grew up alone and forged my own character through my own experiences and revelations.

---

[22] A cooperative community.

I tried to learn and apply everything that I believed was good, and I warded off everything that I believed was negative or bad. I learned from Mother the power of ambition and the virtues of diligence and persistence. I dismissed and forgave Father's indifference, submissiveness, and lack of ambition. Mother also taught me that you can achieve whatever you want as long as you stick to the goals you set for yourself, invest your unwavering energy, and use good judgment.

Our small neighborhood slowly became ultra-Orthodox. There was an influx of new residents from Meah Shearim – bearded yeshiva students in black capotes, and women clad from head to toe, wearing tight scarves to conceal their hair.

Mother, who made the major decisions at home, initiated the sale of our house and we soon moved to 22 Hillel Street in the center of town. Our apartment was on the fourth floor, above the Ron Movie Theater. Along with the invasion of the ultra-Orthodox community, Mother had another good reason for selling the home in Kerem Avraham. My sister Ruttie got married to Yankele, and since Mother felt she had to do whatever she could for her children, she decided to buy them an apartment in Ramat Gan. This financial exercise ended up a complete failure and my parents were forced to take a loan. With the burden of loan payments, we continued living in poverty for a few years.

I was sad to say goodbye to our house in Kerem Avraham. It had been my whole world. I loved the garden, I loved the big pine trees, and I loved to play soccer in the open area on Yonah Street next to our house. I loved all these childhood activities and more, but they all soon became distant memories.

My mother Zippora

My father Shmuel

With Mother and Father, 1945

Left to right: *Aunt Yaffa and her son Zvi, Uncle Loizer, Dr. Biger, Aunt Miriam*

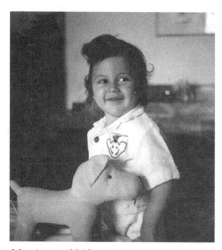

Me, August 1945

Chanukah party, 1950; I am sitting in the right row, fourth from right

The festival of Shavuot (Pentecost), 1949

Me at the entrance to our
house in Kerem Avraham, 1950

With my brother Shlomo (right) in
Jerusalem, winter 1950

My birth certificate. I am an Israeli, born in what was defined by the British as
Palestine.

Chapter 2
WHERE THERE IS A GOOD STUDENT, THERE IS A GOOD TEACHER

After we moved to the center of town, I started fourth grade at Dugma Elementary School, a religious school for boys where I studied through the eighth grade. My best friend, Shmuel Elitzur, was very bright and had skipped a grade. He was the smartest student in the class, while I fought for second or third place.

Shmuel lived next door to Aunt Chava and not far from our house, so it was easy for me to spend hours at his house. It had a nice, homey atmosphere and felt like a home away from home. Shmuel's mother, Rivkah, would sit with us writing poems and knitting. She was a beautiful woman, with dark eyes and black hair that flowed to her shoulders. It may be that my interest in Hungarian women started with my admiration for Shmuel's mother.

Shmuel and I both had a well-developed sense of justice, and we were disturbed and disappointed at how most of the boys in the class, including the popular ones, poked fun of Ovadia, a dark brown Yemenite boy with a severe limp. The boys harassed and ostracized him, showing no compassion. We felt sorry for Ovadia, who not only suffered at school but also at home where his father subjected him to cruel physical punishments, sometimes even burning him with a hot iron.

Shmuel and I decided to form a group. We included Ovadia and defended him against the other boys' persecution. By siding with Ovadia, we were all ultimately ostracized and included in the bullies' torments. It was not only Ovadia that made my popularity in the class sink, but also my brother, Shlomo. Some of my class-mates came to my house for a visit and met Shlomo. He had distanced himself from religion, or as Aunt Chava put it, "gone hypermodern." My brother saw fit to present Darwin's theory of evolution to these religious classmates of mine, and asserted his support of Darwin's proposition that people were descended from apes. Of course my religious friends, who believed that God cre-ated man "in our image, after our likeness" on the sixth day, were horrified at these assertions. As a result of my affiliation to my "heretic" brother, I was ultimately excommunicated.

Most of my teachers were boring, some even annoying, but two of them were entertaining and engaging. One was a math teacher of Hungarian background named Moshe Hershko. He was an excellent teacher, and also unintentionally amusing. He spoke in a heavy Hungarian accent. He would substitute certain Hebrew letters with others, which sounded quite funny to us. He also believed in corporal punishment. From time to time he would bring a rebellious student from another class he had been teach-ing, hauling him by his ear through the corridors of the school. As a punishment he would send him to the corner of the room and make him stand with his back to the class for the full duration of the hour. Hershko could not tolerate disturbances, and he would mete out ringing slaps to the cheek, his face red with anger. Luck-ily, because I was a good student, I was spared from his fury, and I was able to enjoy the entertainment of his lessons and reactions to other misbehaving students.

However, the real star of pedagogic entertainment was Alma-gor, the physical education teacher. Almagor was in his early sixties and had a tanned, wrinkled face, with eyes that frequently gazed far into the distance. He wore a khaki beret tilted to the side, and was always dressed in a blue or khaki blazer with a silver pin adorning the left lapel, an emblem of his contribution to something or other – we never knew what it was. It was rumoured among the students that in his time, Almagor had been an Olympic gymnast, and that one day during practice he fell on his head, with all the problems that this kind of fall entailed.

In the middle of exercise class, as we were running around the yard or performing our routine exercises, he would suddenly yell the words "Kope!" or "Tope!" None of us knew what these phrases meant. In the midst of lessons, he would launch into long lectures, emphasizing that the strong should help the weak and so on, and he would always end this speech with a loud "Kope!"

But Almagor outdid himself when he explained to us that we should learn to swim. Swimming was a strange concept to kids who grew up in Jerusalem in those days, which was far from the beaches, with hardly any pools in the city. He would command us to lie down on the cold stone floor in the Jerusalem winter. As we lay there on our bellies, we had to execute rapid breaststrokes with our arms and legs. With such "swimming," we did not move forward at all, but we did make progress in our prayers – praying that we would not get sick from the cold.

Every time it snowed in Jerusalem, the teachers would go over the same lesson, which was finding where the word snow was written in the Bible. This word, by the way, appears about twenty times in different contexts.

By the age of ten, I was already quite independent. Much to my mother's discontent, I would ride my bicycle by myself from Jerusalem to Tel Aviv. At age eleven, I travelled a great distance alone on the bus to visit my brother, who was serving in NAHAL[23] at Kibbutz Ha'on on the eastern shore of the Sea of Galilee. When I reached Tiberias, it turned out that I did not have enough money for a bus ticket from Tiberias to the kibbutz. I had wasted all of my money on sweets and popsicles during the rest stops. With my last small change I tried to phone the kibbutz, but the operator – in response to my anxious, childish voice – said, "Miss, don't shout at me," and hung up the phone.

---

[23] An acronym for an IDF program called Fighting Pioneering Youth.

Left with no other option, I walked eleven miles in the burning heat of the Jordan Valley summer. When I finally got to the kibbutz, word had spread about how I had accomplished this on foot from Tiberias, and the kibbutz members came to look at me, as a kind of attraction. My brother claimed afterward that I drank "half a tank of water." He was relieved that I had not gotten lost en route; I could have easily taken a wrong path and wound up in Syria, whose border and military outposts were very close to the Sea of Galilee back then.

Dugma was an all-boys school, so by the time I finished studying there, at the age when hormones start to awaken, I was happy to move on to Maaleh, a co-ed school just across the street from our apartment. This too was a religious school with a religious study program, but most of the students were not particularly religious. Some, including me, would stash their yarmulkes into their pockets the moment they left the school grounds.

Our studies were worth taking seriously, but at that age, distracted by the enchanting girls around us, who could focus on studies? And so, while in elementary school I ranked among the three best students in the class, at Maaleh I was just a fairly good student.

The school was run by three teachers that we collectively deemed the Triumvirate, alluding to the threesomes that ruled Rome in the period before the emperors. These three teachers were from the old generation and saw teaching as their mission in life.

One of them, Dr. Mordechai Frankenthal, known as Frankus, was the math teacher. Frankus would give us long lectures in his deep bass voice, watching over us with his cross-eyed gaze. He kept a distance from the students, and when someone urgently raised his hand, Frankus would ask him archly, "Do you want to poke out the teacher's eye?" He was critical, sarcastic, and intimidating. Sometimes he would stare somberly at a student who had irked him and say in his thunderous voice, "What strange creatures has the Holy One created in His world!"

The second member of the triumvirate was Yehuda Greenspan. Of Galician[24] extraction, he mainly taught the Bible. Greenspan was short, wore glasses, and always had a suspicious look on his face. But he was a good Bible teacher. Thanks to him, I was able to memorize large portions of the Bible by heart, most of which I can still recite from memory. My knowledge and expertise of the Bible stemmed mainly from my interest and love of the subject, but also from the need to study seriously enough to perform well on every Bible test. One could not fool Greenspan, and it was impossible to cheat during his tests. He had different groups of questions, which he kept in his jacket pocket, so that almost every student received a different set. We had no choice but to learn all of the material, and learn it very well. The formatting of his questions was generally the same: He quoted an excerpt of about four words from a particular verse, and we had to complete the verse, explain it, and sum up the idea behind it.

Years after I completed my studies at Maaleh, I met Greenspan at a bat mitzvah celebration in Jerusalem. He did not remember me, but when I told him that I owed my exceptional proficiency and understanding of the Bible to him, he replied, "Thank God. All the former students I have met only complained to me about my behavior and my teaching, and you are the first one to thank me!"

The third member of the triumvirate was the history teacher Dr. Azriel Bromberg, whom we called Brems. He was German, and one could say that his grades and his methods directly reflected this. If he gave anyone a grade of 7 out of 10, it was a rare and momentous achievement. His comments on the test booklets were always curt. For example, I once got a grade of 7-plus after getting a 6-plus on the preceding test, and he commented, "An increase is noted." On the next test, when I again got 6-plus, he commented, "A decrease is noted."

---

[24] Galicia is a region in Central Europe that now straddles the border between Poland and Ukraine.

Although Brems wore glasses with lenses as thick as the bottoms of bottles, his vision was still defective. His hearing, however, was perfect, and he would pick up on the tiniest movements of paper, catching cheaters in the act. While he was dry in manner, he never failed to moisten the immediate radius around him, spitting as he spoke. As we were learning about Greece, each time he said "Peloponnese" the letters P and S were accompanied by a spray of thick spittle, to the consternation of those sitting on the first bench at the front of the class.

But the teacher who ultimately stole the show in this high school was Avraham Dgani. I have no doubt that, had he been an entertainer, he would have won all sorts of honors and awards. I personally owe him many outbursts of laughter. Dgani was short and heavyset. His large head sported an expansive bald spot, which would shine when he stood under the light. He sometimes came to class with his pyjama pants poking out and folded over his pants. He taught us literature, and although I loved the subject, I could not force myself to listen to his boring lessons.

Sometimes Dgani, without saying a word, would affix a terrifying, lengthy gaze upon one of the students who had acted up or caused some sort of disturbance. Some students found a way to cope with his penetrating look – they would stare back at him, straight into his eyes. And it was Dgani who would blink first. After a short time he would forfeit and concede, averting his gaze. When he got fed up with our horsing around, he would threaten in his theatrical, dramatic voice, "I will call Dr. Frankenthal!" He looked like a little boy calling his father to help him.

The chemistry teacher was named Yaakov Habusha. He had an elongated head, with protruding eyes and a balding scalp. One day he came to class with a slight limp. Confronted by our surprised looks, he apologized and explained that the taxi he was riding in to Jerusalem had plunged into a ravine, three hundred yards deep. He claimed all the taxi's passengers had been killed, that he was the sole survivor, and that he had climbed back up the ravine to the road and made his way on foot to Jerusalem.

The next day, a report appeared in the newspaper about a taxi that had fallen to a depth of thirty yards. All the passengers, however, were all right, except for one who had disappeared, his whereabouts unknown. If that was Habusha, then at least we knew what happened to him: He had injured his leg, and told us a hugely exaggerated story.

The English teacher, Sheila Sar-Shalom, made my Aunt Yaffa look beautiful in comparison. When Sar-Shalom entered the class for the first time, we rose to our feet to welcome her, as was the school's custom. She looked so grotesque that I could not control myself and broke into loud laughter. Her nose was long and pointed, her eyes mousy, and her lips extended in two thin lines from cheek to cheek. A white hat shaped like a fruit basket sat atop her hair, which was huge and wild like a psychedelic rock star. I looked at her thin, hairy legs, already shaking with laughter. She said to me in English, in a solemn voice: "Do you want to laugh or to learn English?"

Of course I replied, "To learn English." She turned out to be a good English teacher, while I turned out be just an average student.

A serious and well-liked teacher was the bearded Rabbi Moshe Haim Schlanger. He was a previously non-observant Jew who had turned religious, and he taught us Gemara.[25] I loved both the subject and his way of teaching. I was a good Gemara student, but as the wise saying goes, "Where there is a good student, there is a good teacher."

When I finished ninth grade, I decided to transfer to a non-religious school. It was the Hebrew Gymnasium, one of the two best schools in Jerusalem. I did very well there, both academically and socially, and I was sure that I had finally found my niche. But the supervisor of religious education in Jerusalem, Dr. Yosef

---

[25] The second part of the Talmud, comprising rabbinical commentary on the first part, the Mishnah.

Goldschmidt, was not so sure. My mother was now the principal of the religious school near Mount Zion. Dr. Goldschmidt summoned Mother and told her unequivocally, "You have two options: Either your son goes back to study in a religious high school, or you resign from your position."

I did not want to go back to Maaleh at all, and I considered studying independently for the matriculation exams. After a lot of consideration, I concluded that the best way to study for the exams was in school. And for lack of any other choice, I reluctantly returned to Maaleh. Our homeroom teacher, Ms. Yonah Wertheimer, greeted me when I showed up by saying, "I am happy to welcome those who are returning to religion." Of course, that statement annoyed and frustrated me to the extreme.

My plot for revenge against this teacher did not take long to surface. It was implemented from a window of our apartment that was directly across from the classroom. I used a large mirror to direct some dazzling sunlight at the classroom and Ms. Wertheimer. I was pleased with this and did not want to leave out our teacher Dgani, who also received some dazzlement.

School was a necessity, but all the fun was in social life. Having attended a boys-only school in the past, Maaleh was like being in a candy store. During class I would gaze for long periods of time at the girls, which certainly did not help me focus on my academics.

We were adolescents, trying to understand who we were and become popular among our peers. The "queen bee" of the class was unquestionably Tamar Elitzur. She was the sister of my elementary school friend Shmuel, and a year older than him. Tamar was not a stunning beauty, but her deep black eyes and piercing gaze left many casualties pining for her love. The most beautiful girl was Rina Oster, and she was the leader of the group of girls Tamar had rejected.

In those days, we did all we could to impress the girls, from basketball games to brushing our hair, and showing off our skills and talents. Eventually I discovered that there was a good assortment of girls at other schools too, particularly at Beit Haker-em High School. It was there that I met my first serious girlfriend, Mili. We spent most of our free time together. Around that time, I bought my brother's motor scooter, and I would show up at her school during recess riding it like a knight on a white steed.

At the same time, I was enamoured with Iris, another girl from Beit Hakerem High School. She was an attractive girl with beautiful blue eyes. About twenty-five years later I ran into her while living in New York, and she aired out the pent up anger she had against me for my brazen and disgraceful ways in the past. She alleged that when I arrived at the schoolyard riding my scooter, I had the nerve to sometimes ask for her, and other times for Mili.

Along with schoolwork and an active love life, I was involved in a variety of sports, and quite proficient at some of them. Despite my average height, I was a good basketball player, ranking fifth or sixth on the school team. I was athletically gifted, and a good medium-distance runner, placing well in national competitions. I was also one of the best Ping-Pong players in Jerusalem, always hurrying to the YMCA to play every day after school.

It was only in swimming that I was rather undistinguished – I am a Jerusalemite, after all. When I passed the Little Fish test at the YMCA, which entailed jumping from the diving board and swim-ming a single lap, I was very pleased. I could not even dream of passing the Fish test, which required a swift dive from the diving board and swimming five laps. And I could only watch those who attempted and passed the Shark test, admiring their somer-sault jumps from the diving board as they swam twenty times the amount of laps I could.

With the help of my Armenian instructor, Johnny Mistakavi, I excelled at gymnastics – it didn't hurt that Johnny's younger sister was definitely worth looking at. I wasn't bad at tennis either. In retrospect, if I had just concentrated all of my efforts on one sport, I might have excelled, rather than just being good at many sports. Playing so many sports was a form of defiance and my way of proving my ability to succeed at anything I took on.

I would work out alone on the track of the Hebrew University at the Givat Ram campus. To improve my performance in the eight-hundred-meter run, I would break into a sprint on a four-hundred-meter course, then slow down somewhat, then pick up the pace again, repeating this interval sequence. Once, in the midst of a workout, the Hebrew University track coach showed up and asked me, "Do you know your time score in the four-hundred-meters?"

When I said that I had no idea, he explained that he had measured my time and my speed was impressive. Further, he added that if I were interested in joining the university team he would like to be my coach. I told him running was only a hobby of mine, and that I did not want to become a professional runner, especially since I was a student and did not have time for it.

I also kept up one of my favorite hobbies: stamp collecting. I had already accumulated a huge collection, built on the foundation of my father's collection and my brother's additional contributions to it.

During the afternoons, I would spend most of my time at the YMCA. In the summer, between ninth and tenth grade, I worked at a summer camp, first as an assistant at the pool and then as a counsellor. The following summer, I was pleased to be made a counsellor for the oldest group and received a letter of praise for my efforts.

Starting in tenth grade, I began working in gardening. My brother Shlomo, who was going for his master's degree in biology, had financed his studies working as a gardener, and he suggested that I join him by doing maintenance on the gardens that he had created for two apartment buildings in the Rechavia neighborhood. I happily took advantage of the opportunity to earn pocket money, which I later used to buy my brother's 175cc Lambretta scooter. I got great use out of that Lambretta in high school.

Sooner or later, however, like every Israeli after graduating high school, I was drafted into the army.

Me and my brother Shlomo, 1953

Left to right: *My sister Ruttie, me, and my brother Shlomo in front of our house, 1953*

Me with Shmuel Elitzur (left), 1957

At the Dugma school, winter 1957; I am first on the left

My class graduates from the Dugma elementary school, 1957. Bottom row: first from left, *Shmuel Elitzur; I am fourth from right.* Second row: second from right, *Almagor;* fourth from right, *Hershko.* Third row, first from right: *Ovadia.*

With classmates on a class trip, 1958. Bottom row: first from left, *Batya Ben-Yisrael;* second from left, *Naomi Frank;* first from right, *Ruth Nawi.* Second row: first from left, *Gershon Alperovich.* Third row: first from left, *Yascha Siton; I am second from left;* third from right, *Rina Oster.* Top row: first from right, *Herzl Halevi.*

The family at my brother Shlomo's wedding to Keren, 1963. Kneeling, left to right: *me, my sister's son, Ronen. Seated,* first row, left to right: *my brother-in-law Yankele, and on his knees their son, Amir; my sister, Ruttie; my father; my mother; the bride, Keren, and the groom, Shlomo; Kern's mother Yonna and her father Prof. Abraham Kaplan; first from right, Uncle Pinchas. Back row: first from left, my cousin, Yosh; third from left, Uncle Arieh; sixth from right, Uncle Moshe; second from right, Yisrael Diskin; first from right, Aunt Miriam.*

With Rina Oster at the City Garden, 1959

Graduation picture for the Maaleh high school. Top row: third from left, *Avraham Dgani; continuing left are Greenspan, "Frankus," "Brems," and Rabbi Schlanger.* Second row: first from left, *Sheila Sar-Shalom;* second from left, *Tamar Elitzur.* Third row: first on left, *Habusha. I am in the fourth row, second from right.*

JERUSALEM YOUNG MEN'S CHRISTIAN ASSOCIATION

UNDER MANAGEMENT OF THE
NATIONAL BOARD OF Y.M.C.A.'S OF THE UNITED STATES AND CANADA
291 BROADWAY, NEW YORK 7, N. Y., U.S.A.

TELEPHONE : 4437	J. LESLIE PUTNAM
CABLE ADDRESS : WATCHMAN	GENERAL SECRETARY
P. O. Box 294	HERBERT L. MINARD
JERUSALEM, ISRAEL	PROGRAM SECRETARY

ירושלים, 1.9.60

לכל המעוניין בדבר!

הנני מאשר בזה שאהוד דיסקין היה מדריך בקייטנתנו בחודשים
יולי ואוגוסט 1960. על אף הגיל הצעיר שלו מסרנו לידיו את הקבוצה המבוגרת
של הקייטנה, ילדים בגיל 13-14.
אהוד הוכיח את עצמו כמדריך בעל אחריות שהבין לרוחם של הילדים
והיה תמיד מוכן לכל תפקיד.

בכבוד רב

זאב ליבנדל
מרכז קייטנת י.מ.ק.א. ירושלים

WHEN IN JERUSALEM PLAN TO STAY AT THE "Y"
ACCOMMODATIONS FOR MEN AND WOMEN

Recommendation from Jerusalem Young Men's Christian Association.

It reads:

Jerusalem, September 1, 1960

To whom it may concern:

I hereby confirm that Ehud Diskin was an instructor at our camp in July and August 1960. Despite his young age we gave him responsibility for the oldest group in the camp, aged 13–14.

Ehud proved himself as a conscientious instructor with a fine understanding of the children and was always prepared for every task.

Yours sincerely,
Ze'ev Livendahl
Coordinator of the YMCA camp, Jerusalem

Chapter 3

· · · · · · · · · · · · · · · ·

Boot Camp

irst Sergeant Abramov approached us rapidly on the dusty dirt road. A red blemish covered the left side of his face, and with a terrifying gaze, he commanded in a harsh, piercing voice, "You have exactly ten seconds to get off the truck!"

We were frightened recruits, who had just arrived at the desolate Chasah base, which is near the city of Ashkelon, and we clambered noisily down from the rented civilian truck that had brought us to the 82nd Battalion.[26]

Of course, there was no feasible way thirty soldiers could make it off the truck with all their gear in anything less than a minute. When we had all finally disembarked, First Sergeant Abramov bellowed, "Lousy! What's with you people? Now you've got another ten seconds to get back on the truck!"

After two more rounds of this, salvation came from an unexpected source: the truck driver. Frustrated, he turned to First Sergeant Abramov and proffered that the truck was designed for transportation, not for up-and-down drills, which had already scratched it.

All of us were what was referred to in military jargon as "fresh meat," green recruits with very few rights. The kibbutzniks[27]

---

[26] A battalion is a military unit that is smaller than a brigade and is usually composed of three to four companies. Tank battalions like the 82nd consist of thirty-six tanks, eleven armored personnel carriers (APCs), and about five hundred soldiers.

[27] Kibbutnizks are residents of kibbutzim, collective agricultural communities. At that time, the kibbutzim were still considered an ideological vanguard of Israel and contributed disproportionate numbers of elite soldiers and officers to the IDF.

44

among us were better accustomed to this treatment, but those of us who were city dwellers felt our spirits crushed. The combination of the desolate, depressing base, with commanders and NCOs (non-commissioned officers) who abused us during our shifts, made us feel awful.

In those days, the early 1960s, the Israel Defense Forces (IDF) did not enforce minimum sleep requirements. So we found ourselves sleeping very little, and wandering around like lifeless zombies during the day. On our first night, after countless limited-time drills, dashing out of the tents with the right or left boot, or other pointless item, a recruit – whom I later found out, was named Aksenfeld – looked down at his watch. He broke the grim silence of the inspection by exclaiming grumpily, "What's going on here? Isn't it night now? Aren't we supposed to sleep at night?"

Sergeant Yossi, the bully on duty, responded in amazement, "Who said that?" As a collective punishment for this offense, we were all forced to go to sleep two hours later than normally scheduled. As for Aksenfeld, he was sent to the obstacle course to do exercises until daybreak – the hour when the rest of us awoke from our short naps.

A few nights later, as we were hauling hundreds of heavy concrete tiles from one tent encampment to another, Aksenfeld suddenly disappeared. We combed the area for him, and after an hour we found him sleeping out in the field with concrete tiles, padded by a blanket, forming a pillow under his head.

Shortly afterward, Aksenfeld faked a suicide attempt, hoping to be relieved of his duties. He went to the clinic, and when the medic came out to the waiting room, he put a sleeping pill in his mouth and said loudly, as if counting, "Forty-one!" which was followed by a second pill and "forty-two!" However, despite his bluff, he had only taken those two pills.

The medic called an ambulance right away and informed Aksenfeld that when they got to the emergency room at Barzi-lai Hospital in Ashkelon, he would have a tube inserted in his stomach so it could be pumped. Aksenfeld was not expecting his plan to pan out like this, so he hastily announced that he had only taken two sleeping pills. But neither his confession nor any of his pleas helped, and he was rushed to the hospital for the unpleasant procedure.

In the army, you meet people that you would otherwise have very little chance of coming across in daily life. For example, there was a soldier named Dabach. Except for his height, he had a striking resemblance to the actor Anthony Quinn in the movie *The Hunchback of Notre Dame.* Dabach was barely five feet tall, and during inspections, when we had to stand motionless for long periods of time, he would have to fold one leg a bit and tilt his body sideward.

The commander picked up on this habit immediately and barked at him, "Dabach, stand straight!" Dabach would then straighten his folded leg, but fold his other leg and tilt to the other side. When the commander again snapped, "Stand straight, Dabach!" he answered, "Commander, it's not that I don't want to, I can't."

During the summer, we sometimes had to stand for inspection inside the tents. To provide some sort of ventilation, the lower edges of the tent canvas had to be rolled up, which meant that only the lower part of our legs were visible from outside the tent. Standing there in the sweltering heat, we would roll up our sleeves. Shababo, a big, muscular guy who constantly wore an apprehensive look on his face was at his wit's end from the swarms of flies that settled on his thick arms.

To get rid of them, he would fill his mouth with air, pucker his lips, and emit the air in fierce exhalations that scattered the flies. I often stood next to him and had to hear these cannon shots without end, while feeling the shock waves on my face.

Luckily for me, I was able to spend a lot of time with Miki Stark, and he would become my best friend through the following years, including the most unforgettable and unexpected encounter between us in Sinai during the Yom Kippur War.

Miki and I shared a similar sense of humor; he, too, sought out that which was fun and entertaining in life. A common punishment in our basic training was to run a circuit of the camp in full combat gear while wearing personal weapons and shouting a sentence that fit the sin you had committed.

For instance, someone who had whispered something to someone during an inspection would have to run, shouting at the top of his voice, "You are not allowed to talk during an inspection!" A punishment of that kind was meted out to me and Miki.

However, we still wanted to entertain and be entertained. While circling the camp, instead of "You are not allowed to talk during an inspection!" we yelled, "Recruits are not allowed to mess around with female corporals!" You can imagine the looks on the faces of our commanders and fellow soldiers as they watched our defiance.

Miki and I essentially wanted to finish basic training in the least traumatic way possible. There were other soldiers, such as Motti Kaplan, who declared from the start of the training that his goal was to be an outstanding recruit. Motti would crouch in our tent like an Olympic sprinter; eyes wide open, waiting for the order to come out for inspection. When it was given, he would shoot out of the tent like a cannon shell, wanting to be first in line. Unfortunately, despite his enthusiasm and efforts, he did not complete the course as an outstanding recruit.

The outstanding ones were always the kibbutzniks, who looked down upon us city dwellers with an air of superiority. Our conversations were about girls and having fun, while they talked about tractors. It seemed every kibbutznik felt the duty to glorify his kibbutz and himself, continuously discussing their state-of-the-art tractors. A "What do you people know?" look was perpetually stamped on their faces.

Like all recruits, we often had to do guard and kitchen duty. I hated kitchen duty, but I was never able to get out of it. One day, I was tasked with removing the dirty plates from the tables, putting them on a cart, and bringing them to the kitchen for washing. I piled the cart high with plates, and everything was fine, until I reached the entrance to the kitchen, where I bumped the cart on a low step I had not noticed.

In accordance with Newton's laws of motion, the plates kept going, hitting the floor, breaking and scattering leftovers in every direction. The sergeant major of the kitchen, whom no one called by his full name, but only by his post, Kitchen Sergeant Major, decided that the task of clearing the plates from the table was ill-suited for me; instead he assigned me to help the chef with his cooking.

There, he assumed, I would be under close supervision, and thus unable to cause problems, but he was wrong.

The chef, a middle-aged man with a thick Yiddish accent, ordered me to take a large ladle and fill it with white powder from a nearby pot. He then pointed toward a gigantic pot across the huge kitchen, and ordered me to put the powder in it. I walked with self-assured steps toward a huge pot half-filled with oil.

I tossed all the powder into it. Proud of my accomplishment, I carried on. After a few minutes, I heard a cry of outrage from the chef. He came striding toward me, cursing at me for ruining his entire supply of oil, which would not be replaced until the end of that month. It turned out the powder that I had put in the pot was powdered soap (to me it looked like flour!). He exclaimed that he had told me to put the powdered soap in an empty pot right beside the pot of oil. I figured he wanted to bake something with oil and flour.

When Kitchen Sergeant Major heard about my latest mishap, he decided the most I was capable of doing was scrubbing large metal pots, and that was exactly what he ordered me to do. By that point, I was thoroughly fed up with kitchen work, so I went to the clinic, told them I had come down with some illness, and was granted permission to leave for the day.

Kitchen Sergeant Major was an interesting character. He was an immigrant from Eastern Europe, so he was most comfortable speaking Yiddish. His face was round and red, and he spoke with expressive hand gestures. He wore a large, erect black beret that resembled a black pot. He lived in the town of Lod, and was a devoted fan of the Hapoel Lod soccer team. If Hapoel Lod won a game over the weekend, he would come to the base in an exceptional mood and with a positive attitude.

But when Hapoel Lod lost, God save us. We would all keep our distance from him for the rest of the week, and we would pray fervently that Hapoel Lod would soon win again to avoid his wrath. One day, some reserve soldiers said to him, "Kitchen Sergeant Major, we have nothing to eat."

"You are an intelligent person, solve the problem," he replied. "I am not an intelligent person. If I were an intelligent person I would be Prime Minister of Switzerland, not a kitchen sergeant major in the 82nd Battalion." His proposed solution for hunger was, "There is a free barrel of cured fish, and the faucet works twenty-four hours a day."

The commander of the 82nd Battalion was none other than Lt. Col. Shmuel Gonen Gorodish, one of the heroes of the Six-Day War, and after the Yom Kippur War, my good friend. In those days, I was a recruit and he was the Battalion Commander. We saw him as an exalted being, and spoke his name in awe and trembling.

It was difficult for us to take vacation leave, and everyone looked for excuses to go home. I used to make my way to the dental clinic on the neighboring base for a quick treatment, and then – because as a recruit I was not allowed to bring my Lambretta scooter onto the base – I would hitchhike or take a bus to Jerusalem to spend an hour or two there before returning to the base.

Miki, for his part, did very well for himself. On the pretext that he was a skilled pianist who needed to practice, he was fortunate enough to be allowed to leave every weekend, so he could take a Saturday off to play the piano. Other musicians – guitarists, violinists – envied him, and the company commander suggested they bring their instruments to the base to practice. Miki, of course, could not bring his piano, and so he got to go home to Jerusalem.

The transportation to our base from Jerusalem was terrible, and on the weekend, no buses ran at all. Once, right in the middle of an unplanned vacation, which was granted one Friday to only a portion of the company, we were unexpectedly ordered to return to the base the next day, and we all had to hitch rides.

That experience led me to take Miki's recommendation and get in touch with the parents of a recruit nicknamed "Tugi" (his last name was Tugnedreich). Every Saturday they drove to visit Tugi on the base, and I hoped to catch a ride with them.

So that Friday I asked Tugi's parents for a ride to the base the following day. Their faces lit up. They told me that on that particular Saturday they were unfortunately staying put. However, Tugi had an upcoming birthday and they did not know how to send him his birthday cake. The unfortunate result for me was that the next day, I not only had to hitch a ride, but I was also forced to spend a few hours carrying a big cream cake in my hands to deliver to Tugi.

Tugi had a sister named Rivkah who looked as burly and big as a mountain. Miki and I would visit Tugi on Saturday nights and go out on the town with him. When we rang the doorbell, his mother would open the door and ask, in a loud voice so the guests in the living room could overhear her questioning, whether we had come to visit Rivkah.

Before we could answer her, she was already leading us to Tugi's room while talking loudly so we could not, heaven forbid, admit that we had not come to visit Rivkah, but rather Tugi. Once we were in Tugi's room, she went right back to the living room and announced to the whole assemblage of Polish card players, "The door never closes, and boys come to visit Rivkah all the time."

Before the end of basic training, it was decided that part of the company would remain at the base for various tasks, and another part would become the Armored Corps Men's Choir, which would sing on Armored Corps Day at the Charles Bronfman Auditorium in Tel Aviv.

Of course, everyone wanted to qualify for the choir. During the tryouts, a special musical representative of the well-known conductor, Yitzhak Graziani, ordered us to sing in a very high, almost soprano, voice. He then asked who found it difficult, and whoever raised his hand was told to move to the back rows. I decided not to say it was hard for me to sing in a high voice. I thought that if I admitted this, I would not be accepted into the choir.

Only later did I understand that his aim was to properly organize us by voice types. So I had to sing soprano for a few days, until I could convince my commander to let me transfer to the right vocal section.

We attended many rehearsals while living at Beit Hachayal[28] in Tel Aviv. A few days prior to the performance, a letter came to the headquarters of the company. It said I had to come for an urgent meeting at the Education Ministry about my matriculation exam in math.

When I got there, I was told that a student named Shaul Freirich had informed the Education Ministry that I had cheated on the math exam, something that was entirely-fabricated. Indeed, I was amazed that the clerk had mentioned Shaul by name.

He was not a friend of mine, but neither was he an enemy. I was able to resolve the misunderstanding at the meeting. When I returned, I asked Miki if Graziani had made any changes. Miki showed me a few changes but suggested that, instead of singing; I just open and close my mouth. I replied unequivocally that after so much training, it would be quite frustrating for me not to sing.

---

[28] A soldiers' hostel.

The occasion was extremely festive. We took our places excitedly on the stage of the Charles Bronfman Auditorium, and sang before an audience of thousands of people. The program included "Chorus of the Hebrew Slaves" from Verdi's opera *Nebuchadnezzar (Nabucco)*. The whole choir sang the lines, "Our mouths lack the power of song / We can no longer part our lips / As long as we dwell in a foreign land," almost whispering the phrase "our mouths."

I, however, sang that phrase loud and high. To my embarrassment, all eyes were directed at me. It turned out that Miki that had forgotten to update me on a revision of Graziani's – instead of ratcheting up the volume for that phrase, we were to sing it in a whisper.

When I demanded to know from Miki why he hadn't notified me about the changes, he answered matter-of-factly, "Didn't I tell you to just open and close your mouth without singing?"

Our next tour of duty was at the border with Jordan in divided Jerusalem. It was at the end of 1961, during the Jerusalem winter, and we were given guarding and observation responsibilities. Our squad stayed in an abandoned house on the border near Mount Zion, and our lookout point was in front of the Dormition Abbey.

I gazed out curiously at the demolished Jewish Quarter, the Mount of Olives, and the Arab villages. These restricted sites had been completely off-limits since the end of the War of Independence. Israelis were prohibited from visiting the Western Wall, the Jewish Cemetery at the Mount of Olives, or any other sites in the area. None of us dreamed that only a few years later, in the Six-Day War, we would conquer all these places and have the freedom to visit them.

The school where my mother worked as the principal was at the foot of Mount Zion, and was named accordingly after it. I was tasked with guarding the border just a few hundred yards from there. As a soldier, it was a strange experience to go and visit her at the school. Years later, after my mother died, I made a small memorial in a park, in her honor. I also eventually set up a similar memorial to my father close by.

After about a month, we finished our tour of duty at the border in Jerusalem. We returned to the 82nd Battalion at the Chasah base to learn the theory, mechanics, and operation of tanks. Towards the end of the course I injured my hand, and was unable to continue the operational part of the training. Instead, I was given the duties of a storeroom clerk, something that plunged me into a deep depression. Although I got quite a few vacations, I hated the job and I could not tolerate the soldiers that worked around me.

I could not stand the storeroom clerk, named Shimon. He was overweight, with a protruding paunch, and he had a roundish face with staring, calf like eyes. At night he would sleep almost naked, wearing only tiny blue bathing trunks. Every evening he would play Arabic songs on the radio. Each time the renowned Arab singers Farid al-Atrash or Umm Kulthum could be heard warbling in the best Arabic tradition, Shimon would exclaim, "What *breathing!*"

Our complaints and pleading him to stop playing these songs were to no avail. So we had to find a different solution. One night, a few storeroom clerks and I took Shimon, with his cot, while he was still sleeping peacefully on it, out to the obstacle course about a hundred yards from our quarters.

During this night journey, Shimon did not wake up, and it turned out to be a very effective treatment for his festival of Arabic songs; after that we never heard Umm Kulthum or Farid al-Atrash again. He got the hint.

I looked for any possible way to get out of the job in the storeroom. During a family conversation, it turned out that my brother-in-law, Yankele, was a friend of a friend of our new Battalion Commander, Lt. Col. Haim Deem, who had replaced Lt. Col. Gorodish. That sparked a feverish family effort to make the needed connections so that the battalion commander would invite me to an interview, and possibly assign me to a new, more fitting role.

My mother quickly decided that I should serve as a Gadna[29] counselor at the Schneller base in Jerusalem, a role that was less dangerous, and was close to home. I was ambivalent as to what to do. Luckily for me, fate intervened and helped my decision, but it disagreed with my mother as well.

On one of my bus journeys to Jerusalem, I gazed through the window at the gutted iron skeletons of the War of Independence convoys that were set up after the war at Sha'ar Hagai as a memorial. I thought about the heroes who had gone through so much to bring us food and supplies in besieged Jerusalem. Tears came to my eyes, and I felt a lump in my throat. It could not be, I told myself, that whereas they had acted out of a sense of supreme purpose and paid with their lives, I would serve as a *jobnik*.[30]

I did not reveal these thoughts to anyone else, which was not surprising; I was a reserved person in general anyways. I always made a point of investigating, learning, hearing opinions, and then drawing my own conclusions.

In my opinion, advice givers are biased in their views in most cases, their thoughts colored by their own feelings. For example, my mother, who was very astute, gave great weight to the element of my personal security, as in this instance. My mother's concern was always, first and foremost, my safety.

In any case, the contacts and the talks finally paid off, and I was invited to a personal interview with the battalion commander, Lt. Col. Deem. When he asked where I wanted to serve, I replied, "In the battalion reconnaissance patrol."[31] When my mother heard about my request and my decision, she almost fainted. She angrily said I was irresponsible. As far as she was concerned, I had wasted everyone's time, including Yankele's, because the scout's role is the most dangerous in wartime, and only those who were irresponsible volunteered for it.

---

[29] A program that prepares young people for military service.

[30] A term, often derogatory, for a minor, noncombat soldier.

[31] The force that scouts, navigates, and gains information.

To get such an assignment, one did not need to outsource their connections, because only very few people desired such a position. The family, especially Ruttie and Yankele, looked at me as a certified fool who had squandered an opportunity, and they remained mad at me for quite some time thereafter. Looking back, I believe that this defiant and bold move was one of the most important in my life. I had finally found the courage to act on my patriotic feelings, and express my love for my homeland. It also turned out to be an interesting and fulfilling role.

The battalion reconnaissance patrol was composed of four soldiers and a commander. I was the only city dweller; the other soldiers were a *moshavnik*[32] named Yadin and two kibbutzniks named Daniel and Avshalom. I was not able to socialize with them much since their usual conversation topics were about tractors.

Still, we all had a good rapport based on our common missions. Our commander, Sergeant Bloch, was also a kibbutznik and well over six feet tall. With his big green eyes, he always looked at us in a detached, distant way; it was his attempt to create a command hierarchy, but it never worked.

The one in charge of us was the battalion's operations officer, Lieutenant Shamai Kaplan. Handsome and well respected, he had a pleasant temperament, but was also firm and resolute. Lt. Col. Deem assumed direct authority over us, and he cultivated us as fighters under his guidance and patronage.

We lived in a gigantic barracks that was originally intended to house thirty soldiers. There I would also store my Lambretta scooter, which gave me the option of quick sorties to Jerusalem. I would disassemble the Lambretta and service it in our barracks.

One Thursday evening, with an inspection by the battalion commander scheduled for the following day, the commander of the Headquarters Company, Capt. Yaakov Ziso, showed up for a preliminary inspection. His gaze darkened when he saw the parts

---

[32] A resident of a moshav, a cooperative community made up of small farms.

of my Lambretta scattered all over the cabin. When I thought he was about to have a heart attack, I quickly promised that by the morning, everything would be clean and neat.

Since we were more or less under the battalion commander's protection, we were in a safe position. Commander Ziso had another reason to treat us with respect: His navigation and map-reading capabilities were not outstanding, to put it politely, and he always required our services when he had to navigate in the field.

Sometimes, I would take off to Jerusalem on the Lambretta, and only return to the base at dawn. I could not enter through the main gate since I would leave without permission, so with no other option, I would return via the neighboring base, which had no strict oversight at the entry gate.

I would have to drive about one mile on a dirt road that connected the rear parts of the two bases. The road served for tank travel and was saturated with dust, so when I finally got back to the scouts' barracks, both I and my Lambretta looked as if we'd gone through a box of powder. On one occasion, as I was returning to the base at dawn, I saw a soldier trying to hitch a ride on the desolate road leading out of Jerusalem.

I stopped and asked him where he needed to go and what he was doing out here. The soldier replied that he had to reach the base in Ramlah, and had flagged down a taxi. When the driver asked him to pay in advance, it turned out he did not have enough money, and so, the driver abandoned him exactly where I had found him.

I told him he could sit behind me on the Lambretta, and come with me as far as a certain junction, where he would be able to hitch a further ride to Ramlah. The soldier was happy with this arrangement. I talked to him as we rode together, but when the road started climbing between the Sha'ar Hagai junction and Beit Shemesh, it seemed that the Lambretta felt lighter and drove faster.

I turned around, and surprisingly noticed that my hitchhiker had disappeared; for quite a long stretch of road I had been my only audience. I turned the Lambretta around and drove back to where I remembered he had last replied to me. There was no trace of him anywhere. He seemed to have vanished as if he had never been there.

To this day, I do not know what happened to him. Did he simply fly off the Lambretta? Or did I bore him so much that he fell asleep and lost his grip? When I thought back on this incident, I tried to imagine how he must have felt. First he was dropped off by the taxi in the middle of nowhere, and then blown off a mini-bike in the middle of the night.

Although I had to reach my base before the morning inspection so they would not find out I had left for the night, I first drove to the Ashkelon Police Station and reported the incident. I never heard from them again, and the hitchhiker mystery remained unsolved.

While I was at the base, I made many nighttime excursions to Tel Aviv to hang out with girls, but I never stinted on the training and activities. I strove to be a good warrior and scout. We were an elite unit in the battalion, and countless hours of difficult training were invested in us.

We had to do a grueling course in personal sabotage in the mountains of Jerusalem, navigating by vehicle and on foot. We were also included in the final course of the brigade's company scouting patrol. The company commander was Capt. Ben-Tzion "Bentzy" Carmeli, and I got to know him for the first time. I learned to respect him as a soldier and commander, and to love him as a person.

The final course exercise was conducted near the Dead Sea in the summer of 1962 in 105-degree heat. We, the four battalion scouts, were dropped at the entrance to one of the ravines beside the Dead Sea. Our task was to navigate on foot to Beersheba, but they dropped us at the wrong ravine, and we had to start the navigation by scaling cliffs, a grueling task. Within a few hours each of us had emptied his two canteens.

We came to a cistern – with a dead mouse floating on the water. Daniel the kibbutznik was the only one who drank the water; the rest of us preferred our severe thirst. Finally, our group joined up with the rest of the company, and we kept going for two days and two nights without the benefit of sleep.

In the end, less than half of the company made it to the base near Beersheba. All of us scouts from the 82nd Battalion were among those who made it. Having finished the courses, we were given jeeps for patrolling. We now started to play the role of scouts for the battalion. Along with manning lookout points and gathering intelligence, our jobs included navigating for the force.

In one of the battalion-level exercises, I was tasked with leading a tank company through sand dunes in the Negev Desert at night. The navigation was based on aerial photos, and I felt a great sense of accomplishment. In those days, there were no night-vision devices or any such thing as GPS – just your eyes, your compass, and the stars.

Back when we were drafted we had to take intelligence tests, and I had scored highly. As a result of my performance, I was invited to take additional tests for admission into the officer corps. The tests were given over three days at the Tel Hashomer base near Tel Aviv. Our orders were to be back at our encampment every night by midnight because the morning inspection was at seven.

In those days, Tel Aviv, just as today, was a great place for having a good time, and it was there that I preferred to spend the nights. That meant I only returned at dawn, not long before the inspection. As it turned out, part of the testing of our suitability as officers took place on the second night, as they checked to see if everyone had actually returned at midnight. Of course, I was missing.

That morning, the sergeant on duty summoned me and told me that if he were to report me, I would get a failing grade. He looked me in the eyes and asked if I really wanted to be an officer. When I said yes, he told me he would report that I had come back on time. I still do not know if he did me that favor because he liked me, or because I had otherwise excelled in areas that would merit passing.

In any case, my whole future would have played out dramatically differently; had this sergeant decided to report my absence. I would not have had the opportunity to climb the military ranks, and would not have been a commander in the wars. My life path would have taken an entirely different direction, and to this very day, I feel extremely grateful to that sergeant.

The results of the officer-corps tests arrived at the battalion headquarters. I had passed with a high grade. Lt. Col. Deem asked if I wanted to move on to an officers' course and become a platoon commander. I said yes, but emphasized that prior to being a platoon commander, one first had to be a squad commander, and admittedly, I had no such experience.

Lt. Col. Deem summoned the battalion adjutant and loudly ordered him to fill out a form indicating that I had already passed a course for commanders of armored infantry squads. I became a theoretical commander of an armored infantry squad, without knowing a single thing about it.

My next step was to take a course for Operations Branch Officers. It was at the officers' school known as BAHAD 1,[33] which at that time was located at the Syrkin base, near the city of Petach Tikva.

---

[33] BAHAD is the Hebrew acronym for "Training Base."

The monument to my mother that I set up beside the Montefiore Windmill in the Yemin Moshe neighborhood of Jerusalem

The monument to my father that I set up near the Liberty Bell Park in Jerusalem

Chapter 4

. . . .

THE OFFICER'S PATH

S ergeant Fried dashed wildly into the fortified bunker, firing his Uzi into the gulch below him. The tracer bullets shone in the clear night, leaving red trails of fire. Fried dripped with sweat, his thick face red from strain. As he ran, he switched cartridges at a dizzying pace. Acting as the platoon sergeant for this exercise, he scurried ahead of the group firing intensely at the virtual enemy. Our platoon[34] was simulating the conquest of a fortified bunker on a hill in the Ben Shemen area, near the town of Lod in central Israel.

We were cadets in the course for operations officers, given at the Syrkin base near Petach Tikva. After the bunker-conquering drill, we assembled for an evaluation. Our instructor-commanders were Captains Alex Ziegfrid and Binyamin Ben-Eliezer. In later years, Capt. Ben-Eliezer, known as Fuad, became a defense minister and a major Labor Party politician.

Fuad directed a withering look at Cadet Fried as he bellowed in his thick Iraqi accent, "How is it that you, platoon sergeant – you criminal, you fool – fire away blindly into the gulch? Empty another magazine, another one, and another; you'll be paying me a lira for every bullet." It was 1962, well before the advent of the shekel, and the Israeli Lira[35] still maintained its worth. Fuad's anger

---

[34] An infantry platoon is a military unit typically composed of two to four sections of squads. A squad consists of about eight soldiers.

[35] The Lira was the Israeli currency until 1980.

was justified. Cadet Fried had unnecessarily continued his wild running and pointless volleys even after we had already conquered the bunker.

Fuad was a capable officer, and an outstanding teacher. I thoroughly enjoyed his theatrics and admired his professionalism. He would look at us with his usual twinkling, sardonic gaze, and level barbed criticisms that made everyone laugh. Toward the end of the course, Fuad turned to Licht, a cadet from the Artillery Corps, and said, "Listen, Licht, you've made a lot of progress in this course. When we started, you were in the negatives. Now, you're at zero."

The officers' course was difficult for me. I lacked the basic knowledge of a squad commander, and many things that were clear to other cadets were murky to me. True, the adjutant of my battalion, following the orders of the battalion commander, had given me a certified document stating that I was the commander of a mechanized infantry squad. But the piece of paper did not contribute anything to my knowledge, because in actuality I had not taken the course.

When it came to command capabilities and tactical solutions in our exercises, I was average. However, I excelled in navigation; my experience as a scout helped me. As for physical fitness, I was in very good shape. Only Avraham Mukhtar, a cadet from the elite Sayeret Matkal unit,[36] was in better physical shape than I was. Eventually Cadet Mukhtar took part in some secret operations and won citations. Kobi Meron, also from Sayeret Matkal, was in our course as well. He and Mukhtar would exchange secret looks, and sometimes they disappeared for a while without any explanation.

Our squad overflowed with interesting characters. Some were solemn, some funny, and some were ridiculous. Generally, the cadets were nice fellows, and I liked them. Ze'ev Mahnai (whom I called Zaabul) was from the town of Binyamina and came from the infantry. Ze'ev was knowledgeable and capable militarily; he was also a pleasant and sociable fellow. I became quite friendly with

---

[36] The commando unit of the General Staff.

Yaakov Veshler from Artillery; he was a big, handsome fellow. And Rafi Friedyung from Intelligence had a probing, anxious gaze that always awaited instructions.

Shamai Giller, who came from the Armored Corps, suffered from a Napoleon complex. He was short and looked bland for a guy of his age. However, he tried to make a tough impression with curt, blunt-speaking mannerisms like a Mafia member as he gazed sharply through his big horn-rimmed glasses. Giller's clothes were always ironed and starched. As a tank soldier, he was supposed to wear black boots, but he found red paratroopers' boots more impressive, so he wore them instead. Once, before a leave, he proposed that I give him the scout's wings I had pinned to my shirt; while in return, he would give me his paratroopers' boots for the days off. I nixed the idea without a second thought.

Among the intriguing fellows in the course was Adam Weiler, who was also from the Armored Corps. Adam's Zionist family had emigrated from South Africa. He was likable, but inevitably we all got into heated arguments with him over his support for the apartheid regime.

A while later, he served as a company commander in the War of Attrition, and he was killed at the Suez Canal in 1970 when his tank hit a bump, accidentally discharging one of its machine guns. Tragically, his brother Gideon was killed three years later in the Yom Kippur War, when his tank was hit by an antitank missile in the Golan Heights.

Although I liked being with this group of cadets, I did not like the course, simply because I did not like courses in general. I never liked rigid frameworks of any kind; they constantly dictated what to do, and how to do it. I loved freedom, initiative, and individualism, which I rarely found in courses.

Once every two weeks we were permitted to go home. On those weekends that we were required to remain at the base, I simply escaped. I was the only one who did that. Had I been caught, it would have been the end of the course for me, and I would have remained an ordinary soldier until my discharge.

After three months, I was elated when the course finally ended and I was awarded a platoon commander's pin. However, then I faced a new problem: I wanted to command a tank platoon, which required an extra prerequisite course for Armored Corps officers, but I was not eligible because I had neither undergone field training as a tank crewman, nor had I passed a tank commanders' course. In the meantime, I was transferred to the 46th Battalion of the 7th Brigade.[37] It included the brigade's reconnaissance company, commanded by Capt. Bentzy Carmeli.

I settled in with the reconnaissance company. I served as a platoon commander, but I still did not have the rank of second lieutenant (2nd Lt.), just that of an acting officer, so I was assigned an inferior platoon commander. It was decided in the battalion's head office that I would take an Intelligence officers' course, so I could then receive the rank of 2nd Lt.

Quite a few of the soldiers in the company were serious and proficient. One was Amir Nahumi, who went on to the air force, served as a combat pilot, and took part in the 1981 bombing of the Iraqi nuclear reactor. He was also the champion of the air force. When it came to downing enemy planes, he was credited with a total of thirteen Egyptian and Syrian MiGs. Nahumi was head of an air force squadron and was discharged with the rank of brigadier general.

Another soldier in the company, Yoram Mendel of Jerusalem, had been in my high school class, and back then we would spend time together at the YMCA.

I also befriended one of the platoon commanders, 2nd Lt. Eli Ovnat, who joined us a little while later. He was capable, friendly, and kind. He was also good-looking, but shy when it came to girls. During one leave, when we were in Jerusalem together, he told me

---

[37] The brigade consisted of three tank battalions, including about one hundred tanks and three thousand soldiers.

about his shyness problem. When the leave ended, we took the bus together to the central bus station so we could get back to the base. I had already given him a brief lecture on how to act smooth when meeting girls, but I decided he needed a live demonstration.

In the seat in front of us sat two charming girls. To ensure that they heard me, I loudly said to Eli in a loud voice, "I hope this bus makes it to the center of town," even though I knew for certain it was headed the opposite way. The girls were very much interested in helping us soldiers, and after hearing our conversation they turned around to inform us that the bus was going in the opposite direction, toward the central station at the city exit. A conversation then sparked, but unfortunately, it did not lead anywhere.

That is one of the memories of Eli that I carry with me. A few months later he was killed in an accident. He was returning from a reconnaissance mission across the border in Jordan. At dawn, on the way back to the base, the command car in which he was riding crashed into a bridge, and Eli was killed. During war and other military operations, one learns that survival can be arbitrary. Eli was returning safely from a dangerous mission, but was killed in a senseless accident.

The soldiers' training was quite grueling. As a young platoon commander, I learned a great deal from the company commander, Capt. Bentzy Carmeli, who was a wonderful person. As I was preparing the company for a weeklong navigation exercise on foot, I told Bentzy that we were all required to get malaria vaccinations because there was a risk of catching the disease in the area where we would be navigating.

Bentzy replied regretfully, "Then I won't be able to take part in the navigation. I have no spleen, so I can't get shots."

I eventually learned that Bentzy had suffered a series of injuries during his army service. The first occurred during the attack on the Kalkilya[38] police station prior to the Sinai Campaign in 1956. Among other things, these injuries left him with only one lung.

---

[38] A city in the West Bank.

Yet Bentzy did not let any of his disabilities slow him down as a fighter. He saw his military role as a calling. He was a superb scout, and an exceptional IDF commander. On October 8, 1973, Bentzy was killed in the Yom Kippur War while blocking the Egyptians' advance at the forefront of his battalion in Sinai. He won a Chief of Staff Citation for his valor on that mission.

Although the training was not easy, I still managed to experience some good times. On the days that we stayed at the base after training, I would head to Jerusalem or Tel Aviv, knowing I had to be back before the 6:15 a.m. morning inspection. It was a long distance from Beersheba to Tel Aviv, and my Lambretta scooter was getting old, so I had to stop using it for intercity trips. I would spend the majority of these nights hitching rides there and back, and the other half having fun.

One of the girls I spent time with was named Ariela, a pretty flight attendant with dark hair and dark eyes. It was Miki who introduced me to her. Her stepfather was a retired major. During his IDF service, he was in charge of supplying meat to the soldiers. I told him about my experiences as a reconnaissance officer, and he quite liberally told stories about his role as a meat provider. He would describe in great detail how he stopped the kosher inspectors from taking meat for their own personal consumption without any permission. He would get excited telling us about his achievements.

The first time I came to visit Ariela at her parents' house, she told me her father was a major. Her mother, eavesdropping from the kitchen, interrupted with, "But with the status of lieutenant colonel!"

When I told this to Miki, he burst into laughter and said something similar had happened to him, but in reverse. When he visited Ariela, her mother said that her husband was a major in the army, and Ariela shouted from the bathroom, "But with the status of lieutenant colonel!" The mother and daughter had a sort of unwritten pact that when one said the father/husband was a major, the other automatically granted him a higher rank.

When I was a major myself, some time later, I went in my uniform to visit Miki at his apartment. There I was greeted by guests who asked about my role in the army, and before I could answer, Miki asserted that I was in charge of meat. That was his kind of humor. In reality, I was then serving in the office of the financial adviser to the chief of staff. I had an appointment in case of emergency as a company commander, but it was never initiated.

Miki's guests, however, wanted to hear stories about meat, and started inundating me with questions about what I did. Not wanting to embarrass Miki, and wanting to go along with the joke, I told them some of Ariela's father's experiences as if they were my own. Only later did I realize that the guests had seen me as ridiculous and objectionable, wondering why a young officer like me would be dealing, of all things, with matters of meat and putting kosher supervisors in their places, instead of contributing serious military service.

Sometimes I went to visit my sister Ruttie and her husband Yankele, who lived in Givatayim, near Tel Aviv. Yankele had survived the Holocaust in Poland, and was the only member of his family to do so. After his parents were killed, he was left alone when the Germans unleashed Dobermans on his two little brothers. His brothers tried to flee, but the dogs caught up with them and tore them to pieces.

Yankele was fifteen years old when he joined the partisans. He suffered from extreme hunger for months, so he assigned supreme value to food. When I would come to visit them, I inevitably had to eat whether I was hungry or not; it was impossible to decline. Even if I would leave their home at four in the morning to return to the base, Yankele would always wake up and prepare a big breakfast for me, even though he had to start his workday as a taxi driver at seven. The only way to prevent this, and to let him sleep in, was to threaten that I would stop sleeping over unless he desisted.

In 1963, Israel wanted to put its National Water Carrier into service. It would draw water from the Sea of Galilee, which would then be conveyed to the Negev desert via a lengthy canal and pipe system. The Syrians threatened to stop the extraction of the water by force, and part of our company was sent to guard the carrier. The commander was Capt. Bentzy Carmeli and I was his right-hand man.

We established our position north of Kibbutz Ginosar, where the Tzalmon tunnel and other sensitive components of the carrier were located. It was there that I got to know Bentzy better; I learned to love and have great respect for him. Bentzy was the quiet type who only spoke when necessary. He was totally focused on the army and the missions, and he was courageous and resourceful. One day, in an intelligence-gathering operation beyond the Jordanian border, he made out a Jordanian soldier who called to him in Arabic, "*Min hada?*" (Who is that?)

Bentzy answered unflinchingly, "Muhammad ibn Yusuf."

The Jordanian said, "*Tal hon*" (Come here).

Bentzy, cool and calm, replied in a threatening, angry tone, "*Uskut ya chmar!*" (Quiet, you donkey!) The Jordanian soldier fell silent.

On a different occasion, as we made our way to the west of the Sea of Galilee, with Bentzy driving the jeep and me sitting beside him, he suddenly took a detour toward the Amud River. As we were driving, he told me he had a reclusive brother who lived nearby, whom he had not seen in a long time. I stayed in the jeep while the two of them reunited. When Bentzy came back, he did not say a word, which was typical of his restrained, reserved personality.

For the rest of my time in the standing army, I also served as an intelligence officer for the 46th Battalion, to which the reconnaissance company was subordinate. The commander of the battalion was Lt. Col. Itzik Ben-Ari, who was a superb navigator. In the midst of the most difficult topography for navigation, such as sand dunes, he would glance over the aerial snapshots, mentally "photograph" them in his head, and navigate for miles and miles. He did not bother to glance at the map, because he was able to recall the aerial photographs from his memory with incredible precision – he never made a mistake.

Before one of the battalion exercises, I joined Itzik in planning an attack drill, which would be executed south of Beersheba. After we had done the planning, Itzik ordered me to brief the battalion's master sergeant on where to effectively position the targets so that we could assault and initiate fire at them. I did as I was told, but the master sergeant, who was not very good at navigation and field operations, positioned the targets on hills other than the ones the plan specified.

To our surprise, the next day, as the full battalion was moving forward to prepare for the assault, we were stunned to discover that targets were gone.

Itzik contacted me on the field radio and asked angrily, "Where are the targets?"

I replied, "I told the master sergeant where to put them."

Itzik responded in rage, "And did you confirm, or did you not confirm?"

I answered, "I gave the master sergeant a precise explanation of where to position them."

Itzik patiently repeated, "Did you confirm, or did you not confirm?"

When I replied, "I did not confirm," he retorted fiercely, "A three-lira fine and another three liras for the fuel!" Of course, the six liras remained in my pocket; no one ever bothered to collect them.

That incident made it clear to me that following up, and confirming that things have been accomplished, is vital in every domain of life. Those who receive the orders, and those who carry them out, have their own separate agendas and priorities.

Sometimes others also have a different understanding of what needs to be done, as in the case of the targets that were misplaced.

Another lesson I drew from this was that it is always important to learn from mistakes, so that one can apply the right conclusions in the future. Generally speaking, people fall into two types: those who learn and correct the mistakes and those who blame others and keep on making the same mistakes.

In each and every case where we get hurt, lose, fail, or just do not succeed, we need to figure out how we ourselves contributed to the negative outcome so we can derive a lesson for the future and not be disappointed again. Most importantly perhaps, we must always be honest with ourselves, without excuses.

In 1964, the day finally arrived that I was supposed to be discharged from compulsory service in the IDF. As my next step in life approached, I decided to go to university to further my education.

At the time, I was dating a Norwegian girl named Anita, whom I met through my brother, Shlomo. She was Jewish and a Zionist who had moved to Israel to study. Anita was supporting herself by working in the Department of Botany at the Hebrew University of Jerusalem.

Inspired by Anita, I decided I wanted to take a breather and spend some time abroad, so I applied to the Faculty of Natural Science at the University of Oslo, and was accepted. For some reason, I assumed the courses would be taught in English. When I got the registration instructions in the mail, it turned out the courses were taught in Norwegian. I canceled my registration right away, to Anita's disappointment. I decided instead to study at the Hebrew University of Jerusalem.

A cadet in the officers' course, 1962

In the officers' course, before storming a hill, 1962

Intelligence officers' course – a swim in the Sea of Galilee; I am in the top row, fifth from right

Intelligence officers' course (the instructors are wearing sunglasses to remain anonymous), 1963; I am in the bottom row, fifth from right

The brigade reconnaissance company on the march, 1963. At the head of the company, first from right: *Eli Ovant; I am to his left.*

In an exercise in the Negev desert, 1963

Graduates of the reconnaissance officers' course, 1963. Top row: far right, Bentzy Carmeli; I am fifth from right. Third row from bottom, second from left: *Amir Nahumi.* Bottom row, fourth from right: *Yoram Mendel.*

At the base in Camp Natan, near Beersheba, 1964

*The march to
Jerusalem, 1964*

*The group I commanded for the IDF championship
for the ten-kilometer rapid march, 1964; I am first
from left*

UNIVERSITETET I OSLO

UNIVERSITY OF OSLO
Office for Foreign Students
Kontoret for utenlandske studenter

OSLO, July 22, 1964
Univ. jnr. /WKW
Bes oppgitt ved korresp.

Lieutenant Ehud Diskin
P.B. 2825
Israel Defense Army
i.s.K.a.a.l.

Dear Mr. Diskin:

Further to my letter to you of May 9th this year I have
the pleasure to inform you that you have been accepted
in the Faculty of Natural Sciences of the University of
Oslo this Fall. The study will start on August 20th and
you have been placed in Group 6 A. Kindly see the
enclosed papers.

./.
./.

Enclosed you will also find application forms for
matriculation in this University. Kindly return the
forms, duly filled in to this office at your earliest
convenience so as to make sure that you will be in time
for the matriculation ceremony on September 1st, where
personal attendance is necessary.

If, on the other hand your plans of study have changed,
kindly let us know as soon as possible, in order that
your seat in the Faculty of Natural Sciences be given
to another student.

Hoping to see you here in early August.

Sincerely yours,
for Mrs. Guro Nordahl-Olsen
Foreign Student Adviser

Wenche Kielland Wiborg
Wenche Kielland Wiborg
Cand.mag

Letter of acceptance to the University of Oslo, 1964

Chapter 5
"MY BROTHERS, GLORIOUS HEROES"

From a speech given by Colonel Shmuel Gorodish, commander of the 7th Brigade, at the end of the Six-Day War.

Blue smoke rose from the bubbling liquid with a sound that portended catastrophe. The chemistry lab instructor, Yaakov, ran toward us with a look of terror on his face. He ordered me to immediately halt the experiment I was conducting with my friend, Arieh "Golan" Germanski.

Arieh was tall and freckled with reddish hair. He was laconic, never saying a word unless it was necessary. And he was an outstanding Ping-Pong player – I greatly enjoyed our competitive matches. Both Arieh and I had to work full time jobs, and we were by no means good students. All we really wanted was a signed confirmation in the academic registry declaring we had taken and passed the required courses with reasonable grades.

As a freshman, I majored in physics and math, which meant I had to take chemistry as a physics requirement. When we found out we had to do eight experiments in the chemistry lab, Arieh and I hastily copied the results of the first four from other students and began with experiment number five to avoid falling behind.

However, Yaakov not only put a stop to our experiment, but also angrily told us we were dangerous. He said our bumbling could have blown up the whole lab, including everyone inside. Yaakov was basically a good fellow, and he told us that as long as we never showed our faces in the lab again, he would give us the credits at the end of the year showing that we carried out all the experiments to his satisfaction. We were very pleased with this arrangement.

The reason I did not go to lectures, and preferred to copy the homework and exercises, was that I had to work a full-time job to support my family. Upon finishing my army service, I had married a woman named Miriam.

In the army, one of the trainees had been enthusiastic about a pleasant and attractive female soldier who served as an assistant in the dental clinic at the Kastina base near Kiryat Malachi in southern Israel. Intrigued by his enthusiasm, I went to see Miriam for myself, and I was equally excited. She and I were very young and took a romantic interest in each other.

Despite warnings from my mother and my friends that I was too young to get married, my romantic feelings triumphed over reason, and we did it anyway. We promptly had two kids, Yarriv and Anat. My duty as the head of the family was to work hard to keep us solvent. Eventually, in line with my mother's and my friends' warnings, Miriam and I found that we did not have much in common, and within three years we had separated. Several years later, we officially divorced.

I enjoyed some of the courses in my first year of studies, especially algebra and set theory, but I detested differential calculus. I will always remember the tutor in horror, whose name I did not care to remember. He would flood the blackboard with formulas that were comprehensible only to him and a select few students.

His eyes shone with mad intensity, and his whole body swayed with passion as his hand scrawled strange and sundry formulas in chalk. After he filled four blackboards with formulas and reached the end of some proof of a complex differential equation, he would smile with satisfaction, as if he had discovered the perfect solution to one of the most puzzling problems in the universe.

I soon realized I was not cut out for mathematics, and decided to major in economics and statistics. It was not hard to get accepted into the economics program, but at the end of the year there was a selection exam – only 30 percent would pass and go on to the next year. Luckily for me, I was among those who passed.

In addition to our major subjects, we had to choose four introductory electives. Arieh and I opted for the easiest choices, our criteria being that we would not have to invest much time and effort, and easily pass the exams. One class that met our criteria was Introduction to Sociology.

Our plan was to find a female student who regularly attended class, completed the work, and took clear and articulate notes. This turned out to be the charming Shifra, who had taken Introduction to Sociology a year earlier. We photographed her notes, took a few days to memorize them, and went to the exam feeling that we were prepared.

However, when I saw the exam, my face clouded over. Not only did I not know the answers, I did not even understand the questions. I turned my gaze to Arieh, who stared back at me in utter bewilderment and helplessness. After a couple of minutes we got up and walked out. Of course, we both scored a grade of zero. It turned out that our test was in Introduction to Sociology for non-sociologists, while Shifra was a Sociology major, so her course material was completely different from ours.

I also had to take electives for my major, and here too I looked for the easiest breaks. For one of these classes I hit upon Regime Theory. The lecturer was Professor Emanuel Gutmann. After I dozed off during the first of his lectures, I did not return for the second. During that first lecture, I sat as usual on the hindmost bench of the large hall, next to the door, so that if I needed to escape in the middle of the lecture, I would not attract much attention. Sitting so far away, however, ultimately turned out to be a disadvantage when I tried to identify the professor later.

I needed his signature as proof that I attended his lectures, so I went to his office during office hours. When my turn came, I opened the door, and to my astonishment, there were two professors sitting there.

I feared that if I approached the wrong one and said, "Professor Gutmann, I would be grateful if you would sign here and confirm that I was present at your lectures," and the individual were to answer, "Excuse me, but I am not Professor Gutmann," that would be my bitter end. I quickly stepped back, closed the door, and let the next student approach. Only when I found out which one was Professor Gutmann did I return and get his signature.

Another basic course I chose was Economic History. The lecturer was Professor David Flusser. Among the basic courses, it was a popular one. For several years Professor Flusser had not changed a word of his lectures, and one of the students, who had good business sense, printed and sold a notebook containing the lectures word for word. But to be on the safe side, I went and listened to one of his lectures.

To my surprise, out of about one hundred students who were registered for the course, only one student besides me had showed up. The other student even bothered to take notes, and Professor Flusser took comfort from this. After every few sentences, he would ask the student if he had finished jotting down what he said.

While I was at university, I successfully completed a course for GADNA instructors, as well as a course in judo. I worked as a GADNA instructor in Jerusalem's Seligsberg High School for Girls, and with a group of delinquent youngsters through the Hebrew Youth Club. I also passed exams in education and attained a teaching certificate. I went on to serve as a regular substitute teacher for math at Seligsberg. I enjoyed teaching math, but I had to deflect the flirtations of some of the students who, instead of paying attention in class, would stare at me with romantic looks.

בית הנוער העברי   ירושלים שׁל מרץ 1965

ירושלים

הריני לאשר בזה כיאהוד דיסקין הדריך במוסדנו

שׁנת ס/64, והוכיח את עצמו כמדתיך טוב לשׁביעת רצוננו.

הנ"ל עבד בשׂכר שׁל מדריך שׁלב א' בעל שׁתי שׁנות

חק, במוסדנו רכשׁ את שׁנת הגתק השׁלישׁית שׁלו.

בכבוד רב

מנהל/בית הנוער העברי

Letter of appreciation from Seligsberg High School, 1965

The Hadassah Alice Seligsberg Comprehensive High School

Mr. Ehud Diskin was employed at our school as a temporary math teacher. He also tutored student groups in study assistance lessons.

Mr. Diskin performed the job perfectly and contributed to the advancement of the students.

A. Pierst
Principal Deputy for Educational Matters

בית הספר התיכון המקיף של הדסה ע״ש עליס סליגסברג

THE HADASSAH ALICE SELIGSBERG COMPREHENSIVE HIGH SCHOOL

Tel. 25400 טלפון   P.O.B. 1114 ת.ד.

ירושלים

<u>לכל המעונין בדבר</u>

מר אהוד דיסקין שמש בבית-ספרנו כמורה ממלא
מקום במתמטיקה וכן למד קבוצות תלמידים
במסגרת שעורי עזר.

מר דיסקין עשה עבודתו ללא דופי וגרם רבות
להתקדמות התלמידים.

א׳ פירסט
סגן מנהל לעינינים חינוכיים

*Letter of appreciation from Seligsberg High
School, 1965*

**The Hadassah Alice Seligsberg Comprehensive
High School**

Mr. Ehud Diskin was employed at our school as a
temporary math teacher. He also tutored student groups
in study assistance lessons.

Mr. Diskin performed the job perfectly and contributed
to the advancement of the students.

A. Pierst
Principal Deputy for Educational Matters

Me, a GADNA instructor, 1965

In 1966, instead of looking for part-time jobs as a teacher to finance my second year of studies, I decided to commit myself to a two-year career position as an education officer in the army, by the end of which I intended to complete my BA. Initially, I served at the Nachal Sorek base, about an hour's drive from Jerusalem, at the headquarters of the 14th Brigade. The brigade's commander was Col. Moshe "Mussa" Peled, who was later a general and commander of the Armored Corps.

As an education officer I was responsible for all educational programming, including lectures and Cultural Encounter events that were intended to increase unity and develop soldiers' sensitivities to the complex differences within Israeli society. I handled all the logistics and publicity for these events, and I felt as though I could make a difference in the army by strengthening the officers' and soldiers' sense of belonging and commitment to the Land of Israel, and to the people and their legacy.

My job included setting up the brigade's cultural staff, for which I needed to find the right soldiers. One of the candidates I auditioned was a soldier named Avi Toledano, who went on to become a popular singer both in Israel and internationally, even representing Israel in the 1982 Eurovision Song Contest in Europe. Avi had immigrated to Israel only a year earlier from his native country of Morocco, which he left by forging his father's signature on a required form. He served as an ordinary soldier in the brigade's 52nd Battalion. As part of my search for singers, I auditioned him informally in the canteen, and I was immediately impressed by his pleasant voice, self-assured appearance, and singing style. Avi Toledano wanted to be a combat soldier, and he completed his training in the battalion. After that, however, I arranged for him to join the Armored Corps's musical troupe. I would like to believe that I had played a part in getting his career going.

From the 14th Brigade, I later transferred to the Armored Corps Headquarters. My commander was Lt. Col. Moshe Nativ, the Adjutancy Officer of the Armored Corps.

In June 1967, the Six-Day War broke out and changed everything. In the weeks leading up to the war, the Egyptians closed in on us from the south, the Jordanians from the east, and the Syrians from the north. All the Arab leaders had promised to destroy Israel as their people demonstrated in the streets. Those weeks were terrible, and we thought Israel's days were numbered. Amid a cloud of fear and tension, the country prepared for a holocaust. Ordinary citizens listlessly filled sandbags and dug trenches.

The depressed state permeated everything while we waited for decisive action to take place. A muddled, stammering radio speech by Prime Minister Levi Eshkol did nothing to boost morale. Nor did a purposely misleading speech by legendary soldier-politician Moshe Dayan, now serving as Defense Minister, in which he said it was already too late to act. Attempting to use deception, the IDF discharged reserve soldiers en masse. The aim was to trick our enemies into thinking our army had no plans for offensive operations. But I had no doubt war was imminent, and just as I expected, after nearly a month of despondency and despair, we launched a pre-emptive strike. The Israeli air force essentially won the war in three hours, destroying most of the enemy planes and leaving it to the ground forces to rout the enemy armies and conquer territories.

If it's to be said that the air force won the war, it was the Armored Corps that set the tone for the ground combat. The tank forces surged through the Sinai with the aim of destroying the Egyptian army and conquering the peninsula. They included three divisions, and two of these, under the command of Maj. Gen. Ariel "Arik" Sharon[39] and Maj. Gen. Avraham Yaffe respectively, penetrated and took over central Sinai. The third, which I joined, was under the command of Maj. Gen. Israel "Talik" Tal. This division mounted the assaults in northern Sinai, moving past Israel's defensive deployments in the Gaza Strip, pushing to the town of el-Arish, and then on to the Suez Canal. The 7th Brigade executed

---

[39] A major Israeli figure who later became defense minister and prime minister. He died early in 2014.

most of the assaults under the command of Shmuel Gorodish, then a colonel.

Gorodish emerged as one of the Six-Day War's greatest heroes. Later, after the Yom Kippur War, he became my friend. At one point he mentioned to me that as a brigadier general and a major general, he was told more than once that he was en route to becoming the chief of staff. But that was before the Yom Kippur War and the conclusions of the Agranat Commission, which was appointed to investigate the war's failures.

Lt. Col. Moshe Nativ ordered me to head east to the headquarters. However, I made my way in the opposite direction, toward the front in the Sinai desert. It was there that I thought I could contribute more to the effort.

We sat in the cabin of a pickup truck – the driver, Sergeant (res.) Shaltiel, and I, a twenty-three-year-old lieutenant – believing for some reason that we would be active in the combat effort. Sergeant Shaltiel sat tense and ready, gripping his loaded Uzi so tightly that the joints of his fingers were white. He was bent forward, peering into the dark, trying to make out whatever might happen. He seemed to steel himself in advance for a rain of bullets or shells, even though no preparation would help in the face of fire. He wore a look of self-confidence and seemed to tell himself, "I have to know that I'm doing all I possibly can."

We passed supply convoys as the pickup truck jostled its way over potholes. As we got closer to the front, the convoys thinned out, and we saw more and more tanks that had been hit or gotten stuck. My throat constricted when I saw the tank crewmen beside their tanks. Their faces were sooty, eyes red from exhaustion; all they wanted was to do the repairs and return to the front.

We ran into white-haired, wrinkled Master Sergeant Shmulik, riding on an old Sherman tank. He had the smile of someone who has seen the Messiah coming. "I'm bringing a fresh tank to the war," he kept repeating, as if the fate of the campaign depended on whether this tank would join the key battle at the decisive moment.

By morning Sergeant Shaltiel and I joined up with the 7th Brigade at the Jiradi Pass in Sinai. Lt. Col. Nativ received us icily. "I told you to head for the east," he said to me in a grim commander's tone.

"I thought I could do more here," I answered. Nativ did not say another word, but his eyes were angry. Despite his initial displeasure, after the war he promoted me to captain as an outstanding officer.

I do not know if I was punished from above or below, or perhaps given a chance to do a good deed, but the task foisted on me was to guard Maj. Efraim Tzemel, the Military Rabbi of the Armored Corps, and go deep into closed-off zones to extract corpses of fallen IDF soldiers. Rabbi Tzemel was an exceptional person. His face, with its thick beard, exuded kindness and helpfulness toward others.

I was given a squad of soldiers to command, and we advanced by vehicle into the zones, which had been conquered and partially mopped up. Egyptian soldiers still wandered about, but they looked more pathetic than dangerous. Their choice was between death by our soldiers' bullets or surrendering to be taken prisoner. At least in the latter, if they succeeded, they could escape the heat and thirst of the merciless desert.

Part of our operation had to be carried out on foot, with me leading the troops. We crossed trenches and barriers, determined to reach any spot where the rabbi thought we might find bodies of our soldiers. Even in a minefield, we persevered. Naively, I thought they were anti-vehicle mines, and took some extra cautionary measures I learned in the sabotage course I took as a scout. I studied the layout of the rows of mines in the field, and tried to navigate between them. Shortly after this mission, Lt. Col. Georgie Gur, the engineering officer of the corps, informed me that the minefields in the area were mixed and also included anti-personnel mines. His words left me wondering whether it was due to my training as a sapper and my cautionary measures that none of us had been harmed by the anti-personnel mines? Or was it just luck from the heavens that Rabbi Tzemel brought with him? Perhaps it was proof of a saying from the Talmudic sages: "Those who perform good deeds are safe" (*Pesachim*, 8a)?

Each wounded or dead soldier hurt my soul, and I needed all my spiritual strength to withstand this difficult mission. Near the Rafah Crossing, we came to a Patton tank with the commander still propped beside the turret, a fatal wound to his head. His weapon, an Uzi submachine gun, lay by the turret's entrance. I took the Uzi and at first thought of bringing it to his parents as a last memento of their son, but then I decided against it. Nearby, people from the military rabbinate were striving to extract the corpse of a soldier from a jeep that had taken a direct hit. They worked with an axe, a spatula, and other tools. It was a dreadful thing to do, and to watch.

I was stunned in particular to hear of the death of Capt. Shamai Kaplan, who had been a company commander in the 7th Brigade and was killed in battle in the el-Arish area. Shamai was an officer admired by both his commanders and his subordinates. He had been an operations officer for the 82nd Battalion, where I served as a scout while still in the standing army, and he had been my commander. I had developed respect and affection for him as a talented, shrewd commander and a fine, considerate person.

Capt. Bentzy Carmeli, who had been commander of my reconnaissance company during my compulsory service, was severely wounded during the offensives waged by the 7th Brigade. He was given up for lost on the battlefield, abandoned without further medical treatment. His brother-in-law, Capt. Yochanan Magal, who was a munitions officer, saw Bentzy lying "half-dead" on the ground and rushed him to emergency medical treatment, which saved his life.

After the war, I visited Bentzy at the Armored Corps School at the Julis base near Ashkelon, where he was an instructor. It was a frightful scene to encounter. One of his eyes was prosthetic, and he was completely deaf in one ear. But he survived, and he insisted on continuing his combat service. Six years later, he died in battle during the Yom Kippur War. His death was a painful blow.

After the Six-Day War, in my role as education officer, I accompanied the journalist and author Shabtai Teveth as he interviewed commanders and soldiers, gathering material for his book on the Armored Corps in the war, *The Tanks of Tammuz*. It was revealing to hear commanders' stories firsthand. Particularly memorable was a meeting with Col. Issachar "Yiska" Shadmi, who commanded a brigade that fought in the central part of Sinai.

Yiska asserted that in war you have to act wisely, not wildly. "If you charge forward with abandon you suffer unnecessary losses," he said. He denigrated heroic battles that resulted both in numerous heroes and numerous casualties. He believed that if you were clever and used the right tactics, you could have the same achievements with fewer losses. These words made a deep impression on me, and later, when I was a commander, I tried to put them into practice.

Indeed, many of the IDF soldiers and officers were heroes, prepared to sacrifice their lives. However, if the senior officers knew how to plan and conduct the campaigns more efficiently, there would not have been a need for so much sacrifice, or so many casualties. It is no secret that in the aftermath of the Six-Day War, the Yom Kippur War, and the subsequent wars, there was much criticism over battles that could have been waged differently with considerably less loss of life. That, however, is true of every army and every war, not only of the IDF.

When the war was over, I returned to Jerusalem, where I knew that in the battle for the Old City, my good friend and table tennis competitor Arieh Germanski had fallen. Arieh, serving in the reconnaissance company of the Jerusalem Brigade, was riding in jeep along the Old City wall, near the Dung Gate,[40] when he was shot and killed.

---

[40] One of the gates in the walls of the Old City of Jerusalem. The gate is situated near the southeast corner of the old city, southwest of the Temple Mount.

For nineteen years, high walls had protected the residents of Jerusalem from snipers of the Jordanian Legion. Every few years, and for reasons unbeknownst to us, they would fire into the city. Now these walls were down, and it was wonderfully exhilarating. We could see new vistas, previously concealed, in their full splendor. Visiting the eastern part of Jerusalem, seeing the places we could not go in the past, was emotionally affecting. My father, who had grown up in the Old City, was even more moved, and we went together to the Hurva Synagogue[41] where he had prayed years earlier. Jerusalem had changed in other ways too. It had become a noisy tourist attraction and no longer had the intimacy I experienced as a child with my family, my friends, and my fellow students.

After the war, driving to Jerusalem for a visit, I picked up a hitchhiking soldier at the Latrun Junction. He told me he belonged to a combat engineering unit along the main road from Tel Aviv to Jerusalem. Those soldiers had delivered an ultimatum to five Arab villages in the Latrun area: They had to leave immediately as part of the plans for resettling the territories won during the war. When the ultimatum had expired, they came with tractors and "flattened the place," as he put it. Amid all the sorrow about what happened, we have to remember that this action was necessary. In the War of Independence, the Jordanians blocked the main road from Tel Aviv to Jerusalem, and these five villages took over the land in this area. For nineteen years, until the Six-Day War, all Israelis were forced to take an alternative, long, and dangerous route that caused many car accidents.

A few years later, when I was studying for my PhD, I analyzed the issue of the settlements with my adviser, Professor Yoram Peles. We agreed that at that time Israel should have adopted the decisive

---

[41] The synagogue was founded in the early eighteenth century, but it was destroyed by Muslims a few years later, in 1721. The plot lay in ruins for more than 140 years and became known as the Ruin, or *Hurva* in Hebrew. In 1864, the Perushim rebuilt the synagogue.

approach that David Ben-Gurion, prime minister and defense minister during the War of Independence, had taken to ensure Israel's future as a Jewish state: That Israeli settlements should have only been established west of the decided border.

Unfortunately, the prime minister during the Six-Day War was not Ben-Gurion, but Levi Eshkol. During 1966, the year preceding the Six-Day War, his popularity had sunk to an unprecedented low, and a satirical booklet called *All the Eshkol Jokes* made the rounds. Perhaps the most popular of the jokes was one about his apparent inability to make a decision. In it, Eshkol is asked if he wants tea or coffee, and he replies, "Half coffee, half tea."

Eventually he came to be seen more positively, but regardless, he did not make a decision about the borders. At that time, the media was not as powerful and vituperative as today, and every measure the government took was accepted. In retrospect, it seems clear to me that this lack of decision, along with the irresolution of subsequent prime ministers on the issue of settling the territories, made the issue of settlements problematic.

If the various prime ministers, starting with Eshkol, had made firm decisions about the future borders, it would have prevented much suffering for the settlers, a considerable portion of which were Zionists and pioneers who sometimes found themselves deceived by the government and their own leaders.

*Captain Bentzy Carmeli, fighter and
friend*

*General Israel Tal ("Talik"), bent
over a map of the battle with Colonel
Shmuel Gorodish, 1967 (courtesy of
the IDF Spokesperson's Unit)*

Captain Shamai Kaplan

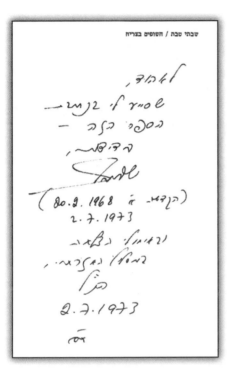

שבתי טבת / חשופים בצריח

A personal dedication from author Shabtai Teveth in his book The Tanks of Tammuz.

It reads:

To Ehud, who helped me with the writing of this book.

In friendship,
Shabtai Teveth
First dedication February 20, 1968

My wishes for your success in civilian life.

[signed]
July 2, 1973
[signature]

Me beside a damaged Egyptian T-34 tank, 1967

Tanks lumbering toward Abu Ageilah, 1967 (courtesy of the IDF Spokesperson's Unit)

Patton tanks of the 7th Brigade entering Khan Yunis, 1967 (courtesy of the IDF Spokesperson's Unit)

Chapter 6
THE WAR OF ATTRITION

The Six-Day War interrupted my university studies, so I decided to take some additional time off to express the patriotic emotions and passions that surged within me. I decided to make the transition from education officer to ordinary tank officer, and become part of the Armored Corps.

I had never taken an interest in tank mechanics. I always preferred to see hills and valleys in their natural, serene state, not as part of a military exercise. However, if you want to defend the country and keep the enemy at bay, you also need to know the technical secrets of the tank and have a tactical grasp of topographical features. It was for this reason that I took a course on operating tanks. We learned about the technical and tactical aspects of the tank, and how best to use it as a mobile force that wields firepower.

I then joined the prestigious 79th Battalion and was made a deputy company commander. The battalion's prestige stemmed from 1964, when it was the first to receive American Patton tanks, which were then considered state-of-the-art weapons. The commanders had their own clique, into which only veteran professionals were welcome. Whoever had been "converted" from another corps, or was not an outstanding professional, was inevitably seen as an outsider.

After the Six-Day War, the Egyptians were unable to reconquer the Sinai territory that Israel had won. Instead, they attacked Israel in hopes of exhausting the Israeli forces. Egyptian President Nasser even advocated for extreme destruction, saying, "We cannot conquer Sinai, but we can wear out Israel and break her spirit." For three years, these battles and incidents of fire between Israel and Egypt were dubbed the "War of Attrition," lasting from 1968 to 1970.

To protect Sinai during that time, two tank brigades of the standing army, the 14th and the 401st, were deployed. One would hold the line at the Suez Canal while the other occupied the rear, and every few months they would trade places.

The 79th Battalion was part of the 401st Brigade, and we were stationed in western Sinai at the southern reach of the canal. The battalion commander, Lt. Col. Haim Erez, was a superb field commander. Every morning he would leave early for patrols with a jeep and driver, not returning until nightfall. The deputy battalion commander, Maj. Gilad Aviram, was a South American immigrant. He was the battalion commander's right-hand man and eventually made it all the way to brigadier general.

There were three companies in the battalion. The commander of Company B was Ilan Maoz, a talented young fellow who treated his dog like a person, and people like dogs. I served as Ilan's deputy company commander. But I wanted to be a company commander, and as time went on, my patience wore thin. I asked Haim Erez if it was possible, but he thought I still was not ready and then coined his maxim, "Better to wait half a year and be a company commander than half a year minus company commander." In other words, a premature appointment would soon get me dismissed from the post. I had no choice but to accept the decision and wait.

Finally, in 1968, the day arrived that I was appointed company commander, replacing Ilan in Company B. I felt I had fulfilled a calling: company commander in the glorious 79th, the first to be given the Pattons, a battalion profoundly influenced by the legacy of the Six-Day War. I was befriended by fellow company commanders Dubi Israeli, who had grown up with tanks and was in charge of Company A, and Rami Cohen, a veteran officer and converted infantry fighter, who was head of Company C.

As a commander of Company B, I did my utmost to retain the post. I still lacked experience. The course I took more than a year before gave me theoretical knowledge but not much practical savvy on how to run a tank unit. I had never taken either a company commanders' course or an Armored Corps officers' course. The only officers' course I had taken was the infantry-oriented operations course, and it would help very little in my new role. My previous service as a battalion scout did not help me either as commander of a tank company, aside from my navigation experience. Still, I devoted myself entirely to the tanks and the soldiers and tried to do my best. In retrospect, I realized my insecurities and lack of experience made my professional progress go much slower.

I will never forget the first exercise I carried out. One tank platoon gave covering fire while another attacked in a flanking maneuver. Haim Erez's face filled with despair when he witnessed the poor execution.

One day a new battalion commander appeared. Lt. Col. Avigdor "Yanosh" Ben-Gal was tall, thin, undoubtedly professional, and a little strange. He was impatient, intolerant of others, with a tendency for hysteria. He also had a nasal, grating voice. Yanosh demanded nothing less than perfection; any mistake, any imperfect execution from me or my company, evoked screams and reprimands. In his nasal castigations he would enumerate and analyze our "catastrophes," as he called them, and leave me completely frustrated. I strove for the best possible result, but he always found fault with something, making me feel like I was causing horrific disasters. When I tried to tell him that while his criticisms were accurate, it would be better if he just stated them plainly instead of getting swept away in pointless and insulting superlatives, he admitted I was right. And yet, right or not, very soon afterward, his nerves betrayed him and he fell back into hysteria.

Five years later, in the Yom Kippur War, Yanosh commanded the 7th Brigade in the Golan Heights. Under his stewardship, the

7th was credited with blocking the Syrians' advance in the Northern Heights during the battle of the Valley of Tears. In 1977, he was appointed head of Northern Command, and in 1982 he became commander of Corps 446 of the Central Command, which fought the Syrians in Eastern Lebanon during the First Lebanon War.

The recruits in my company came from the May draft, meaning that quite a few of them had never even finished high school. Had I not known that Israel had compulsory education, I would have wondered whether some had even completed elementary school. There was Tzion Gatka, a lean guy with an anxious gaze, whom I was supposed to turn into a tank gunner. The loud boom of the tank gun made him shut his eyes with fright. He could not make out where the shells had hit to help him correct his aim for the next time. There was Arieh Baumkler, a loader-signaler who did not send his underwear to the laundry, instead wearing each pair until it was black, then tossing it into the trash. There was also Bar-Ratzon the driver, who would drive his tank straight into another tank if irked. Of course, there were also good crewmen like my gunners Zvi Offgang, Haim Raskanski, Shmuel Segal, and others.

We were given few leaves and life was not easy. We awoke at dawn and would take the tanks out for the day's work under camouflage nets. I imposed strict discipline on the company, but in their free time I would let the men unwind. I recall the weekend when they took cold cuts and other food from the kitchen and had a party. On Sunday, when Deputy Battalion Commander Major Amram Mitzna returned from his leave, he ordered my company to eat nothing but battle rations outside the dining hall for a week.

Eventually Mitzna and I became good friends. Mitzna had served in the Six-Day War as an operations officer in the 79th Battalion. He was wounded three times but kept fighting, and he was awarded a Medal of Distinguished Service. For his service in the Yom Kippur War, he received the Chief of Staff Citation. In the beginning of the 1990s he ended his military career as a major general, having been head of Central Command and head of the Planning Directorate. After retiring from the IDF, Mitzna entered politics and served a few years as mayor of Haifa, later becoming a parliament member.

One day, we returned from an exchange of fire with the Egyptians and had to reload the tanks. My soldiers went to Unger, the ammunition man, for replenishment. He was a bureaucrat just like his boss, Capt. Roland Aloni, Commander of the Headquarters Company. Unger told my soldiers that his commander was at an airfield in Sinai, and he could not honor their request until the commander returned and gave his approval. As a quick and effective solution, my soldiers tied Unger to a post and took the ammunition.

Yanosh did not say a word to me about that until, on another occasion, one of my company's tanks sank into a quagmire and had to be hauled out. He said to me angrily, "Problems in Company B again?"

I asked, "What do you mean, 'again'?"

He shot right back with, "What about the rough stuff?" I knew he meant Unger.

Roland was indeed a classic bureaucrat. He carried his big black book everywhere, treating it like an infallible source of wisdom. One day, when I told Deputy Battalion Commander Mitzna that there was not enough ammunition in the bunker, he summoned Roland for an explanation. I again mentioned the lack of armor-piercing shells. Roland jumped as if bitten by a snake, opened his black book, and read fervently, "Please, there are eighty-five armor-piercing shells in the bunker."

I replied, "I was in the bunker just now, and there were no armor-piercing shells."

But Roland patted his book and said resolutely, "You are wrong, look, there are eighty-five shells." It was his book that determined reality; if reality differed from his book, then reality had a problem. Just as in government ministries, bureaucracy is part of the army, both in headquarters and in field units. It exists wherever there are people like Roland.

Meanwhile, I had to be very tough to maintain my company's discipline. Although my approach may have been demanding, insisting on a high degree of professionalism saves lives. Pinhas Kabasa, a loader-signaler, asked his platoon commander if he could have a talk with me. When he came in for the talk, he saluted and said, "Commander, being a tank crewman is, for me, a very severe burden."

I realized right away that these were words that someone else had put in his mouth. I thought to myself, he could not have known words like "severe" and "burden." I answered him curtly, "So you think I have it easy?"

That caught him completely off guard. I preached Zionism to him, and told him we were defending the homeland. It seemed to calm and boost him. Generally the soldiers in my company, even if some were mediocre, were dedicated fighters who bravely faced adversity. They truly did carry the nation's security and well-being on their backs.

Alongside the ongoing skirmishes, a strange dialogue developed between the Egyptians and us. It was a dialogue of signs. On their side, they would write words on a big blank board on the west side of the canal, and we would respond with a big placard on our side, east of the canal. For example, one of their signs proclaimed, "Sinai will be your grave." We came back with, "Your next grave will be Cairo." Given our eventual numerous casualties in the Yom Kippur War, even though the IDF ultimately turned the tide and won dramatically, their signs had more truth behind them.

Usually the messages were in English, except for one of ours that was in Russian, which was intended for the Russian soldiers and technicians who were helping the Egyptians.

The sign read, "Comrades, it's time to go home." These words were written by the Russian-speaking grandfather of 2nd Lt. Rami Kozlov, a platoon commander in my company.

Every few weeks there would be a shooting incident between us and the Egyptians, until the night when intensive war broke out. One evening in 1968, I was in a bunker across from the hospital in Ismailia, a town on the west bank of the Suez Canal. My company was deployed along the canal from the Al-Firdan Bridge in the north, down to the Tomb of the Unknown Soldier in the south. I decided to carry out a nighttime inspection of my dispersed soldiers, so the command car driver and I set out on a patrol.

It was a moonlit night, and we could see well enough to drive without the headlights. The moon calmly suffused the dunes around us. I started patrolling from north to south, amazed by my soldiers' lack of preparedness. One of the guards had simply gone to sleep beside the canal. He had to be daring, dumb, or both at once to snooze right across from the enemy. I ended my patrol near the Tomb of the Unknown Soldier, where I watched the platoon commander, 2nd Lt. Freddie Cohen, lead his platoon in the morning exercises.

I went back to my bunker and spent the day resting and dealing with routine matters. As evening came, I decided to make another surprise inspection. Who would expect it two nights in a row? I sent someone to fetch the driver, but he was not to be found. So I decided to do the inspection by myself – a bold move, as I would be patrolling at night along the canal with the Egyptian army encamped on the other side. A few minutes after I started driving, I heard shooting from the south, and the whole area lit up with flares.

I stopped short and picked up the field radio wondering, was this an ambush my own company had laid while it was still dusk, and were they now firing mistakenly at the battalion's own patrol When I found out that our own ambush had already been removed, I immediately knew it was the Egyptians who were doing the shooting.

It turned out that, in the southern part of my company's zone, the Egyptians had set an ambush for the two jeeps of our battalion's patrol. One of these jeeps, amazingly, made it through the dense array of mines that the Egyptians had laid on the route. The other jeep hit a mine, injuring its soldiers. The Egyptian ambushers, about ten soldiers, dragged one of these men to the west bank of the canal, where he died of his severe wounds. The sound of shooting came from every direction, and the entire area was aglow with the light of Egyptian flares.

The mines had been planted so densely on the road that the chances of any jeep getting past them at night were nil. And yet the first jeep did just that, while the second jeep hit a mine. One could say the soldiers in the first jeep were very lucky. An officer in that vehicle had fought a year earlier in the Six-Day War. He was in a clash with the Egyptians, I was told, in which both the signal operator behind him and the driver beside him were injured, but he got out unscathed. The probability of an officer making it unharmed through two such incidents is close to zero. Apparently, there are some things human beings cannot quite explain or understand – maybe it is fate, or maybe it is just luck.

The War of Attrition was exhausting, depressing, and a war without direction, lacking purpose or hope. We were drowning in a sea of Egyptian artillery, showered by Katyusha rockets[42] and mortar shells.

It was the end of the 1960s, and in Tel Aviv the people danced to the music of the era. But in the Sinai Desert, on the banks of the canal, there was a different type of music: the sound of noisy tank treads accompanied by mortar and cannon fire, while the stifling sandstorms continuously stung our faces. We were constantly exhausted, sleeping uncomfortably for many nights inside our tanks. We did our best to rest among the shells and instruments. During the day we were exhausted from the desert heat that beat down on our heads and inflamed the steel of the tanks. We wanted to wear out the Egyptians. They wanted to wear us out. And in the end, we were all worn out.

---

[42] A type of surface-to-surface rocket first built and used by the Soviet Union during World War II.

As mentioned earlier, our brigade, the 401st, held the line of the Suez Canal along with another armored brigade of the standing army. Our tank battalion, the 79th, alternated with the 46th, the brigade's other tank battalion. When it was my company's turn to hold the line, we would immediately take our positions, and if there was shooting, we would carry out the rapid-fire destruction of all enemy targets. When we were not at the canal we were about 10 miles to the rear. To maintain the element of surprise against the Egyptians, my company had to move quickly to the central sector of the canal, and each time it was in a different place. At the beginning of the war, I was inexperienced and not particularly competent, but the combat experience I accrued steadily improved my abilities.

As per usual, when my company approached the canal, I commanded my men to spread out, so they could fire from various points along the shore. The results of such surprise volleys were always spectacular, as Egyptian tanks, bunkers, and soldiers were knocked out. However, on one occasion, as we were approaching the canal from behind some sand dunes, we came under heavy Egyptian fire. We took cover behind the dunes, shifting from place to place, but the barrage continued. At first, I did not understand how the Egyptians could have detected my company's presence, until I noticed an Egyptian soldier on the western side of the canal, sitting atop an old electric tower that was very high and made of latticed metal strips.

He was directing the debilitating artillery fire. I immediately turned my tank gun sideways, aimed toward the target, and gave the order to fire. Zvi Offgang was my tank gunner, and an excellent one, but he fired and missed. I ordered him to adjust the sights and continue firing at the tower. After a few more shells, the tower started listing to one side like a tree being chopped down by an ax. The giant pole increasingly tilted to one side, and finally collapsed with a satisfying noise. The Egyptian soldier was thrown from a height of about 30 yards. At last, the Egyptian shelling stopped.

We were short on manpower, and I had to use all of our tank crews for our combat maneuvers, including the crew commanded by Sgt. Mordechai Parasol, which I had originally made a reserve crew. When the company first began training, I realized that Sgt. Parasol was a poor tank commander. In one of the last exercises, he even managed to fire at our own forces instead of the enemy. In another exercise, when I told him on the radio to retrace his steps, he replied that he had lost his traces. Parasol's tank crew included Tzion Gatka, the gunner who so feared the boom of the tank's gun that he would shut his eyes while firing. And the signaler and driver were, to put it mildly, not of the highest caliber.

In debriefings after incidents, Parasol would usually stand up when it was his turn to talk, and with a serious, self-important demeanor describe his crew's actions – firing, destroying targets – as heroics on the order of James Bond. Of course, I did not believe a word of these accounts, but to go easy on him I would say, "Okay, Parasol, we heard, be seated." I could hardly believe that a gunner could hit a target with his eyes closed.

After one incident, when it was Parasol's turn to tell his tale again, he stood up and said, "I went to the dugout and two Egyptian tanks fired at me immediately. I got down and crept to another dugout. I fired at the first tank and slightly missed, so I adjusted the sights, hit it, and destroyed it. I then immediately knocked out the second tank." Parasol didn't stop there. "Suddenly I was under fire from four Egyptian bunkers. I fired at the first bunker, just missed, made the adjustment and hit it. I kept firing and destroyed the other three bunkers."

I was, of course, very skeptical about such an exploit, and as usual I said to him in a dubious tone, "Okay, Parasol, we heard, be seated."

To my surprise Deputy Commander Lt. Shlomo Ginzburg, an outstanding officer and professional, stood up and backed up his claim, "What Parasol says is true. I was beside him and saw that he did exactly as he described."

I was taken aback. I looked into the matter, holding a private debriefing with Parasol and his crew. Yes, indeed, Gatka was still closing his eyes while firing, but Parasol had not used his gunner at all. Intensely ambitious and determined to be a good commander, he had learned to perform what was called "commander's fire." In other words, he would aim the tank gun at the target, pull the trigger, and adjust the sights as needed all by himself. So in that way, Parasol transformed himself from a lousy tank commander to an outstanding one who worked wonders.

The case of Parasol taught me an important lesson in life: Sometimes things seem inconceivable and we immediately dismiss them, though they may be worth considering. Years later, when I entered the business world, I did not forget Parasol. Sometimes there were deals that seemed totally unfeasible to me, not even worth thinking about. I would tell myself it could be a "Parasol case." On at least two occasions, such deals did turn out to be "Parasol cases," and had good outcomes.

While we were crossing some hills on the way to the canal to take positions near the Al-Firdan Bridge, my tank's engine died just as I crested a hill. "Start it up!" I told the driver on the radio, but nothing happened. I shouted again, "Start it up!"

The driver responded back to me: "Commander, the tank's not starting." It turned out that the fuel injection pump had stopped functioning, just as we rounded the summit.

The Egyptian army suddenly had us in a turkey shoot. Shells from the other side of the canal exploded all around us. Of course, I fired back rapidly. When I thought about it later, I was surprised that I never once considered abandoning the tank and letting the Egyptians demolish it as it remained idle and deserted. Instead I contacted one of the platoon commanders on the company radio, and requested a tow. There was no reply. I assumed that he was simply scared and pretending not to hear me. Luckily another platoon commander, the courageous and capable 2nd Lt. Ron Yishai, did hear me. He showed up as fast as he could with tow cables, and hauled us back down the hill.

Ron Yishai was killed a few months later when his platoon heroically attacked an Egyptian unit that had raided our forces; he was honored posthumously with a Distinguished Service Medal.

When approaching the Suez Canal, we would scout around to find unexpected hiding places to surprise the Egyptians. At nightfall, my company and I would come within a few miles of the canal. We would find a place to park the tanks, spend the night, and at dawn we would take positions near the canal and open fire at the Egyptians. For a few nights we were encamped beside a small oasis, not far from the canal.

One evening I was returning to the oasis, and I could not shake the feeling that I should move the company somewhere else. I acted on that instinct, and that night around midnight, we suddenly heard the roar of artillery fire. It was not directed at us, and it lasted for about an hour. In the morning, we returned from firing at the Egyptians, and we passed the oasis. We could not believe what we saw. It was pulverized, black, and sooty, with all the vegetation destroyed.

The barrage of Egyptian fire we heard the night before was indeed directed at the oasis. Apparently the Egyptians discovered where we had been camping and attempted to annihilate us. If we had still been there, we most certainly would have suffered major casualties. I asked myself more than once why, specifically on that night, had I sensed that we should leave the oasis? It could just as well have been the night before or the night after. Again, I found myself face to face with fate, or luck.

I learned of several such random acts of fate. There was the case of my friend, Capt. Yitzhak Dagan, who had taken the tank-operating course with me a few months earlier. I heard that during the War of Attrition he was making his way along the Northern part of the canal to rescue a wounded tractor driver and found himself under a heavy Egyptian artillery barrage. Dagan and the driver jumped out of the jeep and dashed to take cover. An artillery shell fell exactly where they hid, killing both of them. The jeep remained standing, intact.

There was also a case in which a group of officers from the Armored Corps Headquarters arrived to visit us just as the Egyptians started shelling. We were standing by the company's command bunkers. The officers split into two groups, each dashing toward a different bunker. One officer called out to another officer who was in the other group, he shouted, "Come over and join us, so we'll be able to talk."

So the second officer went and joined his friend's group. A few minutes later a delayed-action mortar shell slammed into the bunker that the officer had just left, killing everyone in it. The officer who joined his friend was – by that seemingly trivial decision – saved from certain death.

These incidents remind me of an ancient legend about fate I read many years ago, in the introduction to John O'Hara's novel *Appointment in Samarra*. One morning, a servant came to his master in Baghdad and asked for his fastest horse. When the master questioned why he wanted the fastest horse, the servant explained that, in the market that morning, he had seen the Angel of Death, who had given him a strange look. The servant saw the look as a sign that the Angel of Death's intention was to take his life, and he needed the fastest horse so he could flee to Samara. The master was convinced and gave the servant his light-footed steed, and the servant rode it to Samara, arriving at nightfall.

That afternoon, when the master was in the market, he too encountered the Angel of Death. He asked him why he had so badly frightened his servant. The Angel of Death replied that he had not intended to scare the servant, and that he, the Angel of Death, had simply been surprised. That evening, he was supposed to take the servant's soul in Samara, yet he had seen him here, in Baghdad, this morning! So the servant, it turned out, had ridden directly to the bitter fate he was trying to escape.

Unlike those who only believe in statistics and probability, I also believe in fate and luck. One has to let the events of life flow and the ramifications fall as they will. In certain cases though, you can tell in advance that events are moving in a direction that will lead to a bad or unintended outcome. If so, you need to divert the flow. Choosing between the two options is often hard, as the decision depends on a blend of intuition and logic. We do not always understand intuition, but it exists.

Along with our offensive activity during the War of Attrition, we planned a defensive strategy in case the Egyptian army was to cross the Suez Canal, which indeed happened a few years later in the Yom Kippur War. I was amazed to discover that, according to the plans, my company was supposed to fend off at least an entire Egyptian tank brigade. Given the balance of forces, I saw no way in which we could accomplish that, especially when our side included soldiers like Gatka the gunner. Yet, if I had expressed that concern to someone like Battalion Commander Yanosh, it would have resulted in nothing but a torrent of insults about my cowardice. A few years later, during the Yom Kippur War, we found out how sadly deficient those presumptuous plans actually were.

We strove to survive the war not only physically, but emotionally as well. I was twenty-four, just a few years older than my soldiers, but I had to set an example of maturity, strength, and confidence in front of them. Deep down, I was falling apart from too little sleep, the pressure of my tasks, and from the fact that my wife and I had recently separated. As a child during the War of Independence and as a teenager too, I was afraid of all sorts of things. Now, I did not fear the hazards. During shooting incidents, when I wanted to aim our artillery guns more accurately, I would get off the tank and run some distance from it, even as shells fell around us. I did this so that the compass, which tells you where the fire is coming from, would not be thrown off by the metal of my tank.

Sometime later, I ran into one of my former soldiers in Tel Aviv. I cannot say I remembered him. He shook my hand and told me that, when he was under my command, I was an exemplary figure for him because I would get off the tank and locate the sources of fire with the compass without fear amid artillery fire.

That does not in any way mean I was unaware of the dangers, or threw caution to the wind. I was always careful about my company, and my tank crew. When I considered my own safety, I particularly took my mother into account. If something happened to me, it would have been the end of the world for her. I never told my parents, especially not my mother that I was in the thick of the War of Attrition. It would have caused both of them – but mostly my mother – sleepless nights. At one point, I even told her I was stationed at a base near Beersheba, and I expressed how worried I was about my friends who were serving at the canal. She answered, "Good, it's best that way."

One night, after we had barely survived one of the clashes, I called home and spoke with my mother. There was a bad connection, and I had to tell her I was out in a field near Beersheba. She replied, "I hope you're wearing a sweater." I laughed to myself. If she had known where I really was, a sweater would have been the least of her worries.

I always tried to keep my parents from worrying about me or getting involved in my problems, especially as they got older. To me, it seemed selfish for an adult child to overburden parents with his own problems, not taking into account that his parents may also have issues to deal with. I believed it was better to help parents cope with their difficulties, than to give them more to worry about.

So, for quite a long time, I kept both of my parents in the dark about the fact that I was now a combatant in the War of Attrition. That is, until the day the news reported that the IDF had suffered 10 casualties at the Suez Canal, and my cousin Hanna, who is my age, saw fit to call my mother and say, "I wanted to know if Ehud is all right." I had no idea how Hanna knew I was serving at the canal. At any rate, her intentions were good; she was calling out of concern.

My mother, though, was dumbstruck. "What do you mean, is he all right? Ehud is stationed near Beersheba."

Hanna, replied with sincere bewilderment, "What are you talking about? Ehud is serving at the canal." From that day on, my parents no longer slept well.

In any case, the War of Attrition was rough. The soldiers of my company were given leave once every two months, sometimes only once every three months. As a captain and company commander, I took time off every two or three weeks. I would fly to an airfield in north Tel Aviv where my driver, Nissim, would wait for me with his jeep. When he asked where we were headed, I would say, "Drive straight." I honestly did not know the answer. My marriage had recently come to an end, and I had neither a home nor a serious relationship. I could not call from Sinai to ask for accommodations, so after leaving the airfield, we would stop at a pay phone, and I would call to check which of my friends felt nice enough to let me stay at their home. Fortunately, I always found a female friend who was willing.

I have fond memories of one of those volunteers. Her name was Dorit, and I met her as a hitchhiker when I picked her up a few months prior to the war. When I asked what her hobbies were, she said, "sex and music." I mentioned that I could only take part in one of those, since music was not my forte. Dorit was a soldier-instructor, and served at one of the kibbutzim near the Gaza Strip. One night I came to visit her, and the guard at the gate said I could not enter with my jeep. Although I flashed my officer ID, it still did not convince him; he said I could potentially be a Jordanian officer. When I asked him to read what was written on the ID, he said he lacked the ability to read. I had no other option, so I left the jeep outside the kibbutz and climbed the fence at a point far from the gate.

Another girl I spent time with was the pleasant, pretty Adela. After a few months, I got tired of our relationship, but I wanted to end it without hurting her. So, on one of my free weekends, as we were walking to the sea, Adela said, "I don't like your bathing suit." I seized the opportunity and replied, "You're always insulting me. I want to break up. I don't want to put up with these insults anymore." Adela, with tears in her eyes, said, "I didn't do anything wrong. I just gave my opinion!" In her time of distress, she turned to my friend Miki Stark, who for some reason told her I was a sensitive guy, and that she should hold onto me no matter what. So I was forced to be with her for another month.

During one of my leaves I drove to Jerusalem in my jeep and decided to go to Machane Yehuda, Jerusalem's large, popular open-air marketplace. When I was about 200 yards away, the jeep got a flat tire, so I went into a gas station beside the marketplace to take care of it. While there, I heard a massive explosion. It turned out terrorists had left a car bomb on Agripas Street, inside Machane Yehuda. The blast killed 15 people and about 50 were wounded. I usually parked on Agripas. If it had not been for that flat tire, I could have been among the casualties.

Immediately, all sorts of riffraff started harassing Arabs. I was still at the gas station, and one of the workers, a bearded, bespectacled man in his fifties, told me solemnly, "Beating them up is wrong." I thought I had found a real saint, but he added, "The right thing is to kill them."

As a child before the establishment of the State of Israel, I remember that Jews and Arabs in Jerusalem somehow coexisted peacefully. I remember an Arab man in a keffiyeh,[43] a permanent smile plastered across his face, who came to our street with a monkey on a chain. I enjoyed watching the monkey dance as the man sang, "*Urkud, urkud, ya zalame*" (Dance, man, dance).

There, on the street outside the gas station, I saw an elderly, keffiyeh-wearing Arab with a bleeding head. A group of teenagers

---

[43] A keffiyeh is a traditional Middle Eastern cotton headdress worn mostly by Arabs.

were chasing after him with sticks and stones. I started up the jeep, and hurried toward the man, slamming on my brakes very close to the teenagers. I told him to get in, trying to save him from a lynching. The teenagers stared at me with uncertainty. Then they saw I was holding a loaded Kalashnikov, and settled for shouting, "Arab-lover!"

I took my passenger to the eastern part of Jerusalem, which was predominantly populated by Arabs. His voice choked with sobs, he asked, "What have I done? I finished work at a building site. I have ten children. Why do I deserve to be attacked?"

On the way to the eastern side of the city, I passed a local hospital. I saw families of the casualties of the terrorist attack standing outside, some were weeping in obvious distress. I thought to myself, this is exactly what happens on both sides of the conflict – the ones who pay the price are mostly innocent. I have always believed that if someone attacks you, you should hit back as hard as you can, even if he throws a stone. But harming someone who has done nothing wrong is out of the question, and when innocent people are attacked, someone has to defend them.

A few months after the War of Attrition began, a cancerous tumor was discovered in my father's brain, and he died a few months later. During this time, I began to have the nagging thought that perhaps I had done enough for the homeland. A lady in Tel Aviv helped me reach a decision. After a shooting incident at the canal, my deputy Shlomo Ginzburg, as usual, turned on the radio while smoking one of his expensive cigarettes and drinking a Coke. It was a question-and-answer show, and we heard a Tel Aviv woman present a "very serious problem." She had put her flowerpot out on the balcony, but the plant's leaves were not getting green enough. I was struck by the contrast. This was what preoccupied the people in Tel Aviv? At that moment I concluded that I had my fill of the War of Attrition. In addition, I resolved that as soon as my term of service with the IDF would end in 1970, I would leave the army and finish my BA.

For the remaining two years in the standing army, I managed to serve at the Armored Corps Headquarters (as always, I knew how to get what I wanted). I served there as an aide to the training officer, Lt. Col. Yigal Reuveni. I was responsible for coordinating the training programs for the different units. We worked smoothly together, and I learned a lot from him.

Before I was discharged, however, the Armored Corps Headquarters decided to award me with an early promotion to the rank of major for having been an "outstanding officer," as Maj. Gen. Avraham "Bren" Adan, Commander of the Armored Corps, wrote in a recommendation letter on May 29, 1970. The officers' personnel administration approved the new rank and the early promotion. However, the adjunct officer at the Armored Corps Headquarters had an entirely different idea. He said I would only be able to get the new rank if I committed to another three years of duty. I explained to him that, after completing two years of BA studies in economics and statistics, I had already taken three years off, and according to the university's regulations, I would lose the two years unless I resumed now. I told him I already had to study for an additional year to get the BA. I was not made a major. Even my interview with the chief of staff, Lt. Gen. Haim Bar-Lev, did not help. I protested to him that, as an outstanding officer, I should be promoted to major without having to stay on for three more years, but he was not persuaded.

So I went back to the Hebrew University for the third year of economics and statistics to finally complete the BA. To support my family I worked at Kiryat Yearim, a youth village near Jerusalem for children with learning difficulties. I was in charge of after-school activities. Teachers and nannies helped me out. It was interesting and fulfilling to deal with teenage boys and girls who came from dysfunctional homes and had missed out on education.

Once I finished my degree, I decided to go back to army service. I realized that I could apply the academic knowledge I had gained to my military experience.

My company, Company B, 1968. I am at the left of the top row; those who fell in battle appear in black frames.

On the bank of the Suez Canal, 1968. First from left, *my deputy, Shlomo; I am second from left.*

A festive meal in Sinai, 1968. Second from right, *Dubi Israeli, commander of Company A; I am second from left.*

With Dorit on a desert outing

Agripas Street after the terror attack at the Machane Yehuda marketplace, 1968

Chapter 7
· ·
HE WHO PAYS HAS THE SAY

W hen I received my BA in economics and statistics, I figured that the Financial Adviser's Office to the chief of staff
would be an ideal place for me. The financial adviser operates
simultaneously within the IDF and the Defense Ministry. After the
IDF defines its requirements to the Defense Ministry, the Defense
Ministry determines the budget. The Financial Adviser's Office
advises the IDF chief of staff, facilitates communication between
the two institutions, and is responsible for designing and control-
ling the defense budget. I thought that, in this office, I would be
able to apply what I had learned and deal with military matters
with which I was already experienced.

Maj. Gen. Avraham "Bren" Adan, commander of the Armored
Corps, opposed my working in the Financial Adviser's Office and
wanted me to continue serving in the corps, once again offering
me a promotion to the rank of major. Despite this attractive offer,
I wanted to work in the field I had studied, while still contributing
to the country.

Brig. Gen. Nehemiah Kain, who in 1971 was the financial
adviser to the chief of staff and head of the Budget Division of the
Defense Ministry, fought for me.

"We beat Hitler, we beat Nasser, we will also beat Bren," was
his reaction.

General Kain summoned the head of the Administration
Department in the Defense Ministry and ordered him to sign a special civilian contract with me that gave me exactly the same terms

as a major in career service, though this status came without the social prestige that a ranked military position carried in those days. His order was carried out immediately. Even in the Defense Ministry, the maxim, "He who pays has the say," coined by a Jewish sage, remained true.

I was put in charge of the Defense Ministry's budget for the research and development department and it's entities. The latter included RAFAEL, the Armament Development Authority, which was responsible for developing cutting-edge defense technologies. It was very interesting work, and for the first time I felt I was really putting my qualifications to good use.

My direct superior was Lt. Col. Yaakov Hai, a man of great knowledge and experience, who was also kind, affable, and always ready to help. I also had direct and ongoing interaction with General Kain, who gave me support, a good deal of authority, and showed his appreciation for my work.

Kain was an interesting sort, exceptionally shrewd and worldly, but with a sharp tongue. He was not – to put it mildly – an easy person to get along with. Once, in the middle of a meeting, he turned to one of the lieutenant colonels and asked, "Why are you sitting like a monkey?"

His knowledge of Hebrew and its grammar was amazing. During meetings, when he was supposed to be listening to speakers, he would pass the time by adding vowel points to the text of some document. Once, after I had given him a memo, he asked, "Where were you born?" When I answered, "In Israel," he asked, "So why don't you know Hebrew?"

Previously, General Kain had been the military attaché at the Israeli embassy in Italy, and he was also in charge of Israel's defense-related activities in Switzerland. He played a key role in an operation that involved smuggling engine plans for the French Mirage 5 warplane from Switzerland to Israel. Israel used the plans to manufacture the Nesher (Eagle), which was almost identical to the Mirage 5, overcoming the embargo on weapons exports to the

Jewish state that France imposed after the Six-Day War. Years later, when Kain was a major general and we met in a social context, he told me the details of the operation. I was utterly impressed by his skill, daring, and cunning.

I wanted to perform my duties as an officer, which was seen as more prestigious within the ministry, rather than work as a simple civilian clerk. My civilian contract with the ministry could be terminated at any time, so I was glad when – after I had served half a year in the Financial Adviser's Office – the adjutancy officer of the Armored Corps, Lt. Col. Georgy, called to tell me that General Bren had withdrawn his opposition to my transfer. I could now join the office officially. Georgy requested that Nehemiah call Bren. I immediately relayed that request to Nehemiah Kain, who responded, "Bren needs money from me now, so he can call me. I'm not going to call him."

The standoff continued for a few days until Bren and Nehemiah chanced upon each other in a meeting with the chief of staff. In Nehemiah's telling, he budgeted one million pounds for a project Bren was interested in. In return, Bren approved my signing on to the Financial Adviser's Office.

Nehemiah brought me this news and said, "You have to sign on for three additional years." I told him that I only wanted to sign on for one more year.

Nehemiah gave me a harsh look. If physical violence had been an option, he would have landed a few punches to my face. Instead he fumed, "Are you out of your mind? After I fought for half a year so you could sign on with me, this is the gratitude you show me?"

We compromised on two years – up to July 1973.

I was given the rank of major retroactively, along with half a year's retroactive salary. At the same time, to satisfy my patriotic feelings, I insisted on receiving an emergency appointment, which meant I was on call for active duty. In case of war, I would serve with the Armored Corps at the front, in a field unit.

General Bren appointed me commander of a tank company, and I was amazed to find out that the deputy commander of the 421st was Haim Erez. I saw it as much more than just coincidence that, of all the companies, battalions, and brigades in the Armored Corps, Bren had sent me to none other than Erez, who had been my battalion commander when I was a company commander in the 79th Battalion during my compulsory service. That was improbable enough. Then, as a volunteer during the Yom Kippur War, I was really surprised when I was assigned to the Sde Teiman base and, once there, discovered that the brigade was the same 421st and the commander was, again, Haim Erez. I found myself randomly under Haim Erez's command three different times in my military career. Eventually, we became good friends.

Nehemiah, however, tried to make sure I didn't leave the office for any operational activity or field training as an on-call company commander. He claimed my work in the office at the time was too important. I heard through the grapevine that Nehemiah managed to make sure that I was never actually summoned to the field, despite the emergency appointment.

Toward the end of my term in the Financial Adviser's Office, Brig. Gen. Yitzhak Elron replaced Nehemiah Kain. Yitzhak Elron was not without talent, but in my eyes he did not come close to Nehemiah. What did impress me was his spitting ability. We were situated on the seventh floor of the Defense Ministry building in the Kirya, the governmental and military complex in Tel Aviv, and sometimes Yitzhak would stand by the window and, to the amazement of all present, execute a long-range spit.

Around that time I met my future wife, Nili. It was my friend Miki Stark who introduced us. Nili was a successful probation officer and an intelligent woman. Having divorced not long before, I was not keen on getting married at that point. But Nili wanted to start a family, and I thought she was special enough to wed. We soon got married and had three children, Dana and the twins, Lior and Tali. I have always had close, warm ties with them. After seven years, however, Nili and I decided we should go our own ways, and we divorced.

As for work, I was heavily involved in research and development in the defense domain, including the budget for RAFAEL. I was responsible for approving the budgets for various projects and overhead costs.

I worked closely with Bentzy Bezalel, then the deputy director general of RAFAEL, and Mordechai Kikayon, then the head of its computer center. Kikayon, in his fifties, was tall, serious, always practical, and addicted to his computers. I was amazed by the huge room where RAFAEL kept its gigantic computers, each nearly the size of a room itself. Today an ordinary PC, or even a state-of-the-art cell phone, has calculating and data-processing capacities much greater than those giant computers.

Nehemiah Kain gave me extensive powers well beyond my job description and my rank as major. He would send me personally to meetings of the Defense Ministry's director general and other senior officials. It marked the first time in my life that important public bodies awaited my decisions and recommendations. Having previously served in some public roles, I always took care not to accept any sort of perk, not even the smallest, so as not to abuse my status. I even returned all the Passover gift baskets I received to their senders.

As for my approach to work, I was tough about disbursing the ministry's budgets and tried to save money for the IDF and the Defense Ministry. And yet, somehow, I got along with the recipients of these budgets. It may have been because each time I trimmed and saved, I justified it. That was apparently what kept the disappointed from turning hostile.

Meanwhile, I was studying for an MA at the Rehovot branch of the Hebrew University. Although my subject was officially agricultural economics, I took only general economics courses. The courses were very high level, thanks to the fine quality of the lecturers and the dedicated students that came mostly from kibbutzim and had been specially chosen for their motivation and ability.

Sometimes I had trouble understanding the kibbutznik mentality. For example, Professor Dan Yaron, in a class on pricing, stressed the importance of following the rules of pricing and said, "And I don't mean the cowshed at Givat Hashlosha"[44] – and the kibbutzniks burst out laughing. For my part, I did not – and still do not – have the faintest idea what he meant or why it was so funny.

Among my lecturers were Professor Pinhas "Siko" Zusman, who was also the economic adviser to the Defense Ministry, and Professor Ezra Sadan, who became my friend. A few years later, Ezra was appointed director general of the Finance Ministry, and a dozen years after that, he tried to help me when I decided to go into private business.

Professor Zusman was an impressive person of unusual quality. Fortunately for me, he agreed to be my MA thesis adviser. My thesis was on the application of various budgeting methods, and Siko's guidance was of great help. Studying for an MA with Siko at the Rehovot branch of Hebrew University put me in close contact with the Economic Adviser's Office in the Defense Ministry. Some of those who worked in the Economic Adviser's Office were also taking courses at Rehovot. People in that office, which held special sway over the ministry's director general, the deputy defense minister, and the defense minister, did not think too highly of those working in the Financial Adviser's Office; they saw them basically as technocrats who watched over the budget. Because of my courses at Hebrew University, though, they regarded me as someone like them, knowledgeable in the fine points of economics – someone closer to their mold. Their attitude toward me proved helpful in calming the tensions of the ministry's internal politics and handling conflicts of interest between various projects, especially during the transformation of RAFAEL from a unit administered by the ministry into a separate entity that had to balance its own budget and expenses.

---

[44] A kibbutz in central Israel.

Siko continued as my thesis adviser after the Yom Kippur War, which interrupted my studies. For his part, he was a lieutenant colonel in the reserves, and during the war he served as commander of Ariel Sharon's tactical headquarters. As a twenty-four-year-old company commander in the War of Independence, Siko had suffered a serious trauma. On July 17, 1949, his company was sent to block Jordanian troops from advancing toward the site where a major attack had been planned. Of the eighty-two fighters who went with Siko, forty-five were killed in a fierce battle. Feeling personally responsible, he thought of taking his own life. He came out of it sad, or as his friend Maj. Gen. Israel Tal put it, "Siko remained in a state of shell shock." A detailed description of that battle later appeared in Yosef Argaman's *Pale Was the Night*, a biography of Siko published in 2002.

Siko was later appointed director general of the Defense Ministry. I enjoyed every moment of the meetings he held. Without fail, the military and Defense Ministry people present had loud and fierce disputes. Everyone put forth his arguments in detail, and Siko the director general had to reach a decision. He would propose solutions in a quiet and decorous voice, solutions that were often completely different from the views that had been expressed.

Siko would also pleasantly ask those present, "What's your opinion on this?" He would then calmly explain why his solution was logical and smart. And, lo and behold, almost all those who had been noisily wrangling would accept his solutions and explanations, quietly expressing their assent. King Solomon was right when he said, "The words of the wise are spoken in quiet" (Ecclesiastes 9:17). In these meetings, Siko knew how to ward off antagonism and soothe inflated egos.

While I was working in the Financial Adviser's Office, various people and units needed my approval for their budgets and would behave ingratiatingly toward me. I would often try to figure out who was behaving genuinely toward me, and who was just buttering me up. I came to the conclusion that just four out of all these people were real friends who would remain friends after I was discharged and they no longer needed me. I was off by 50 percent; only two, Bentzy Bezalel, and Mordechai Kikayon, remained my friends.

Kikayon kept after me all the time, saying I was wasting my talents and had to get out of the army. It was he, an authority on computers who had been the first commander of the IDF's Center of Computing and Information Systems, who recommended me to Advanced Technology Ltd., a company dealing with information systems and software engineering, which was founded in 1969 by Yossi Vardi, Meir Burshtein, and Yoram Rosenfeld. They were among the first people in the world to realize that software development is a type of engineering, and they coined the now widely used term.

When my agreed-upon discharge date arrived, I left the Defense Ministry and joined the company's management with an excellent compensation package, almost the same as that of the director general, Meir Burshtein. The company's mainstays at that time were Burshtein and Rosenfeld, both of them products of the IDF's Center of Computing and Information Systems and extremely talented. Both of them were also kindhearted, but whereas Meir had great patience, Yoram lacked it completely. Sadly enough, Yoram died of cancer in 1997 at the young age of fifty-three. He and Meir were men of vision and enterprise. When they founded the company, they recruited a group of outstanding professors from the Israel Institute of Technology in Haifa (the Technion) and Tel Aviv University to lend it prestige and academic standing. While I was working at Advanced Technology, our flagship project was "Torch of the Maccabees," the creation of the Israel Air Force's control system, with Advanced Technology subcontracting for Hughes Aircraft. I mainly dealt with information systems and sales management.

The company had twelve professional employees and a secretary. The employees' level of intelligence and knowledge was truly impressive; working with them involved constant brainstorming.

They were all in software and systems analysis, and somewhat looked down upon the masses for their ignorance of computers. Whenever the name of a successful businessman was mentioned, it was with a tone of disdain because the person had succeeded in construction or commerce, below the lofty stratum of computers.

I have noticed that systems usually develop their own inner mystique, and people not involved in their development are looked down upon. I witnessed the same thing in the university world. The professors, because of my uniform, saw me as a military type, a "square." Years later one of them gave me his greatest compliment: "You're not a typical military person."

There was a reciprocal attitude toward education within the military world itself, particularly in the combat sphere. Years later, when I was deputy commander of a reserve brigade, we had to conduct a call-up drill and needed a plan for picking up the reserve soldiers at various bus stops. That raised questions of how many buses were needed, and at what frequency to send buses to each pickup station. I suggested to the deputy division commander that we use a model derived from queuing theory to determine the right allocation of buses to the various pickup stations, according to the number of soldiers expected to report to duty. His reaction, in front of a large group of people, was to dismiss the idea contemptuously. "We don't need any doctors around here," he said. (Actually, I only had an MA at that point!) Of course, the results of his planning were that the buses left some of the stations empty, while at others they picked up so many soldiers that fights broke out among those present.

A few years later, when I was a candidate for financial adviser to the chief of staff, at the rank of brigadier general, Chief of Staff Lt. Gen. Rafael "Raful" Eitan was against it. He told me bluntly, "You're too educated." (I then had a doctorate in business administration.) It reminded me of a remark in Sholem Aleichem's book *Tevye the Dairyman*, which Tevye attributes to the sages: "Don't take a bride whose eyes are too pretty...."

In another instance, the same Raful told a colonel from the air force who was requesting to study for a BA, "I became chief of staff with merely finishing high school. You finished high school and can become the air force commander; you don't need to go to university."

With all due respect to Raful, I believe in education. And so, alongside my ongoing MA work, Advanced Technology sent me to a one-year systems analysis course at the Institute for Work Productivity. It was an intensive course and I learned a great deal.

And yet, even with my high salary and the interesting projects in the software field of which I was now part, I felt bored. We were developing systems that would provide a computerized alternative to human systems. I was more interested in the human systems themselves. I preferred to deal with planning, building, and practical applications. Still, even though I did not find my work at Advanced Technology all that fascinating, the pay was good and I learned a great deal about computerization. If I had not had to do so much reserve duty after the Yom Kippur War, I would have stayed at Advanced Technology a few more years and kept gaining knowledge. Later on, I was happy to hear how the company was growing. By 1988 it employed four hundred people, and ten years later, in 1998, Advanced Technology was acquired by a group of American investors and became the administrative nucleus, with considerable influence, of Ness Technologies.

In my personal life I became something of a square. On Friday nights Nili and I would get together with a few couples to gripe about things. Each person would analyze the political situation and criticize current events. I was always amazed at how these know-it-alls would base their passionate opinions on so little. Once I even impolitely asked one of our friends how she could know what Egyptian president Anwar Sadat was planning and thinking; of course, she was offended.

The Yom Kippur War put a stop to everything. When the siren sounded on October 6, I dropped all that I was doing and hurried to the front.

צבא הגנה לישראל

31   יולי   1973

רב-סרן אהוד דיסקין

אהוד היקר,

השלמתי עם שחרורך .מטרות קבצ בידעי. שבכך
תצליח להתקדם יותר בתחום הסקצועי והכלבלי, לולא
כן הייתי עושה כל סאסז, שחיסאר עסי בעבודה.

נהגיתי לעבוד עמך במשותף, ושתי השנים,
שעברו בצוותא, היוו תקופה של עבודה פוריה, עשירה
בהישגים וסלאת חוויות.

הסטידות והדביקות בסטרה איפיינו אותך,
וביצעת עבודתך ביעילות לסוטחיות הראויים לציון.

בסגעך עם אנשים ידעת את הדרך שתוביל ללבם
ורכישת אסונם, ראוסנם סעידים על-כך החיבה וההערצה.
שרכשת עם כל אלה. שנאם עסם במבע.

ברכתי ואיחולי, כי תצליח להגיע לסילוי
כל שאיפותיך בחיים ונהקדם, אשמח לסייע לך בכך
בכל עת.

עלה והצלח!

יעקב חי, סא"ל

יח/חג

A letter of appreciation upon my leaving the financial advisor's office, from Lt. Col. Yaakov Hai, 1973.

The text reads:

Israel Defense Forces   July 31, 1973

Major Ehud Diskin

Dear Ehud,

Although your discharge from career service saddens me, I am encouraged by my knowledge that you will make greater professional progress in the field of economics, though I would make every effort to have you keep working here with me.

I enjoyed working with you, and the two years spent in your company have been a period of productive work, rich in achievements and experiences.
Your dedication, resolute pursuit of objectives, efficiency, and expertise are worthy of praise.

In your contact with people you find the way to their hearts and win their loyalty, as is well evident in the affection and esteem felt toward you by all those you have interacted with.

I wish you success in rapidly fulfilling all your aspirations in life, and will be happy to help you at any time.

Onward to success!

Yaakov Hai, Lt. Col.

During my service in the office of the financial advisor to the chief of staff, 1972

Brig. Gen. Nehemiah Kain, financial advisor to the chief of staff

Professor Pinhas Zusman ("Siko"), 1978

צבא הגנה לישראל
המטה הכללי

ב אב תשל"ג
31 יולי 1973

מ/1603-842

רס"ג אהוד דיסקין

עם שחרורך משירות קבע לאחר שתי שנות שירות ביחידה,
ברצוני להביע לך בדרך זו הערכתי על עבודתך.

ביצעת עבודתך תוך גילוי יכולת ויסודיות הראויים
לציון.

עם שחרורך מ-צה"ל הנני סאחל לך הצלחה בהמשך דרכך.

יצחק אלרון , תא"ל
הרועץ הכספי ל-רמטכ"ל

A letter of appreciation upon my discharge from career service, from Brigadier General Yitzhak Elron, 1973.

The text reads:

Israel Defense Forces, General Staff   July 31, 1973

Major Ehud Diskin

With your discharge from career service after two years of service in the office, I would like to express my esteem for your work.

You carried out your work with skill and thoroughness that are deserving of praise.

Upon your discharge from the IDF I wish you continued success in life.

Yitzhak Elron, Brig. Gen.
Financial Advisor to the Chief of Staff

Chapter 8

"WHO SHALL LIVE AND WHO SHALL DIE"

From the Yom Kippur liturgy

I often wondered how I ended up in the tank brigade that spearheaded the crossing of the Suez Canal during the Yom Kippur War, all the while pelted by heavy Egyptian fire. Only two weeks earlier I had been an ordinary citizen, director of a software company, with challenging work and an attractive salary. The future seemed clear and certain.

And then suddenly, it all changed.

On Yom Kippur in Israel there is almost zero traffic on the roads. Even those who do not go to synagogue prefer to stay home, either to avoid offending those who do, or because they fear troublemakers who throw stones at cars, thinking they are doing a *mitzvah*, a good deed.

That morning, Saturday, October 6, 1973, I saw a surprising sight from my apartment on Katznelson Street in Givatayim, a town that neighbors Tel Aviv. Military vehicles were on the move. I wondered what was going on, so I called my former commander Lt. Col. Yigal Reuveni, then the deputy brigade commander of Northern Command, who lived nearby. His wife Adina answered the phone.

"Hello," I said and introduced myself. "Is Yigal home?"

Adina updated me in two laconic sentences that sent a shiver down my spine.

"Yigal is with his brigade in the north. Yesterday he told me to prepare the shelter because we're about to be at war."

In retrospect, it is a pity that Yigal did not call Prime Minister Golda Meir, Defense Minister Moshe Dayan, Chief of Staff Lt. Gen. David Elazar, and in particular Maj. Gen. Eli Zeira, head of Military Intelligence, to update them on this important piece of information. It seems fitting that they too should have been preparing for the war that would break out the following day.

On second thought, considering they had not listened to the multiple indications they had received over the previous month that war was imminent, including the explicit warning of Jordan's King Hussein and signs of Egyptian and Syrian advances in the Sinai and Golan Heights, instead sticking with Military Intelligence's assessments of the "low probability" of war, they would not have listened to Yigal either.

At two o'clock in the afternoon, the Syrians and the Egyptians simultaneously attacked. The sirens began to wail; war had begun. I did not think twice. Nor did I wait for the phone to ring, or for an emergency call-up order to reservists. I bid farewell to my wife Nili and hurried to the home of my ex-wife, Miriam, in nearby Petach Tikva, where my military equipment (fireproof overalls, combat boots – or as we called them, "hero boots" – and a combat harness) was stored from the time we were married. I had put it in safekeeping for a call-up.

I kissed my young children Yarriv and Anat goodbye, got into my blue Volkswagen, and drove off to the war. At this time I did not yet know the extent of the fighting, and no one knew how long and bloody this war would be.

On the first day of the Yom Kippur War, the Syrians and the Egyptians launched surprise attacks on IDF strongholds. In the Golan Heights, in the north of Israel, the Syrians attacked with a force of three divisions, including seventeen hundred tanks, twelve hundred artillery cannons, a large quantity of surface-to-air missiles, and hundreds of aircraft. The IDF presence in the Golan

Heights consisted of only two armored brigades that included 177 tanks and two infantry battalions. In the south of Israel, the Egyptians crossed the Suez Canal, attacked our strongholds, and entered Sinai with an enormous power of two armies, which included two thousand tanks, a lot of artillery, aircrafts, and antitank missiles, plus five infantry divisions, including commando forces. Against these forces, the IDF had merely one armored division which included three hundred tanks and small infantry forces.

The results of the first day's battles were catastrophic for the IDF. Syria launched a heavy artillery barrage on the outposts and settlements in the Golan Heights and took over most of the IDF strongholds. Commandos captured the Mount Hermon post and took its soldiers captive. In the south, the Egyptians took over most of the IDF strongholds on the east bank of the Suez Canal. Many Israeli soldiers were killed or captured. Out of three hundred IDF tanks, only one hundred remained. On the second day of the war the reserve forces began to arrive at the front and tried to change the outcome.

A few months earlier I had been discharged from the IDF at the rank of major, and I had not yet been assigned a position in the reserves. So I drove to the Armored Corps House in the Yad Eliyahu neighborhood of Tel Aviv, where I met with a liaison officer from the Armored Corps. Quickly realizing that he would not be helpful, I drove on to the Armored Corps Headquarters near Kiryat Malachi in southern Israel. There, I reported to the staff officer at the Personnel Administration Office. He looked through my file and saw that I had been a tank company commander during the War of Attrition in the late 1960s.

"Do you still know what to do and how to operate?" he asked me.

I answered him in the affirmative, and he sent me to the Sde Teiman base near Beersheba to be assigned a role in the 421st Reserve Brigade.

I arrived on the afternoon of Yom Kippur and presented myself to the brigade commander. To my surprise, the commander was Col. Haim Erez. We had met a few years earlier in the War of Attrition when he had been commander of a battalion in which I had served – first as deputy company commander, later as company commander. It was nice to see Haim again; he was an amiable and talented commander.

When Haim saw that I was a major, he said, "Ehud, I'm afraid I don't have a post for you as a major or company commander, but I have an available role as brigade operations officer. The reservist who was filling this role is currently in England. Does that suit you?"

"I'm here to help," I replied, "and I'm prepared to be a simple driver if necessary. I want to contribute; I don't care what I do."

I wasted no time and began to organize the half-tracks[45] and APCs (armored personnel carriers), as well as the soldiers and officers who formed the fighting force of the brigade command. We tried to stock up with as many supplies as possible from the storerooms and ammunition bunker, but they were greatly depleted. We hastened to outfit the armored vehicles, though it was difficult because chaos prevailed all around us. Since there was a shortage of military vehicles, the roof rack of my Beetle served to transport arms and equipment from the storerooms to the armored vehicles. Once we had taken all there was to take, we set off, though still desperately lacking in supplies.

Most crucially, we lacked standard machine guns to mount on the half-tracks and APCs. If we had to fight Egyptian infantry, the only weapons at our disposal were our personal, short-range Uzi machine guns. Not encouraging.

We made our way to the battlefield in Sinai, toward Tasa, east of the city of Ismailia. On the road west toward the Suez Canal,

---

[45] A vehicle with regular wheels in front and rear wheels on treads, enabling cross-country driving.

before we crossed the Green Line,[46] we passed the Shivta base, a branch of the 460th Brigade. I stopped our convoy of vehicles – about a dozen half-tracks, APCs, and off-road vehicles – and walked into the base alone. The military storeroom was full of supplies and I turned to the logistics sergeant and said in a commanding voice, "Show me your 0.3-caliber machine guns."

He showed them to me, mentioning that he had four machine guns for each tank. I was dumbfounded. A tank needs only two machine guns, and sometimes a third is kept for backup, yet here in the 460th there was also a fourth machine gun – a backup for the backup. We desperately needed the supplies, yet I knew that even if I asked for the backups of backups, they would only be granted if I were commander of the 460th Brigade. That is how it was in the IDF.

Time was of the essence. We had to reach the battlefront as quickly as possible, with machine guns and ammunition. I again turned to the logistics sergeant and said in an authoritative tone, "I'll take all the fourth machine guns."

The sergeant, realizing that he was dealing with a self-confident major, gingerly asked, "Are you from the 460th?"

No sooner had I replied with a decisive, "Of course," than he filled out the receipt, had me sign it, and handed over about fourteen "fourth" machine guns. We were finally on our way to fight, equipped with what we needed.

There were no available tank transporters, so we were forced to drive directly on tank treads. This slowed us down, wore down the tanks, and damaged the road – but what choice was there? On Sunday afternoon, October 7, a day after Egypt's surprise attack, our brigade reached the area of the canal.

The Egyptians held the eastern side of the canal along the Bar-Lev Line.[47] Their defense was now effectively organized along a six-mile-wide strip. We, with our high self-confidence, naively

---

[46] The commonly used term for the previous Israeli borders, before the Six-Day War.

[47] A line of fortifications built by Israel in the late 1960s.

believed we could easily take them out. Our aim was to push the Egyptians back to the western side of the canal, join up with our existing deployments, and pull out whichever of our forces still dangerously lingered in the field.

We soon learned the hard way that wishing for something to happen is not the same as making it happen. We surged ahead into well-organized Egyptian deployments that greeted us with deadly fire, inflicting heavy losses on our troops. We realized this was not the Six-Day War, in which Israeli forces had quickly routed Egyptian forces in Sinai. This was an entirely different story.

During those first two days of fighting I did not sleep a wink. Only on the third day, in the midst of battle, while speeding and bouncing in an armored vehicle with Egyptian shells landing all around us, could I no longer hold out and nodded off for two hours. I woke up feeling like a new man. As far as I can remember, nothing but water crossed my lips during the first two days of fighting.

A day and a half later, on October 9, our division attacked Hamutal, an elongated sand dune about five miles east of the canal in the Ismailia area that overlooked a vital crossroads. Our aim was to capture Hamutal, advance toward the line of Israeli deployments, and try to link up with our Purkan position east of Ismailia.

The Hamutal site was controlled by Egyptian infantry and backed by antitank artillery. Some have called Hamutal the "Latrun of the Yom Kippur War" because the site sustained no less than eight failed Israeli assaults.[48] All the brigade's battalions took hits. Most of the dead and wounded, however, were from the 2nd Battalion under the command of Maj. Ami Morag, who was given a Medal of Distinguished Service after the war, and later appointed chief Armored Corps officer at the rank of brigadier general. Meanwhile, though, thirty-three of our soldiers stranded in Purkan were evacuated in a daring infantry operation.

---

[48] Latrun is a strategic site near Jerusalem that Israeli forces tried to conquer repeatedly and futilely, with heavy losses, during the 1948-1949 War of Independence. Since 1967, Latrun has been part of Israel.

The commander of Company H of the 2nd Battalion, Lt. Shraga Bar-Nissan, was seriously wounded during the battle. I heard Ami on the two-way radio, begging for a helicopter to evacuate him, as Shraga was losing blood and in critical condition. I spotted a medical evacuation helicopter nearby, which kept landing on different hills. It could not stay in the air long for fear of antiaircraft fire, nor stay on the ground long for fear of Egyptian artillery.

My attempts to alert the helicopter via wireless did not succeed. I decided to take a chance and try to catch the pilot's attention during one of the brief landings. I jumped into a jeep and sped off toward the hill where I expected the helicopter to alight next. The gamble paid off; the pilot caught sight of me as he landed. When the helicopter door opened I was surprised to see that the doctor inside was my longtime best friend, Miki Stark. He had come straight from Shaare Zedek Hospital in Jerusalem, still wearing his flip-flops!

I handed him a map, showed him where he needed to go, and gave him the radio network frequency. Miki's helicopter reached the 2nd Battalion but was unable to land at Hamutal because of Egyptian fire. Instead it landed in a more remote area behind a sand dune. Meanwhile the battalion doctor, Lt. Dr. Michael Toaff, skillfully operated on Shraga in the field and saved his life. Later Miki told me that Shraga was transferred to Tasa, where many injured soldiers were treated with the limited wound dressings at the doctors' disposal. Miki served as a captain in a medical company throughout the war, and we crossed paths frequently. My battalion quartermaster gave him a more soldier-like getup, as he had come straight to war from the hospital without any equipment. At that time Miki was still a young and inexperienced doctor. Yet, later in the war, while crossing the canal under heavy fire, he treated more than eighty wounded soldiers, some seriously, and he was helped by only a small number of medics, most of them also inexperienced, while in short supply of dressings and medications.

I never spoke of the helicopter incident with anyone from the brigade, just as I did not discuss with them, or exchange experiences from, any other incidents of the war. Why did I keep it all inside? I think the answer lies in the fact that my experiences were very traumatizing. When I first set out for the war with the aim of helping as much as I could, I knew it was not going to be easy. But I had not foreseen the extent of the carnage and constant mortal danger.

My official commander was the operations officer Capt. Tzvi Kan-Tor, a talented and professional officer who was later appointed division commander at the rank of brigadier general. But I worked more closely with Lt. Col. Israel Potash, the deputy brigade commander directly in charge of me. This was made possible by the fact that I was released from my post as operations officer after Capt. Reuven Rothstein, the brigade's appointed operations officer, managed to catch a plane in London at the onset of the war and return to Israel.

Not long after the war broke out in Sinai, and shortly before we crossed the canal, Potash contracted erysipelas, an acute bacterial infection marked by a red rash that spread to his legs. On some days he suffered high fever, chills, fatigue, and headaches. That, of course, made it very hard for him to function, and I became his "prompter." He trusted me completely. I usually had to tell him what to say on the radio, since the illness made it difficult for him to concentrate. I knew full well that he was the commanding officer and the one to give the orders. Since he was my senior in the hierarchy, I did things in a way that would not offend him and would conceal from others how much he needed me. He acknowledged this and told me several times that once the war was over he would recommend me for a citation and a promotion. On October 25, 1973, he wrote in an official evaluation, "Maj. Ehud Diskin carried out his duty as operations officer and other duties with courage, tenacity, and leadership deserving of special praise. He is an outstanding officer worthy of special note, and I recommend an immediate promotion."

Those days were like a boxing match. You knew you could not knock out your opponent, but there was still hope of defeating him, so you kept throwing ineffective probing punches at his face. Even though we were close to the canal, we knew we could not drive the Egyptians out from its eastern side, and we were still far from carrying out the plan to cross it, which would ultimately turn the tide of the war.

The Egyptians wore us down. We could not budge them from the positions they had occupied, and we continued to suffer casualties. Every night there were alerts and warnings of Egyptian FROG missiles and commando attacks.

I have always been moved by the sacrificial courage and devotion of the soldiers and commanders. I will never forget the night I was charged with reassembling tank crews from those teams that had been hit. I felt a choking sensation in my throat and tears well up in my eyes when I had to team up uninjured members; one gunner was the only soldier from his tank who had not been hit. Soldiers who had miraculously survived had to get back in their tanks and keep fighting. On one of the tank turrets there were still bloodstains of previous crewmen who had been hit.

One night, in the parking area, the lookout guard saw troops approaching us and discreetly informed me. We were sitting in our armored vehicles at the time, wary, ready to open fire. According to the rules of engagement, I should have given an order to fire. The approaching troops were out in the open and none of our forces were supposed to move at night in the area. Nor had we been notified of anyone passing through.

The order "Fire!" was on the tip of my tongue; yet I hesitated a while, then a while longer. Something inside me told me to hold back. So I waited. Only when the approaching troops came close did I recognize them as IDF soldiers. I later learned that they were paratroopers on the move in the area. For some reason they had not notified anyone that they would be passing through our forces. Fortunately for them – and no less fortunate for me – I did not go by the rules. Intuition is undoubtedly important, not only on the battlefield but in everything in life.

When we destroyed enemy aircraft during firefights, our armored vehicles plunged toward the wreckage to capture pilots who had abandoned their planes. On one occasion I raced to capture an Iraqi pilot (Iraq assisted the Egyptians during the war) whose plane had been shot down. When I reached him, another APC had gotten there before me, and I saw an IDF major beating the living daylights out of the hapless pilot. When I asked the major if he had lost his mind, he snapped at me, "I was born in Iraq, and it wasn't enough that they made our lives hell over there, they had to come here and attack us again."

As he spoke, he kept pounding the pilot with his fists. There was nothing I could do against a claim that I had never heard before, and besides, my rank was no higher than that of the angry major. The sight of an Israeli officer beating an Iraqi pilot in the pristine desert was surreal.

We also shot down an Egyptian MiG-21, but the pilot escaped the plane and parachuted to the ground. As we surrounded him, one of our soldiers dug his hands into the pockets of the pilot's overalls and pulled out his money. I approached the soldier and, without saying a word, snatched the money from him and shoved it back into the pilot's pockets. But the soldier did not stop there; he again motioned toward the pilot's pockets. I had never been violent toward soldiers, but now I slapped this soldier across the face with the back of my hand. His head shook wildly, but more importantly, he gave up any hope of filching the pilot's money. Someone who had filmed the event later gave me a photo that I have kept to this day, along with the Egyptian pilot's ID card.

Despite our hunger, the arrival of food mingled with a twinge of fear. The maintenance officer would notify us by radio a few minutes in advance of the food arriving, and would specify the pickup location on the code maps. The problem was that the Egyptians had our code maps and would target their weapons at us. We got hold of our food amid artillery shells.

The code map the IDF used in Sinai was called the Sirius Code and came into use in 1968. The Egyptians, apparently with the help of Soviet experts, did painstaking work in listening to our transmissions and cross-referencing them with our movements on the ground, and they succeeded in decoding the map. At the end of 1970, after the War of Attrition ceasefire, the Signal Corps issued a document saying IDF forces should assume that the Sirius Code was no longer a secret. When using various code words (for routes, strongholds, etc.) via radio, the enemy knew exactly what they referred to, and so the code should be treated as a regular map. Our forces, out of habit, ignored this instruction and continued to treat Sirius as a code, with results like the one described above. It is highly likely that Maj. Gen. Albert Mendler, commander of the 252nd Armored Division, was killed in the war as a direct result of not heeding such instructions.

In those first days of the war, after the surprise attack, the IDF suffered heavy casualties and many losses of tanks and aircraft. In planning the strategy for the rest of the war, it was important to avoid additional losses, and at the same time to push the Egyptians back from the Israeli territory they had taken, about six miles along the east side of the Suez Canal. Leaving the situation as it was would have meant that Egypt won the entire war; to change it, it was necessary to take the initiative and attack.

Attacking the well-organized Egyptian infantry strongholds on the east side of the canal would have caused more heavy casualties. On the other hand, the Egyptian army on the west bank of the canal did not expect an Israeli ground attack, since the Egyptians knew their troops were holding the entire east side of the canal and they believed they could block any of Israel's penetrative attempts. The IDF believed that if they could succeed in crossing the Suez Canal and attack the Egyptians at the western bank, the Egyptian army might withdraw most of its forces from the east to the west bank in order to protect the way to their capital, Cairo, which is about eighty miles from the canal.

Very cleverly, the IDF found a gap between the Egyptian Second Army at the north and Third Army at the south, in the area of Deversoir. The IDF troops planned to penetrate the Egyptian army at the east side of the canal, cross the canal, and go deep into Egypt from the west side. It had to be carried out as a surprise, in a short time, in a very complicated way, and with very limited crossing equipment. The execution of this mission was given to Maj. Gen. Ariel "Arik" Sharon, commander of Division 143.

Crossing the Suez Canal between both Egyptian armies was a "mission impossible." Scanning our last set of orders a few hours before crossing the canal, we were skeptical as to whether we could make it. The uncertainty was so great that some soldiers and officers wrote their wills before the operation commenced. Yet, though many of us clearly had a slim chance of surviving the war, no one felt the urge to flee the battlefield. For my part, it did not occur to me to write a will. I had adopted the attitude that in times of war, or during an operation, one must focus only on achieving the objective.

We had pinned all our hopes on the roller bridge, which was built of large metal rollers joined together to form a chain that was towed by tanks. The rollers served as wheels on land, and on water they became a floating bridge that APCs and tanks could cross to the other side of the canal. However, on that day, October 16, one of the rollers broke while being towed to the canal, despite meticulous planning.

On October 16, 1973, my tank arrived in the Deversoir area at the "Yard," a marshalling area at the Suez Canal where heavy equipment had been deployed for Israeli troops so they could build a bridgehead to its western side. There were scores of IDF troops in the Yard, and they suffered heavy shelling from the Egyptians.

Dozens lost their lives in this deathtrap, which the troops nick-named "the Death Yard."

I stood in the turret of a Patton tank belonging to the first tank brigade that was supposed to cross the canal. The night sky turned blood red from the heavy Egyptian fire. Shells exploded all around us, spraying shrapnel in all directions. The Egyptian artillery guns grew more accurate all the time, causing more and more casualties. Radio calls for medical treatment were in vain; the brigade doctor, Capt. Dr. David Robert, was stuck in his half-track between other vehicles and could not make his way through.

I pinpointed the doctor's location, but I was in a similar predicament; my tank was also stuck between armored vehicles, unable to reach the doctor and take him to the wounded, by then in desperate need of help. Seeing no other option, I leapt from my tank and ran toward him. Each second was a matter of life and death. As I ran, artillery fire pounded the area I had just abandoned.

Thoughts raced through my mind. Realizing that I needed shelter, I turned around and ran frantically back to my tank. No sooner had I climbed into my turret and closed its steel cover than a bomb exploded next to my tank and shrapnel flew everywhere, striking the turret at the exact spot where I had been standing a second earlier. A split second, less than the blink of an eye, had separated me from death.

I crossed amid heavy Egyptian artillery fire to the other side of the canal with the tank operations officer and the rest of the tanks atop amphibious rafts, instead of the roller bridge. Though the Egyptian guns continued to harass us, we felt the euphoria of having finally crossed the canal.

Once we had crossed the canal, things became much simpler. The Egyptians were unprepared for us because they had not expect-ed the crossing. They probably thought that, in the worse case, we would drive them from the east side of the canal and be satisfied with that. We destroyed antiaircraft missile bases with tank and artillery fire to give our air force greater freedom of movement.

WHO SHALL LIVE AND WHO SHALL DIE | 141

The Egyptians' resistance was as weak as their surprise was strong. Haim Erez even weighed the possibility of continuing to Cairo. He thought we would encounter no more than seventy Egyptian tanks on the way, which we could easily deal with. He figured that if we threatened Cairo with tanks, there was a good chance the entire Egyptian army would break and retreat westward.

We spread out west of Fayed Airport facing the Egyptians. We were short on ammunition, and the command had a plan to move General Bren's 162nd Division across the canal and encircle the Egyptian Third Army. That was accomplished, and we received orders to stop and reorganize. The ceasefire was declared as we fronted the Egyptians on the western side of the canal, just sixty miles separating us from Cairo.

I was very fortunate that Haim Erez was my brigade commander in the war. He was self-assured, intelligent, and levelheaded, which is why Division Commander Ariel "Arik" Sharon had him carry out the division's key missions. In crossing the canal, the 421st Brigade, commanded by Erez, was the division's spearhead brigade and the first tank brigade to ford the waterway. After the war, I worked closely with Maj. Gen. Shmuel Gorodish, who was head of Southern Command during the war. Gorodish told me that Erez was the best brigade commander in the command. Many years later, while writing this book, I heard further praise for him from Operations Officer Zvi Kan-Tor. He told me that during his studies at the Command and Staff College in 1975, his lecturer Maj. Israel "Talik" Tal, who had been deputy chief of staff during the Yom Kippur War, had told the students that Erez was the best brigade commander in the war.

Later, in 1982, Erez was appointed head of Southern Command and promoted to major general. In that capacity he commanded the withdrawal from Sinai as required by the Israel-Egypt peace treaty.

After we crossed the canal, Erez had promoted me to deputy commander of the brigade's third battalion, the 257th. The relationship in the 257th Battalion between battalion commander

Yehuda Cohen and the company commanders was troubled. If you had to rate the mutual respect between them on a scale of one to 10, it would not exceed two. As deputy battalion commander, I was viewed as an outsider. The company commanders thought the task of deputy battalion commander should only go to one of their own. Some of them even showed signs of malicious pleasure whenever there was a problem.

I remember one night when we lost our way in the dark while returning to our battalion by jeep from brigade headquarters. Our driver was Avsha, the battalion scout. Avsha pointed to one of the stars and said that every night on his return to our battalion from brigade headquarters, he navigated by it. Doing so, he claimed, would take us straight to the battalion parking area. Since it was very late and I was exhausted after a day of nonstop activity, I went along with his claim, despite my rule as a commander not to trust anyone's navigation and to constantly check if we were on course. In this case, Avsha had not taken into account that we were returning to the battalion a few hours later than usual, and meanwhile the earth had rotated, causing us to veer off course. Suddenly we found ourselves facing a group of tanks. Machine guns opened fire on us; I did not know if they were our tanks or Egyptian ones. All I knew was that we were being shot at.

My greatest fear in the war was not so much getting wounded or killed as falling prisoner. At the time I knew a lot of information that had to be kept from the enemy, and I realized there was little chance of keeping secrets in captivity.

I ordered Avsha to turn around and move in zigzags. We drove like crazy, being thrown in the air by potholes on the road. Luckily we were not hit, and later we found out that the tanks firing at us had belonged to a neighboring battalion. When we got back to battalion headquarters and the cause of the shooting became clear, I saw the derisive and gloating looks of the company commanders.

This nocturnal journey, especially the fact that we came out of it unharmed, is engraved in my memory for another reason. One of the drivers who had left Sde Teiman told us that regular soldiers who had remained at the rear base had broken into the private cars left by reservists, stealing radios and tape recorders. I too had left my private car at that base, and said, "This is outrageous. We were fighting and barely survived, and they were stealing from us."

Haim Erez, who was present, said in his quiet and sober voice, "Look at you…you have two legs and two arms, you're alive…and all you're worried about is that your radio may have been stolen?" I thought about it, calmed down, and told him he was absolutely right. I had lost perspective; it happens to all of us. I have never forgotten this lesson, and have tried to apply it throughout my life. In the end it turned out that nothing had been stolen from my car.

The reality on the ground forced us to do things we would never have done in civilian life. For example, we were sorely lacking equipment to outfit our vehicles, yet we had a surplus of fuel, a commodity that the infantry units needed. I took advantage of this situation and paid in fuel for two Russian BTR[49] vehicles, then provided our battalion's reconnaissance with an operational APC. We also traded fuel with the well-equipped anti-aircraft battalion to get all sorts of luxury items.

One night, our sergeant major tried to "adopt" a command car from a neighboring unit. When he began driving off in it, he realized that he was dragging the tent next to it, and the soldiers from the tent started running after him. We later found out they had been worried about theft and had tied the car to the tent to prevent it.

In another example, since we did not have showers, I asked the maintenance officer, Benny, to build us some. Benny, a disciplined officer who exuded willingness to help out for a greater cause, asked me, "What exactly would you like me to build the showers with?" I replied that I did not really care how they were built, but if he wanted a few days' leave, he had better get cracking on it. The result, of course, was that Benny built showers.

---

[49] A kind of armored personnel carrier (APC).

On a similar note, I ordered the battalion master sergeant, Zvika, to set up a recreation room. He looked at me as if to say, "Why are you bothering me with this?" Later he approached me and asked, "What would you like me to build it with? I don't have materials. I don't have anything."

I gave him the same answer, "I do not care how you build it – just make sure a rec room gets built." I carried on with my business, and when I returned to battalion headquarters that afternoon I saw a magnificent rec room built entirely from doors.

I summoned Zvika. "What's with the doors?" I asked.

"Well, it's like this," he replied. "I went with a few of the guys to the nearest Egyptian village and took down all their doors."

"Are you out of your mind?" I asked.

He answered, with obvious impatience, "When I told you I had nothing to build a rec room with, you said you didn't care how I built it...."

Our sages teach us in the Talmud that the true character of the individual is revealed in how he responds when drunk, in how he spends money, and in how he behaves in moments of anger (Eruvin 65b). I have no doubt that a man's true colors are also revealed in times of war, when all signs of hypocrisy vanish. If an individual is brave, kind, practical, sensible, it will manifest itself in times of war. And if an individual is cowardly, mean, and inefficient, that also will come out clearly. It is hard to hide the truth in combat conditions.

One of the soldiers, whom everyone called Shemesh, was the phlegmatic type. One day, artillery fire landed on the battalion headquarters and everyone quickly ran for cover – except for Shemesh, who continued to fill sandbags with a look of indifference.

"What are you all so hysterical about?" he dryly asked all those who were lying on the ground.

And then there was Turgeman, nicknamed Turgi, a driver who threw himself flat on the ground the moment he heard the distant whistle of a mortar shell. His friends would tease him by imitating that sound, and poor, startled Turgi would immediately lie flat. But Turgi had a great sense of humor and entertained everyone with his stories.

After the ceasefire agreement, we secured the line in the Fayed Airport zone. The Egyptians occasionally shelled our frontline observation posts – in the Middle East this qualifies as a ceasefire.

One day, a replacement doctor, who was also a psychiatrist and had been my classmate at school in Jerusalem, joined our battalion. Although the war had ended and there was a ceasefire, he would walk around carrying his combat harness, loaded gun, and helmet. Several times a day he would ask me to show him on the map and on the ground where the Egyptian forces and we were deployed. Since patience for pointless requests is not my strong point, I repeatedly put him off. Finally one morning, unable to keep deflecting him, I showed him where Egyptian troops and our forces were concentrated. I then left the battalion to deal with other matters. When I returned that afternoon, I saw the medical unit with all its APCs lined up and facing east toward the area held by our forces. I called the medical clinic's sergeant major and asked what was going on. He explained that the doctor had assembled the unit and told them that up until that morning he had believed we were encircling the Egyptian Third Army, but after talking with me he had realized – or so he thought – that the Egyptians were actually encircling us. He had told the medical troops that, in the event of an Egyptian attack, they would have to escape immediately in a convoy and return to the east bank of the canal.

At that moment I realized that the doctor's strange behavior and apparel were a combat-stress reaction. I discharged him immediately and replaced him with another doctor.

Although the Yom Kippur War ended on October 25, we stayed in the Fayed zone from the end of October until March. We had time on our hands, and I was curious to find out what had happened to all the reservists who had not reported for duty. I discovered, among other things, that because of the chaos at the start of the war, most of our missing troops had been sent to serve in other units. But I found ten of our reservists who had not shown up at all. One of them, for example, was a battalion chef who continued to attend the Tadmor Culinary School in Herzliya as if nothing had happened. Another continued his studies at the Israel Institute of Technology.

We sent them to the military court, but they were acquitted because, with all the disarray at the beginning of the war, it was impossible to prove that they had received their call-up orders. And yet, to be fair to the fighting, wounded, and killed troops, I decided we had a moral duty not to make allowances for the draft dodgers. I made sure that my decisions were implemented. For example, the Israel Institute of Technology student was called up for reserve duty a few months later in Ras Sudr, a town in Sinai on the Red Sea coast. By chance, I caught him one day violating a ban on swimming in the sea between one and two o'clock in the afternoon when there was no lifeguard on duty. I told the master sergeant to file a complaint against him.

I sentenced the student to thirty-five days in jail, to begin at the end of his reserve duty. His family created a stir and complained to the head of Southern Command. Deputy Brigade Commander Potash approached me in a fluster and asked, "Tell me Diskin, are you nuts?" He thought thirty-five days in the cooler was too strong a punishment for the crime. But once I explained that the student had evaded duty during the war, Potash was furious and said, "Listen, before he finishes his reserve duty, I want you to go to the jail where he'll be serving his sentence, and tell the commanding officer to give him special treatment."

I was shocked by these draft dodgers. A year later, when I talked about it with Gen. Shmuel Gorodish, I told him how sorry I was not to have served in the War of Independence when all the soldiers were enthusiastic patriots. I was taken aback when he told me, "You don't have to be sorry about that; there were also many draft dodgers in the War of Independence." Historians who wrote about that war have confirmed what he said.

In the period after the ceasefire, I tried to devote some time to my academic studies. Luckily for me the head of Ariel Sharon's division command post was Lt. Col. (res.) Professor Pinhas "Siko" Zusman, who was also my thesis adviser for my MA. During military routine I managed to talk with him, among the APCs, about various issues of my thesis.

During the little leave I had, I went to the Hebrew University in Rehovot to hear the occasional lecture and hand in exercises. I was perturbed to see that there were students who simply spent their time studying, while most men between the ages of twenty-two and forty-five were doing reserve duty.

The computer company that employed me was very supportive and treated me wonderfully. They tried to help as much as possible and paid me a full salary even though I had only started working for them a few months before the war began.

During those five months after the ceasefire we had visits and inspections. Gen. Ariel Sharon came by frequently. On one of his visits, at which the brigade commander Haim Erez was present, Sharon asked the officers, "How are you doing?"

The patrol officer stood up and said, "The Egyptians are advancing, creeping up to their line."

"Why don't you shoot them?" Sharon asked.

"Because we don't have permission from the brigade commander," replied the officer.

"Don't you know how to act?" Sharon asked. "First you shoot, and then you ask for permission."

That was Sharon's philosophy – if you think it is the right thing to do, you do it. The question, of course, is how to determine what is right and wrong when you are contravening orders.

On one of Sharon's night visits he arrived with his group without prior warning and went straight to the battalion command. At the time, I was the acting battalion commander because Yehuda

Cohen was on leave. Sharon, who wanted to check our state of readiness at all levels, ordered me to replace the company stationed along the line with a backup company from a nearby battalion. In general we did all this well, but with some failings. And here I saw the greatness of Sharon. After the order was carried out, he shook my hand and said, "Overall, it was fine. You saw the shortcomings and I'm sure you will make it your duty to fix them." Obviously I did fix the flaws. The important thing, though, was that Sharon had not ignored them, yet knew how to leave me with a good feeling.

Another inspection, carried out by Sharon's deputy Col. Jackie Even, was quite different. Jackie visited the company of Capt. Oded Megiddo, a war hero and exemplary commander. He asked Oded, "How long have you been a company commander?"

"Five years," Oded said.

"Well, you may have been a company commander for five years, but you don't know how to get your company into position," said Even.

Oded was not only left with an unpleasant feeling, but he also thought Even was talking nonsense and took no remedial actions. I am not belittling Jackie Even; he was a skilled commander and reached the rank of major general. But when it came to relations between commanders and subordinates, he – like many other senior commanders – had a lot to learn from Ariel Sharon.

Among the officers and soldiers there was a lot of grumbling about the way the senior officers and politicians handled the war. After the war, Moshe Dayan visited us. We all thought that, as defense minister, he had been a main cause of the disaster of the Yom Kippur War. There was a cold atmosphere during his visit. When he asked if there were any questions, no one raised a hand, except for one fool who asked why God's name was not mentioned in the war.

Moshe Dayan replied in astonishment, "What were you expecting…that we would say 'With the help of God' more often?"

In March, before our discharge from reserve duty, Maj. Gen. Bren also paid us a visit. He had been appointed head of Southern Command in January. Bren told us that we needed to hold a training session immediately. I liked some of the officers' reactions to this. One officer remarked: "We, the officers and enlisted men, fought well. Those who didn't fight well were you, the generals, so you're the ones who should be training."

Those of us who served in Sharon's division disapproved of Bren, mainly because of his division's ineffective counterattacks on October 8, and the mistaken and misleading reports it sent afterward to Southern Command and the General Staff. We did, however, admire Ariel Sharon. He read the battlefront accurately and relentlessly urged a crossing of the canal until his superiors finally acceded. It was a decision that turned the tide of the war. Sharon was deeply intuitive, could rightly assess the course of a war, and knew how to instill confidence and determination. It was moving to hear him one evening in the parking area, talking by radio to his wife Lily and telling her in a resonant voice, so that all the soldiers in the vicinity could hear him, "Lily, you can do anything with these guys."

Later, when I worked closely with Maj. Gen. Gorodish and we became quite friendly, I tactlessly told him that Ariel Sharon was the only general in the Yom Kippur War who knew what needed to be done. To my surprise, Gorodish agreed, but added that while it was good to be Sharon's subordinate, it was impossible to be his commander. Of course, Gorodish had replaced Sharon as head of Southern Command only a few months earlier, and relations between a predecessor and a successor are often highly charged.

However, many years later when I read books about the Yom Kippur War, especially Amiram Ezov's *Crossing*, I realized just how tactless I had been. I learned about the deep-seated resentment Gorodish and Haim Bar-Lev harbored toward Ariel Sharon.

For my part, I saw Sharon as having changed the fate of the campaign on the southern front. In my eyes he will always be a great commander who understood the arena, and who had the military talent and intuition to initiate the right moves that led to victory. I felt great personal satisfaction at having taken part in crucial battles with commanders like Haim Erez and Ariel Sharon.

Once the Interim Agreement with Egypt had been signed, and our forces discharged, Brigade Commander Haim Erez and his deputy, Potash, wanted the deputy battalion commanders to spend two weeks at Sde Teiman putting the warehouses in order. I had already abandoned my civilian job for five months to volunteer in the war effort, and I did not consider it my task as a reserve officer to tidy up warehouses. The IDF had career soldiers for such jobs. So, to the dismay of the brigade commanders, I went home. I suppose this was a form of insubordination, but I was not censured for it, probably because of my performance during the war.

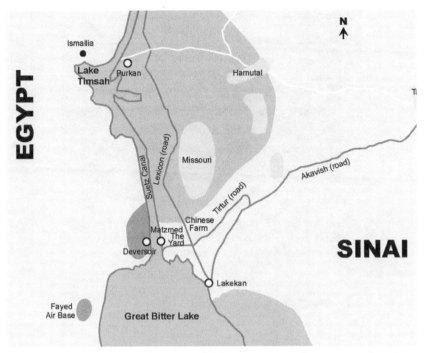

Map of our brigade's area of activity and the crossing point. Some names of roads and some positions are according to the Sirius Code.

Israeli Patton tanks damaged during the war in the Central Zone (photo: Ron Ilan, courtesy of the IDF Spokesperson's Unit)

*Colonel Haim Erez (*center*) at a briefing with officers of
the brigade reconnaissance company before an operation
(courtesy of the IDF Spokesperson's Unit)*

*Israel Potash, deputy brigade commander (*left*); Giora Lev, First Battalion
commander (*center*); me (*far right*)*

Maj. Gen. Shmuel Gorodish (right), *Maj. Gen. Ariel
Sharon* (left) *at a briefing during the Yom Kippur
war, 1973 (photo: Shlomo Arad, courtesy of the
Government Press Office)*

Last set of orders before crossing the canal, October 15; standing, center*:
Operations Officer Zvi Kan-Tor (photo: Ron Ilan, courtesy of the IDF
Spokesperson's Unit)*

IDF forces immediately after crossing the canal, October 16 (courtesy of the IDF Spokesperson's Unit)

Centurion tanks of Division 162 crossing over the roller bridge, October 19 (photo: Ron Ilan, courtesy of the IDF Spokesperson's Unit)

Exposed in the turret at the height of battle (courtesy of the IDF Spokesperson's Unit)

Shaving after the fighting with a piece of a broken mirror

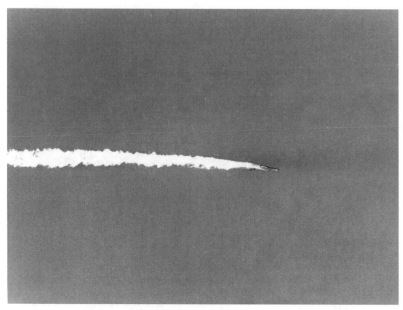

The Egyptian MiG that was hit (photo: Ron Ilan, courtesy of the IDF Spokesperson's Unit)

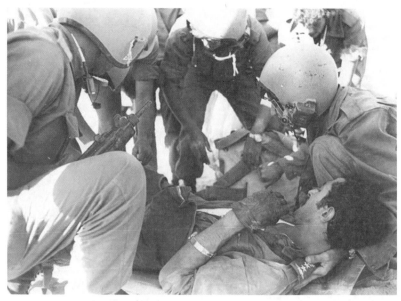

Mamduch Almlet, the Egyptian pilot whose plane was shot down; I am in the center background (photo: Ron Ilan, courtesy of the IDF Spokesperson's Unit)

ID of the captured Egyptian pilot, Mamduch Almlet

The Egyptian pilot who was shot down, Mamduch Almlet, twenty years later as an Egyptian commercial pilot

Interrogation of Egyptian prisoner; I am on the left; the interpreter is on the right (courtesy of the IDF Spokesperson's Unit)

Me with Battalion Master Sergeant Tzvika (right)

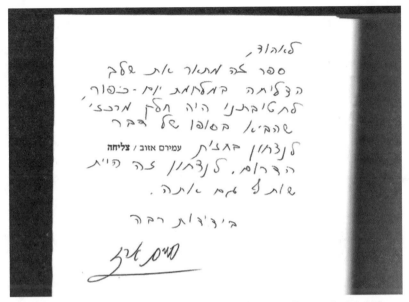

An inscription I received from Brigade Commander Haim Erez in the book The Crossing, *which he gave me as a gift. The inscription reads: "Dear Ehud, This book describes the canal crossing in the Yom Kippur War, in which our brigade played a central role and ultimately led to our victory on the southern front. You too were a part of that victory. Your friend, Haim Erez."*

A combatants' gathering after the war. In foreground (left to right): *Defense Minister Shimon Peres, Haim Erez, me.*

פקודת יום מיוחדת

מטעם

אלוף אריאל שרון

מפקד אוגדה 143

לוחמים,

לפני שלשה וחצי חדשים יצאנו יחד למלחמה. היתה זו מלחמה קשה ועקובה מדם.

ביום הכיפורים נזעקנו, אנחנו אנשי המילואים, ויחדיו חשנו אל החזית המתמוטטת. אוגדתנו הוצבה מול המרכזי שבמאמצי האויב.

תוך לחימת גבורה ומאמץ עליון של כל אחד מכם, עצרנו את הכוחות המצריים.

היתה זו האוגדה שלנו שיזמה ולקחה על עצמה את ביצוע הקשה, המורכב והאכזרי שבמהלכי המלחמה — מבצע צליחת התעלה. צליחת התעלה היא שהביאה את השינוי ואת התפנית במלחמה. צליחת התעלה — היא שהביאה את הניצחון במלחמה. עלינו לזכור שניצחוננו במלחמת יום הכיפורים הוא הגדול שבניצחונות שהיו לנו.

אם — למרות מחדלים וטעויות, למרות כשלונות והכשלות, למרות אבדן עשתונות ואבדן שליטה — הצלחנו להגיע לניצחון, טוב שנדע כולנו, שהיה זה הנצחון הגדול ביותר שנחל צה"ל מעודו.

אנחנו נלחמנו, מאות מטובי לוחמינו נפלו בקרב ורבים יותר נפצעו במהלכי המלחמה — אך ניצחנו!

אתם, למרות הכל, ניצחתם ועשיתם זאת במסירות, בהקרבה עצמית, בעקשנות ובגבורה.

לאחר המלחמה המשכתם באותה התמדה ובאותה רוח טובה לשאת בנטל היומיומי, לעמוד בעבודות התבצרות אדירות, לעמוד מול אש ולהשיב מלחמה שערה.

עם סיום המלחמה הודעתי, שאשאר איתכם כל עוד ידרש שרותנו במילואים. הבטחתי להישאר איתכם. אך היום אני נאלץ לעזוב אתכם.

לכם החיילים, שהנכם הגיבורים האמיתיים של המלחמה הזאת, אני חייב הסבר. המלחמה נסתיימה, נסתיים שלב בדיונים על הסדר עם המצרים, ואני חש שהכרחי להילחם היום בחזית אחרת. הכרחי להילחם, ובכל הכח, כדי למנוע מלחמות נוספות בעתיד. לכן אני עוזב.

רצוני שתדעו שמעולם לא שרתתי במחיצת לוחמים כמוכם. אתם הייתם הגדולים שבכולם! מעולם לא חשתי באחוות לוחמים ויחסי רעות רעות כפי שהיו באוגדה שלנו. היה זה בית חם שנתן לי תמיד את הביטחון בכוחנו וביכולתנו.

אני עוזב אתכם היום בצער. איחולי לכל אחד מכם שיחזור במהרה לביתו, אך אם נצטרך לשוב ולהילחם — אני מבטיחכם לחזור ולהילחם איתכם יחד.

אריאל שרון, אלוף

מפקד האוגדה

20 ינואר 1974

כ"ז טבת תשל"ד

Special Order of the Day from Maj. Gen. Ariel Sharon, January 1974.

It reads:

Special Order of the Day
on behalf of
Gen. Ariel Sharon, Division Commander 143

Dear Combatants,
Three and a half months ago we went to war together. It was a hard and bloody war. On Yom Kippur we reservists were called to duty and together we hurried to the collapsing southern front. Our division was stationed in the central region of the front, opposite strong enemy forces.

With the brave fighting and supreme effort of all of you, we held back Egyptian forces.

It was our division that initiated and took it upon ourselves to carry out the most challenging, complex, and brutal operation of the war: crossing the canal. The crossing of the canal was the turning point of the war, and we need to remember that this victory in the Yom Kippur War was our greatest victory.

If – despite our oversights and errors, our setbacks and failings, our confusion and loss of control – we were triumphant, then we should all know that this victory was the IDF's greatest victory ever.

We fought hard, hundreds of our best soldiers fell in battle and many more were wounded in the war – but we won!

Despite everything, you won and you did so with dedication, self-sacrifice, commitment and bravery.

After the war, you continued to bear the daily burden with the same diligence and good spirit, to build massive fortifications, and withstand fire and fight back.

When the war was over I told you that I would remain with you as long as our service in the reserves was needed. I promised to stay with you, but today I must leave you.

I owe all you soldiers, the real heroes of this war, an explanation. The war is over, the talks with the Egyptians have ended, and today I feel I need to fight on a different front. I must fight with all my strength to prevent another war in the future, and to do that I must leave you.

I want you to know that I have never fought alongside soldiers such as yourselves; you are simply the best. I have never felt a comradeship and closeness among soldiers like in our division. It was a warm family that gave me confidence in our strength and ability.

Today, I sadly leave you. I hope that each and every one of you returns home speedily – but if we should need to fight again, I promise to return and fight with you.

Maj. Gen. Ariel Sharon
Division Commander
January 20, 1974

Chapter 9
. . . .
YOM KIPPUR SCAPEGOATS

Tanks moved mechanically in the field like ducks at a shooting range. The helicopter rose into position above the hill, ready to open fire on them. As a lieutenant colonel in the Systems Analysis Center of the Planning Division, I sat behind the pilot. Beside me sat an air force captain who was also taking part in the war game, an exercise to test the helicopter's ability to destroy enemy tanks.

My job was to do the research and recommend to the air force which helicopters it should buy, both in terms of cost and effectiveness. I had to go all-out to get the air force's cooperation. I also involved people in the project whose job it was to research performance in the field. They built a special model to test the helicopters' vulnerabilities and effectiveness in hitting different enemy targets.

We came up with clear results and straightforward recommendations for the type and number of helicopters to purchase. I wrote a proposal on the topic and submitted it to the planning chief, Maj. Gen. Avraham "Abrasha" Tamir. He read it, told me I had done good work, and ordered me to circulate it to the heads of the relevant IDF divisions so a discussion on the matter could be held. I did as he said, and a few days later Abrasha called me in a panic, ordering me to recall the proposal and put a freeze on the whole matter.

Of course, I looked into what had really happened. It turned out that air force commander Maj. Gen. Benny Peled had received my proposal and angrily declared, "The Planning Division is not going to tell us whether to buy helicopters or which ones to choose!" He ignored the fact that the project was conducted in full collaboration with his people. Abrasha, who was not only a smart general but also an experienced politician, opted to shelve the issue rather than get into a bitter fight.

Eventually the air force decided to purchase its new helicopter, the U.S. AH-1 Cobra, which had the same design and capability that we had proposed. But I was disappointed to discover that politics and narrow interests prevailed, rather than the merits of the case. Unfortunately, this was a typical occurrence.

I had gone back to the IDF after finishing my work at Advanced Technology, realizing that a job in the private sector did not work well with a great deal of reserve duty. It was Col. Uri Rabinovich, head of the Budgets Department in the Quartermaster's Division, who got me back into the army. We had met while both of us served in the office of the financial adviser to the chief of staff. Uri introduced me to Maj. Gen. Arieh Levi, head of the Quartermaster's Division, who proposed that I join his department at the rank of lieutenant colonel and deal with financial and economic issues.

Not yet certain I wanted to return to the IDF, I hesitated. What finally made up my mind was yet another call up for reserve duty, this time as supervisor of an exercise.

Once I decided to sign on, I had to find the best niche. At some point I heard a new unit, the Systems Analysis Center, had been added to the Planning Division. This unit sounded like a good fit for me because I had military experience in the field, as well as the academic background to carry out cost-benefit analyses of military units and weapon systems.

The head of the center, Col. Simcha Maoz, was happy to have me on board. I started the official induction process, but quickly ran into trouble. Uri Rabinovich got angry when I decided not to serve in his unit in the Quartermaster's Division. Uri claimed that since I had already met with General Levi, head of the Quartermaster's

Division, it had first rights to me. This was not the private sector, he said, but the IDF, and one could not simply pick and choose where he wanted to serve. With the help of the deputy head of IDF Manpower Administration, he waged a struggle to prevent my induction.

This reminded me of my earlier battle to serve in the Financial Adviser's Office instead of the Armored Corps. In neither case could I say what I really thought: "Gentlemen, I have always, even as a conscript, served where I wanted to serve, because it is important for me to live my life as I want to live it, and not as you want me to live it. What you want is actually of no interest to me."

I was also reminded of Brig. Gen. Nehemiah Kain, who told me as I was joining the Financial Adviser's Office, "We beat Hitler, we beat Nasser and we will beat Bren." I substituted Bren's name with Uri Rabinovich and Arieh Levi, and after a difficult struggle, I took my place in the Planning Division.

I started work there full of enthusiasm. I dealt with important and interesting projects such as "Homefront Vulnerability" and "Planning and Building of Units." I recruited scientists and operations researchers for these projects, and we received compliments on the results. The only hitch – as in the case of the helicopters and the air force commander – was that nothing was applied in the field. I discovered that a very high percentage of the activity on the General Staff centers on internal politics and frictions between the various divisions. Sometimes these divisions even conceal data and otherwise mislead one another, all in the name of gaining prestige and proving their superiority and power.

I was also disappointed with my immediate commander, Simcha Maoz. Although his name, Simcha, means "joy" in Hebrew, for me he was only a source of grief. Maoz was an intelligent and highly knowledgeable person, but he suffered from multiple complexes, and I found that much of his activity was aimed at his own advancement. For example, when I did some work on optimal structure for tank brigades, Simcha took the work, attached a personal letter to it, and brought it to Maj. Gen. Herzel Shafir, head of Southern Command, because he thought it would win him points with Herzel.

One day, Abrasha Tamir informed me that Maj. Gen. Shmuel Gorodish had been appointed to plan a new unified headquarters for the ground forces, to be called the GOC Army Headquarters. It would take all the ground forces, which so far had operated separately, under its wing. Because the Agranat Com-

Shmuel Gorodish at the 1967 war

mission, set up in the aftermath of the Yom Kippur War debacle, had ruled that Gorodish could no longer serve in a command position, he was now mostly involved in planning. Abrasha told me I was to join Gorodish's team.

Although he had commanded the 82nd Battalion while I served in it during my conscript days, I did not know Gorodish personally. They said he was a tough, difficult commander. I recalled how, in the vicinity of the headquarters of the 7th Brigade, of which Gorodish was commander, you could drive no faster than 3.5 miles per hour. Anyone who drove faster and got caught ended up in military lockup for thirty-five days. I heard horror stories about Gorodish's rants and reprimands, and how he sent soldiers and officers to jail at the drop of a hat. My answer to Abrasha was, "I am not going to work for that person."

Today, in retrospect, I am amazed that I, as a lieutenant colonel, dared to give such an answer to a major general, and that the general did not send me to the gallows. Maybe it had to do with my reputation as someone who did not do things he did not want to do, my steely tone, or Abrasha's regard for me. Maybe it was all those factors combined. In any case, he replied, "Let's compromise. Go work with Gorodish for two weeks, and if at the end of those two weeks you're not happy, come back."

I agreed on the spot.

So I went to Gorodish and joined the team. I was completely taken aback by his personality. He turned out to be a clever person, polite and respectful toward me. My first task was to prepare a proposed structure for the training and R&D units at the Ground Forces Command. To do so, I drew on my military knowledge and used systems analysis methods.

Ten days later I gave Gorodish a paper analyzing the issue and proposing two alternatives. Of the two, I recommended option B.

Gorodish gave me his response the next day. Gazing sternly at me through his horn-rimmed glasses, he said, "I read your paper. It's good, but you have to make one change: Instead of recommending option B, recommend option A."

I promptly replied, "I'm sorry, but in my opinion option B is the right one, so I can't recommend option A. But you're a general, and you're entitled to choose whichever option you desire."

The next day Gorodish told me, "I showed the booklet to Talik (Maj. Gen. Israel Tal) and he said you're right to recommend option B." It was no secret that Gorodish saw Talik as an oracle and admired him. But he added, "Both you and Talik are wrong."

At that moment I decided that, since the two weeks I had agreed to work with Gorodish would end in two days, I would part from him right then. It seemed my fears were right; Gorodish was bullheaded and did everything his own way without regard for the merits of the matter.

After the weekend, I returned to the office prepared to tell Gorodish goodbye. Before I could open my mouth, he turned to me and said, "You know, I thought about the issue all weekend, and you're right. Make it option B." Right then and there I decided to keep working for him. After all, he was able to admit when he was wrong.

Over the next several months, I discovered Gorodish's personality was completely different from what people had led me to expect. I found him to be an extremely astute person, who knew how to logically analyze both military and everyday issues. He was also sensitive to people, even though he used that to achieve his own goals.

I was further impressed by his knowledge of the Bible. Since I was also knowledgeable in this area, we would sometimes wrangle over biblical fine points. Maj. Eli Narkis was Gorodish's bureau chief, and usually the one who ended meetings. In one meeting, Gorodish turned to him and called him "Shebnah the scribe." Shebnah was biblical King Hezekiah's scribe who conducted negotiations with Rabshakeh, envoy of King Sennacherib of Assyria, during the siege of Jerusalem. Gorodish wrote the name Shebnah on the board with the Hebrew letter *heh* at the end. I corrected him, telling him that the name Shebnah ends in the letter *aleph*. Gorodish said I was wrong, and we bet on it. He opened the Bible and showed me where the name Shebnah ends in *heh* (II Kings 18:18). I opened the Bible and showed him several other places in II Kings and Isaiah where the name ends in *aleph*. We were both right. The other officers at the meeting were amazed.

Beyond the fact that Gorodish was pleased with my work, there was personal chemistry between us. And though he was fourteen years older than me, and a major general, we became friends. On more than one occasion he took me into his confidence. Our conversations were frank, but for my part, I now regret that I was sometimes too outspoken. Gorodish always behaved graciously toward me and never raised his voice. Undoubtedly most of those who knew him, upon reading this, will think I am talking about someone else.

Once when I asked Gorodish why he had built such a terrible reputation for himself, he said it was because he wanted his underlings to be in great fear and awe of him, and that it had taken him years to create this image.

The army was everything to him. Before the Yom Kippur War, he told me, he was led to believe that he was on his way to becoming chief of staff. He had emerged from the Six-Day War as a successful commander and hero. Then came the Yom Kippur War. He was head of Southern Command, but his string of successes came to an end. The Israeli public was distraught over the war's surprise opening and the large number of IDF casualties, and the Agranat Commission was appointed to investigate these issues. One of their conclusions was that, in the south, Gorodish had fouled up. His main mistake, the commission claimed, was that he had not deployed his forces properly on the eve of the war. They said he needed to deploy an additional brigade from the armored division to the Sinai front to join the brigade regularly stationed there. He failed to do so, leaving only one brigade instead of two to face the Egyptian army at the opening of the war.

In 2012, the Israeli historian Yigal Kipnis published *1973: The Road to War*. Based on confidential reports from that period, it shows clearly the extent to which the Israeli leaders at the time, Prime Minister Golda Meir and Defense Minister Moshe Dayan, were responsible for the Yom Kippur War. Several months before the war, Egyptian president Anwar Sadat conveyed to U.S. Secretary of State Henry Kissinger, via Sadat's personal envoy Hafez Ismail, his ideas about an Egyptian-Israeli peace agreement. The proposals were forwarded to their ultimate target, Meir and Dayan, who ignored them. Sadat's proposals strongly implied that, were they to be rejected, he would launch a war. Not only did Meir and Dayan reject the peace offers, but they also did not brief the top military brass; as a result, there was a high probability of war. If they had informed this top echelon, Israel would undoubtedly have been more prepared for the war.

The reports also indicated that the Americans cooperated with Israel in return for Meir and Dayan's promise not to launch a preemptive war. As a result, at the brink of war, Meir and Dayan rejected recommendations for a preemptive strike by the chief of staff, Lt. Gen. David "Dado" Elazar, and the air force commander, Maj. Gen. Benny Peled.

Documentation of Dayan's opposition to a preemptive strike and to a reserve call-up, despite Elazar's urging, came my way while writing this book. A transcript of a conversation between Dayan and Elazar on the morning of Yom Kippur, October 6, 1973, was cleared for publication by the defense establishment in March 2013. According to the transcript, Dayan opposed a preemptive strike and reserve call-up on the grounds that it would enable the Arab states to claim that Israel, despite its promises to the United States, had initiated the war. In retrospect, it is absurd that the Agranat Commission was not given a mandate to investigate the political echelon, which, without a doubt, was entirely culpable for the mistakes made in the run-up to the war.

Furthermore, the commission's mandate was limited to investigating the steps taken up to October 8. It only addressed the beginning of the war and the catastrophe that resulted from the flawed conception of both the political and military leaders. From October 8 until the end of the fighting, the IDF succeeded in turning the tables and achieved a brilliant victory. So the Agranat Commission, by not extending its purview beyond October 8, was unjust to those it censured. The greatest injustice was done to Chief of Staff Elazar, who performed very well during the remainder of the war.

The commission also ignored Elazar's request for a preemptive strike. As mentioned, if the politicians had complied with that request, the early phase of the war would have gone very differently. The commission, by turning a blind eye to the army's accomplishments after October 8, gave the Israeli public a picture of unrectified failure and catastrophe, while paying no heed to the turnabout in battle and the resounding victory that ensued, of which the Israeli public should have been made more aware.

Gorodish saw that the commission was biased. After it summoned him to a hearing, one of the lieutenant colonels on the General Staff sent him a stenographer's copy of the orders from the "pit"[50] as they had come down in real time. Gorodish showed me where it said he had been ordered to deploy two brigades for the outbreak of the war at 6 p.m. The Mossad chief had been informed that the war would start before sunset, and the IDF had interpreted this to be 6 p.m. Of course, the Egyptians and Syrians did not stick to this schedule and launched the war at 2 p.m. At that time, the second standing-army brigade was making its way to the front line. According to Gorodish, he had carried out the order he received. He told me that, when he requested to show this document to the Agranat Commission, they said that they already had his testimony and did not want to hear any more from him.

Moshe Dayan, Gorodish said, made him and Elazar out to be the scapegoats because the public was looking for someone to blame. Making use of the only two military men on the commission, Lt. Gen. (ret.) Haim Laskov and Lt. Gen. (ret.) Yigal Yadin, Dayan conspired to have his people ensure that the slates of all the political leaders were wiped clean. According to Gorodish, Haim Laskov was unemployed at the time, and Dayan arranged to place him in the post of ombudsman of the defense establishment. As for Yigal Yadin – a noted Israeli archeologist, general, and politician – Gorodish claimed he was one of Dayan's people and acted on his behalf. If one considers the failures of other generals who got through the Agranat Commission unscathed, Gorodish seems convincing.

For example, Maj. Gen. Peled, commander of the air force during the war, was considered, like Gorodish, to be an accomplished military man with an impressive record. Like everyone else, though, he was capable of making mistakes. In fact, he functioned very poorly during the war, particularly at its outset. The previous air force commander, Maj. Gen. (ret.) Motti Hod, said Peled's whole approach in the beginning of the war was flawed. Before it broke out, Peled rightly favored a preemptive strike on the Arab armies and hoped to carry it out up to the last moment, despite the politicians'

---

[50] A slang term for the command bunker in the Kirya, in Tel Aviv.

opposition. The strike would have included bombing the enemy's airfields and surface-to-air missile batteries. The Israeli planes designated for this mission were equipped with time-delay fuses for their bombs, which explode only after penetrating a bunker, along with special cones to help penetrate the bunkers.

On October 6, at 1 p.m., about an hour before the war started, Peled finally concluded that the political leaders would not approve a preemptive strike. He then ordered that the munitions in the planes be replaced with types better suited to defensive warfare, such as assisting the ground forces and intercepting enemy planes. Peled ordered that the time-delay fuses be replaced with regular ones, so that bombs would explode above the ground and strike soldiers and armored fighting vehicles. The bunker-penetrating cones also had to be removed. These complicated operations took time and required special security measures.

Col. Giora Forman, who was head of the air force's Operations Department, opposed Peled's decision to replace the munitions and said they could still be used for defensive operations to help the ground forces. However, Peled insisted, and the Phantom squadrons started dismantling the bombs and loading air-to-air missiles. The result was catastrophic. When the Egyptian and Syrian armies attacked Israel's borders, the air force lacked the capabilities it required, and the Phantom fleet was almost completely useless for hours because it did not have the necessary munitions.

As my high school teacher, Greenspan, used to say, "When a fool makes a mistake, it's a foolish mistake; when a smart person makes a mistake, it's a sophisticated mistake that could cause a catastrophe." Had Benny Peled not given this shortsighted order, the air force could have attacked the Arabs' offensive deployment effectively at the outset of the war. True, both Egypt and Syria had an umbrella of antiaircraft missiles. But a massive aerial attack on their field units and command posts could have altered the course of the war and prevented many Israeli losses.

Moreover, when the Egyptian-Syrian assault began, Peled pointlessly sent the whole Phantom fleet into action to defend the country, even though a few hours before the war, he had decided that just fifty-seven Mirage and Nesher planes, along with only twelve Phantoms, would suffice. This mistaken decision also contributed to the inefficient use of the air force's power and its effective removal from the balance of forces. Yet Benny Peled got through the Agranat Commission unscathed. An insightful analysis of these events, and criticism of Benny Peled, can be found in the book by Col. (res.) Dr. Shmuel Gordon, *30 Hours in October.*

Just as the Yom Kippur War was traumatic for the Israeli people, the Agranat Commission was traumatic for Gorodish. He did not stop talking about the commission and always brought up different aspects of its conclusions, showing me documents that backed up his claims.

One of the more striking stories concerned General Laskov. Gorodish said that, while he was giving his testimony, Laskov asked him if the soldiers' rifles in the outposts had affixed bayonets. Of course, no one has attached a bayonet to a rifle since World War II. When Gorodish answered in the negative, Laskov banged his fist on the table and proclaimed angrily, "Now I know why the outposts collapsed!"

After I heard Gorodish out, I told him that, in my opinion, the Agranat Commission had indeed gone wrong, but not in the way he thought. As I saw it, a good many of the generals had indeed bungled their duties – some more and some less – but the head of Military Intelligence, Maj. Gen. Eli Zeira, was a major cause of the failure. It was he who made the inaccurate assessment of a low probability of war. He contemptuously dismissed the views of other intelligence officers, including those who thought war was imminent. To this day, Zeira is alive and well, and never admitted his failures in the war.

And apart from Zeira's grave culpability, I believed the commission made a mistake by selectively censuring or sending home certain generals who had slipped up in certain regards, while other generals who had also made mistakes, even if to a lesser extent, got off scot-free without even a reprimand.

I then told Gorodish that I thought the Agranat Commission should have focused on revealing what went wrong and how to fix the deficiencies. As for personal responsibility, it should have taken one of two options: Either tell the generals that they had messed up and that they should continue to serve in their jobs while incorporating the lessons. Or tell them that, as commanders, the responsibility for what went wrong was theirs and they would all have to go home. I then added my own – not very tactful – recommendation and told Gorodish that, in my opinion, all the generals should have been sent packing because they had "screwed up big-time."

To my surprise, he responded, "You're right, but I would have had to go half an hour after everyone else."

I continued in my tactless vein. "Arik Sharon was the only one in command who knew what to do. He read the battle correctly, and he was the one who changed the course of the war in the south." As mentioned, during the war I served in the Southern Command, in Sharon's division. I saw Sharon in all his greatness as a commander, as the one who pushed for crossing the canal.

Gorodish again surprised me by replying, "You're right. The problem is that it's impossible to be Arik Sharon's commander. One can only be his subordinate."

Gorodish had an aggressive streak that he could not always control. During meetings, as he sat at the head of the table, he would sometimes draw his commando knife and, with a toss of about ten yards, embed it in the office door. This was the office of Maj. Gen. Abrasha Tamir, and when Abrasha saw the damage, his gaze would darken and he would tell me gloomily, "Look at how Gorodish wrecked the door."

As a young lieutenant colonel, the interactions between the generals amazed me. One day Gorodish came to the office upset and told me that the driver of Maj. Gen. Herzel Shafir, then head of the Operations Division at General Headquarters, had a lot of gall. Gorodish had been in a meeting with Chief of Staff Lt. Gen. Mordechai "Motta" Gur, and had parked his military car in Shafir's space. Shafir's driver had pulled up in the general's car, seen that the place was taken by another general's car, and decided to block the car by parking behind it. Gorodish saw this move as a blow to his honor. He went to Shafir's car, which was locked, and knocked lightly on the small side window to open it without breaking it, so that he could get the door open and move the car. Gorodish was particularly strong. His hands were like sledgehammers, and the window broke anyway. Gorodish proceeded to open the door and move Shafir's car out of the way.

Gorodish went on angrily that Shafir's driver apparently knew it was his car that was parked in the space, and that was why he blocked it. Had it been a different general, he would not have dared to do it. And the story did not end there. Gorodish told me that Shafir had submitted an official complaint against him to the chief of staff. Personally, I found this behavior immature.

One day while I was working with Gorodish, I was called in for an interview with the commander of the Armored Corps, Maj. Gen. Moshe "Mussa" Peled. He told me, "You became a lieutenant colonel while in the Planning Division. In the Armored Corps, you should be a battalion commander with that rank. What do you think of being an on-call battalion commander instead of a deputy battalion commander?"

This was 1974, not long after the trauma of the Yom Kippur War, a war in which inexperienced or unskilled commanders headed units, with disastrous consequences.

I replied, "My status as on-call deputy battalion commander is good enough for me. All I want is that, if a war breaks out, I can contribute as a fighter at the front. I'm sure I could be a battalion commander at the level of mediocre ones now serving in the Armored Corps. I'm not sure I have the knowledge, talent, and experience to be a good battalion commander."

Mussa Peled, clearly agitated, said, "What do you mean, mediocre battalion commanders? We have excellent battalion commanders!"

At the end of the interview, he said he would look into it further and inform me of his decision. He lost no time turning to some of my former commanders, including Haim Erez, and they told him I could be a battalion commander. He called me for a second interview and told me that I would be appointed to the post. When I mentioned my lack of experience and knowledge, he said that a supplementary course and other training would be arranged for me.

I vacillated about becoming a battalion commander and taking responsibility for people's lives. I also hated all courses and had tried to dodge them in the past. I had passed the officers' course without having obtained the full requirements for the Armored Corps, had gotten out of taking a company commanders' course, and had managed not to take a command and staff course.

Although I waited for the supplementary course and training promised to me, it never materialized. Instead, I received a letter telling me that I had been appointed as battalion commander in Central Command, and that in two weeks my battalion would have its first training session. I quickly realized that no supplementary course and training would be coming my way.

Since the War of Independence, the IDF has sometimes had the problem of blithely giving orders without actually implementing them, sending people into battle without having trained them, or worst of all, appointing commanders who did not have enough training or experience to lead their men into battle. I could not help thinking of the War of Independence and the unfortunate soldiers who recently survived the Holocaust. They had just arrived in the Land of Israel, only to be promptly dispatched to the battle of Latrun. They barely knew how to use their weapons, barely understood their orders, and the dire outcome of the battle was largely due to their lack of training as combatants.

I decided to call Lt. Col. Avigdor Kahalani, who was about to lead an exercise at the Tze'elim training base in the Negev desert, and ask him if I could observe it. Kahalani, an experienced Armored Corpsman, had received a Medal of Distinguished Service in the Six-Day War. And he earned a Medal of Valor in the Yom Kippur War after his battalion achieved the amazing feat of blocking a Syrian advance on the Golan Heights. He readily agreed to my request.

I also turned to Gorodish and told him I was at a loss because I had no idea how to be a battalion commander. He calmed me down by saying he would give me private coaching for a few days. Of course, it was ridiculous to learn how to be a battalion commander while sitting in an office. But thanks to Gorodish's enormous knowledge and great ability to explain detailed concepts, I learned a great deal that later helped me in my post.

As my friendship with Gorodish deepened, he began confiding in me about intensely personal issues. Those, of course, remain between the two of us. But what I can reveal is that he felt persecuted. He had a collection of about two hundred antique pistols and other weapons. Once Gorodish asked me to come with him on a patrol in Judea and Samaria, and he armed me with an ancient double-barreled rifle that he pulled from the trunk of his car and that looked like something they used in the Wild West about 150 years ago. Gorodish further informed me that, in case I needed to fire it, I should not hold it too close because the gunpowder could singe me.

Gorodish told me that one day the police raided his house and confiscated the collection. He claimed that the Shin Bet[51] was behind this action. He had owned the collection for many years and never covered up its existence. In his view, Moshe Dayan ordered the confiscation at precisely that time to paint him as a guilty party in the Yom Kippur War, and also to try and incriminate him.

Gorodish's bitterness toward Dayan was fierce. Once he even told me, "The only thing that will stop Dayan is a bullet in

---

[51] Israel's internal security service.

the head." Gorodish said that to other people as well, and they concluded that he indeed wanted to murder Dayan. For my part, I never thought so. I believed Gorodish had a deadly hatred of Dayan, but no plans to effectuate his demise.

He was not the only one full of bitterness toward Moshe Dayan. Col. Gideon Mahnayaymi, an intelligence man and Palmach[52] veteran who, along with his staff, had been officially appointed adjutant of the Ground Forces Command, voiced his opinion of Dayan at a conference of General Command staff that was held at the Chatzerim air force base in February 1974. Dayan and Prime Minister Golda Meir were present. I myself was not there because the conference was only for those with the rank of colonel and higher, but Gideon told me what happened.

At one point in the conference, he stood up and said that every organization resembles a pyramid, and every pyramid has a head, and the head is responsible for everything that happens below. In other words, Dayan needed to take responsibility for the Yom Kippur War and resign. Gideon went on to tell Dayan that he did not have confidence in him. The outcome: Gideon was requested not to attend the second day of the conference and his military promotion was blocked. He was made a brigadier general only in 1985 as a personal gesture by then defense minister Yitzhak Rabin. Gideon died in 1986 at only fifty-nine years old.

Meanwhile, we finished the preparatory work on our proposed structure for the GOC Army Headquarters. Gorodish presented it to a forum of officers who were brigadier generals and higher, and discussions were held in which the whole IDF elite gave opinions. When I learned of the comments and criticisms, I was shocked. I suddenly realized that some of the most senior IDF officers behaved like politicians, meaning that interest trumped everything else. Some of them gave an opinion that meshed with the interest of the department they headed, while some just pushed their own personal agenda. Only a small number of senior officers offered an opinion based on what was good for the IDF.

---

[52] An elite fighting force in the pre-state period and War of Independence.

It is intriguing to look at the political domain in this light, to see what priorities the various prime ministers assign to their hold on power on the one hand, and to the country on the other. In the rather distant past, prime ministers from the right, left, and center – such as Ben-Gurion, Begin, Shamir, and Rabin – based their decisions mainly on the needs of the country and the people. In later years, prime ministers' personal needs, popularity, and desire to remain in office have assumed greater weight in their decision-making.

Brig. Gen. Nati Sharoni, who was then chief artillery officer, and whose powers would also be circumscribed by the new setup, opposed the new headquarters. In my view, and also that of Gorodish, what drove him was not the good of the IDF but his own personal considerations.

There was another general who had supported the proposed headquarters in preliminary meetings, but afterward changed his tune and opposed it. I had the impression that he thought he would be appointed chief of the new headquarters, but it would be just another job for him, not a real promotion. He feared it would actually detract from his chances of getting the chief-of-staff position, on which he was already closing in. I admire this general for his other accomplishments and will not mention his name.

One of the only upstanding officers to give an opinion at that conference was Brig. Gen. Dan Shomron, who became chief of staff a few years later. Until that time I had no connection to him, but I was deeply impressed by his patriotism and leadership qualities. Shomron was then commander of the Infantry and Paratroopers Division, and he knew that if a general was appointed head of the Ground Forces Command, he would have to be his underling and lose some of his own authority. And yet, nevertheless, Shomron expressed support for the proposed command structure.

On the other hand, Maj. Gen. Rafael "Raful" Eitan, then head of Northern Command, despised Gorodish. Some said it went back to clashes of command during firefights in the Six-Day War. In any case, when his turn came, Raful mounted the stage to give his opinion. He said the research and work Gorodish had done were not to be taken seriously. He did not address the issue itself, just disparaged the quality of the work.

I knew Gorodish and his stormy temperament, and at the intermission I asked him to come outside with me for a walk. He was stone silent as we paced, but I knew his blood was boiling inside. I said, "I'm not sure you'll listen to my advice, but don't sink to Raful's level. Don't attack him personally; just counter him calmly and substantively. Explain why the work is good, what it's based on, and so on."

Gorodish, like an angry child, raised his right hand, flung it down sharply, and emitted the fierce words, "Leave me alone."

When we went back inside, and Gorodish's turn came to respond to Raful, I was happy to see that he did it quietly and logically. The next day in the office, I heard him tell someone on the phone that, while he had intended to let Raful have it with both barrels, a young lieutenant colonel had advised him against it and he had taken the advice.

Gorodish, for his part, was not – to put it mildly – fond of Raful. In January 1978, when he had already returned to civilian life, Gorodish came to my son Lior's *brit milah*.[53] Also present was Col. Ben-Ami Cohen, who was part of our social circle. In our Friday night gripe sessions, Ben-Ami always loudly laid down his views, and you could barely get a word in edgewise. The *brit* was held on a date close to Raful's appointment as chief of staff. On this celebratory occasion, Ben-Ami asked Gorodish what he thought of Raful's new job. At first Gorodish did not respond. But when Ben-Ami went on to proclaim that Raful was a fine soldier in the field, it was too much for Gorodish and he came back with, "I'm not sure attacking and conquering enemy positions is what's needed on the General Staff."

[53] Circumsion ceremony.

When we discussed setting up the GOC Army Headquarters, naturally my commander, Maj. Gen. Abrasha Tamir, took part. But Abrasha did not give an opinion, and since it was well known that he favored setting up such a headquarters for the ground forces, many wondered why.

Brig. Gen. Yitzhak Elron, financial adviser to the chief of staff and one of my past commanders, was not shy in addressing the issue. Once, while I sat eating lunch with Abrasha, Elron joined us and said sardonically, "Abrasha, why don't you tell us your opinion? You don't know what the chief of staff thinks yet, so the cat's got your tongue?"

That really was the problem with Abrasha. He was intelligent and had worthy achievements as a fighter and a commander, but he lacked a backbone. Since he never ruffled any feathers, he was able to get along with all the chiefs of staff and defense ministers.

The deliberations on the matter were concluded by Chief of Staff Motta Gur, who said the time was still not right for such a headquarters. It was finally established only several years later, in 1983, in a format similar to the one proposed by Gorodish and his team.

At Gorodish's request, I would accompany him to various meetings, both civilian and military. He asked me to come with him and view an exercise supervised by Maj. Gen. Mussa Peled, commander of the Armored Corps. Mussa affably told Gorodish how he planned to carry it out, and when Gorodish suggested some improvements, Mussa readily agreed. At that moment I thought to myself, "What a shame that the IDF lets Gorodish's wisdom and experience go to waste."

Gorodish indeed realized that they were letting him mark time, and since they were not offering him any serious position, he decided he had had enough. He had a farewell parley with Yitzhak Rabin, then defense minister, and afterward he called and asked to meet with me. He told me Rabin had said, "With me you'll always find an open door." Gorodish added, "I'm not sure what one does with an open door."

The injustice that the Agranat Commission inflicted on Gorodish never stopped gnawing at his heart. We talked about it often, and I later came up with the idea of writing a book that would reveal the truth that the commission had ignored. I thought Shlomo "Nakdi" Nakdimon, an experienced political reporter and commentator for the *Yedioth Ahronot* daily, was the right man for the job. I had been very impressed with the work he did for the Libi Fund while I was its director in the early 1980s. I set up a meeting between the two of them, and Gorodish gave Nakdi reams of documents and detailed information.

Gorodish was discharged from the army in 1976. We remained friends and continued to meet regularly. At that point he decided to become a businessman. He hoped to earn large sums that would enable him to clear his name from the aspersions that the Agranat Commission had cast on it.

Gorodish began by setting up an arms-trading company with some South African investors. After that, he decided to mine for diamonds in Africa. He befriended Jean-Bédel Bokassa, the leader of the Central African Republic, who had appointed himself "emperor," and Bokassa gave him a concession to mine diamonds. Gorodish recruited investors and a group of Israeli workers, and the mining endeavor began. For my part, I was hurt that he did not ask me to join him. During one of his visits to Israel, when we met in a social context, I told him how I felt. He answered, "I wasn't sure I could pay the people working with me all that I would owe them; that was why I didn't offer you anything. You're a friend and I didn't want to take a chance."

Gorodish kept at it in Africa. After he had accumulated a certain amount of wealth, a flood destroyed his quarry and the surrounding buildings, and he had to start again from scratch. We continued to meet when he came to Israel for visits. Meanwhile, the work on the planned book came to a stop. Nakdi returned all the material Gorodish had given him to his brother Brig. Gen. (ret.) Yoel Gorodish.

Gorodish suffered a sad demise. A poisonous insect stung him in Africa, resulting in a permanent limp. His attempts to get rich and clear his name did not succeed, and in 1991, at the relatively young age of sixty-one, he died of a heart attack – and perhaps a broken heart.

As I mentioned previously, I greatly admired his intelligence. Being around him was always an experience. We were open and honest with each other, and despite the differences in age (fourteen years) and rank (he a major general, I a lieutenant colonel), he was a real friend. Today, when I think of him from time to time, I miss him, and regret that he wasted his last years in a futile attempt to expose the errant conclusions of the Agranat Commission.

With the end of our parleys on setting up the GOC Army Headquarters, and with Gorodish's retirement, I felt I was wasting my time in the Planning Division – just treading water. Of all the elegant analyses and reports, nothing was actually implemented. At best we just talked about the proposal; at worst, not even that.

In addition to my work in the Planning Division and my role as on-call commander of a tank battalion, I lectured on the topic of markets and capital at the College of Management in Tel Aviv. If asked to give myself a grade for my lectures, I would have given myself no more than "average." Pressed for time as I was, I simply did not prepare them at all. I would come to the college in my uniform, change into civilian clothes in the car, and hurry to the lecture. My main reason for lecturing at the college, which paid academic lecturers relatively well, was to earn more income. After about two years, when I realized I simply did not have the time, I resigned. As for the army at that point, I mostly applied myself to my role as on-call battalion commander, and later decided to serve in a field unit until my discharge.

A special appraisal by Haim Erez as requested by the commander of the Armored Corps, Major General Moshe ("Mussa") Peled.

It reads:

Central Command/Adjutancy Officer
Re: Appraisal of Major Ehud Diskin

1. Major Diskin served under my command several times as a deputy company commander and company commander in the 79th Battalion of the Armored Corps in 1968–69, and as a brigade-level operations officer and deputy battalion commander in the Armored Corps in the Yom Kippur War and afterward. In these roles he acquired great experience and professional knowledge.

2. He carried out his duties to my satisfaction.

3. In my view, the series of positions in which he has served along with his professional knowledge qualify him for the position of Armored Corps battalion commander.

Sincerely,
Col. Haim Erez

אישי

לטכ"מ ראש אגף תכנון
בא - 150 - 576
על' 2428
ודר תכ"ה
פנר' 75

ר' מנהל המשב

הנדון: ק/ 471056 רס"ג דיזנהיר אהוד
עלי : בג - 1 - 2025 מה - 13 דצמ' 74.
שלכם : בא - 50 - (4) 53076 מה - 13 דצמ' 74.

1. הקצין הב"ל החל מעלא ומקידד, בהתאם לתיגדיו מה- 7 יגו' 75.

2. הרא מעלא את תפקירו נהצלחה רבה ובוהבטייצות המהרדיב הסמך גאום לדרך הילדי תפקיריו נצבא קקבע בעבר.

3. אני מעליץ נזאח לקצר את פרק הזמן הסיבישטלי לפלייזמר לדרגת סא"ל, ומבקשך לטפל בהצלאאנו לדדגה זו בתועי מ - 1 אפריל 75.

א. מסיר. אלוף
ראש, אגף הכנון

Maj. Gen. Abrasha Tamir's recommendation to promote me to lieutenant colonel.

It reads:

Personal

Office of the Head of the Planning Division 1975

Head of the Staff Administration

Re: Major Ehud Diskin

1. The above officer has begun performing his tasks in accordance with his appointment on July 1, 1975.

2. He performs his tasks excellently and very successfully just as he did in the standing army in the past.

3. I hereby recommend shortening the minimum time span for his promotion to the rank of lieutenant colonel, and request that you carry out his promotion to this rank by April 1, 1975.

[signed]

A. Tamir, Maj. Gen.
Head of the Planning Division

Maj. Gen. Shmuel Gorodish

Maj. Gen. Abrasha Tamir, head of the Planning Division

A letter of appreciation from Major General Shmuel Gorodish (Gonen) that was sent to the chief of staff and the head of the Staff Administration in 1975.

It reads:

Head of the Staff Administration   October 22, 1975

Office of the Chief of Staff
Office of the Head of the Operations Division at GHQ
Office of the Head of the Manpower Division
Office of the Head of the Planning Division
Office of the Head of Military Intelligence
Office of the Head of the Operations Division at GHQ/Division of Planning and
Organization

Re: A praiseworthy officer

As part of the team for preparing the ground forces, I worked with several officers directly
and in daily contact for about half a year under difficult conditions of time pressure, and I
came to appreciate their high quality, character traits, and abilities – and here I find it my
duty to express to you my appreciation of one of them.

Lt. Col. Ehud Diskin (Planning Division Data Center) – an outstanding professional in the
field of organizational systems analysis, independent and assertive about his views, clear-
thinking, with broad horizons, showing an original approach to every issue, with a very
developed sense of responsibility and a systematically critical attitude toward every matter.

Shmuel Gonen – Maj. Gen.

Defense Minister Moshe Dayan (right), *Maj. Gen. Shmuel Gorodish* (Gonen)
(middle), *Maj. Gen. Rechavam Zeevi* (left) *in the Yom Kippur War, 1973 (photo:
Shlomo Arad, Government Press Office)*

חל-אביב 29 באוגוסט 1977

המדרשה למינהל
מיסודה של הסתדרות הפקידים

המכללה

לכבוד
מר אהוד דיסקין
מוריה 38
רמת-השרון

אהוד היקר,

<u>הנדון : התפטרות ממשרת מרצה.</u>

הצטערתי לקבל את מכתבך, בו אתה מודיעני
שלא תוכל להרצות יותר מחוסר זמן.

התחבבת על התלמידים ועל סגל העובדים
וצר לי על ניתוק החוט בינינו.

אני מבין שעברת לצבא-הקבע במוחלט
ואני מאחל לך הצלחה בכל לב.

בברכה

ברוך גבוביץ'
ראש השלוחה

A letter acknowledging my resignation as a lecturer at the College of Administration, 1977.

It reads:

College of Management   Tel Aviv, August 29, 1977
To:
Mr. Ehud Diskin, Moriah 38, Ramat Hasharon

Dear Ehud,

Re: Resignation as a lecturer

I was sorry to receive your letter in which you informed me that because of time constraints you will not be able to continue as a lecturer.

You were well liked by the students and the staff and I regret that we will lose our connection.

I understand that you have begun full-time military service and I wish you success with all my heart.

Sincerely,
Baruch Gabovich, Division Director

Chapter 10
A COMMANDER'S CALLING

"And every Hebrew mother should know that she has put her son's fate in the hands of worthy commanders."

David Ben-Gurion

My long-wished-for service as a battalion commander began with a strange event: Our ammunition was stolen.

In December 1975, my reserve battalion – Battalion 9320 of the 395th Brigade – assembled for its inaugural training exercise in the Negev. It was arranged by the division of Brig. Gen. Amnon Reshef, and I realized right away that we had been given very little ammunition.

I brought this to the attention of the operations officer at the division headquarters, Lt. Col. Natan Ben-Ari. His answer was, "That's the allotted amount."

I could see no logic in providing so little ammunition for a tank battalion's first training exercise. I took the problem directly to Major Shmil at the General Staff. He served in the Training Division at the General Staff Headquarters, and he was in charge of ammunition allotments. I knew him from my days as an assistant training officer at the Armored Corps Headquarters from 1969 to 1970, after I served as a group commander in the War of Attrition.

Shmil, who was heavyset and would spice his sentences with Yiddish, ran limping to the book on ammunition allotments for training exercises. He opened it to the page on providing ammunition for a new tank battalion, photocopied it, and gave me the copy. I read it and was shocked. The division headquarters had not just cut back on some of our ammunition, it had given us only one-third the quantity that was designated for us.

All I wanted for my battalion was the ammunition to which we were entitled. It was important that these soldiers be as well trained as possible in case a war broke out, and a training exercise without ammunition is simply not effective. I went back to the division's operations officer, Natan, and showed him the page photocopied from the book on ammunition allotments. I told him that we had to have the ammunition, and that we were entitled to receive the full allotment that the division headquarters had received for us.

I assumed the decision was not his to make, and that it was in the hands of General Reshef.

Natan promised me a response in a few hours. He called me back to say that our allotment would not be changed. I realized that General Reshef had decided to keep the ammunition for his own division. Later I found out that the missing two-thirds of my battalion's allotment was supposed to be used by the division for a drill that involved crossing a water obstacle, an exercise for which no ammunition at all had been provided to the division headquarters.

I did not give in. I used my contacts to get the General Staff to review the situation, via the Training Division. They confirmed that the amount of ammunition we had been given was grossly inadequate. My deputy, Rami Matan, had a meeting already scheduled with the commander of the Armored Corps, Mussa Peled, and I asked Rami to raise the issue with him.

In other words, we had designed a pincer movement. The interim result was that Brig. Gen. Moshe Levy, head of the Operational Division of the General Staff, was asked to look into the matter. I was never informed of the results, but just before the battalion's concluding drill we received the full allotment, and in that drill we fired an enormous quantity of ammunition.

The drill was set for 2 p.m. I took my place in the commander's position of my tank's turret, ready to move forward, looking at the dozens of tanks and other armored fighting vehicles (AFVs) of my battalion – and I felt fear. I asked myself if I would indeed be able to command this battalion. At the division and brigade head-quarters, there were also some who had their doubts about me. I was not one of the stars of the Armored Corps, one of those whose whole life centered on tanks. I had not performed brilliantly as a company commander or as a deputy battalion commander. I was a patriot, I strove to do my work responsibly, and no more. Later, in talks with people after the exercise, I learned that everyone had expected me to fail because it was such a difficult exercise.

The exercise was scheduled to run from afternoon until the following morning, and a few minutes before it began, I realized that my deputy, Rami, had mistakenly sent all the nighttime path markers back to headquarters. That meant we had no path illumi-nation in the dark – a serious problem.

At 2 p.m. I gave the order to move out. As long as there was daylight, we moved and accomplished our tasks well. After night-fall, a heavy fog with drizzling rain set in. We seemed not only to be fighting the hypothetical enemy, but nature as well. Under the cover of darkness, we practiced overrunning enemy positions in hilly terrain without night-vision equipment, when the operations officer's tank strayed from the path and flipped over. Fortunately no one was hurt.

We had to make our way in the dark, in a column, along a path that was difficult for movement and navigation. I put the company commander, Capt. Ron Dor-Sinai, at the head of the column. He was tall, handsome, blue-eyed, and a good commander and navi-gator. I let Ron navigate for the battalion, his company out in front. I joined up with his company as the eighth tank in the column. However, despite putting Ron in charge of navigation, the lesson of Avsha, the navigator from the Yom Kippur War, was still fresh in my mind. I had almost let him lead us into Egyptian territory, so I monitored our movement with the help of a map, making sure we stayed on the right path.

A battalion commander riding in a tank has many other tasks besides navigation. He has to guide the driver, give orders by radio to the whole battalion, and keep in contact with brigade headquarters. If you get lost when moving along a narrow, dangerous path through hilly terrain, correcting the error and bringing the battalion back on course can be a very complicated endeavor. It is not like driving on a road where you just have to reach the next intersection and turn around.

We came to a fork on the hilly path, and I realized that Ron was continuing straight ahead. According to my calculations, we needed to turn right on the ridge. I stopped the battalion, called Ron to join me on foot, and showed him that he had gone off course and needed to bring his seven tanks back to join up again with the battalion. It felt good to prevent a foul-up. Staying on the wrong route would have caused us to fail the exercise.

By dawn we made it to the enemy's main outposts. We were to attack them in the next stage of the exercise. The attack was well coordinated and successful. And since we were able to use the large stock of ammunition that had previously been taken from us, our barrages were impressive too.

After the exercise, Col. Moshe Verbin, acting commander of the brigade, came to me and said, "Show me your hands."

They were a bit blue from the cold, and Verbin said, "You spoke calmly and soberly on the radio despite the tough weather conditions. I thought about you and said to myself, either the guy is exceptionally level-headed, or he's just sealed off inside the warm tank and giving orders by remote control. When I see your hands, blue from the cold," he explained, "I know you were giving the orders from outside the turret." Verbin, who was intelligent and sharp, also took note of Ron's navigating error and said merely, "You let your ace company commander do the navigating, and the ace was a disappointment."

The exercise won praise from the headquarters of the Training Division. Compared to all the standing-army battalions that had carried it out in the same format, they said it was the best they had seen.

I was overjoyed. With all my fears, and given my inexperience, I had not expected such success. I felt I had found my place, and if I may say so, I was proud of myself. That exercise solidified my status as a reserve on-call Armored Corps battalion commander.

A few months later, the time came for another exercise. About two weeks before its scheduled date, I went to observe a similar battalion exercise led by Lt. Col. (res.) Yehuda Arazi. It was near Maale Adumim,[54] where our drill would also be held. And on hand to watch this one was the chief of staff, Lt. Gen. Motta Gur.

A short time after the drill began, Motta Gur put a stop to it, ordering that the battalion commander be dismissed and the reserve battalion be sent home. I was in shock. Motta Gur was not Shmulik Gorodish; he was not known for such things. This was an extraordinary, one-off event. But there was a reason for his decision: Yehuda was not fully in control of the battalion, and in Motta's view that could have endangered the soldiers.

Lt. Col. Yehuda Arazi was a kibbutznik and an Armored Corpsman who had seen many battles. In the Yom Kippur War, he was deputy commander of the 377th Reserve Battalion of the 9th Brigade. Along with his battalion commander, Lt. Col. Bentzi Padan, he fought effectively and heroically in the Golan Heights. In a do-or-die attack on a Syrian armored division's outpost, their battalion overwhelmed the enemy. The media and the historical accounts make reference to my acquaintance Avigdor Kahalani's important role in blocking the Syrian advance on the Golan, and about that there is no doubt. But if one sifts through the events of the war, one finds that the efforts of the 377th Battalion under Bentzi Padan and Yehuda Arazi were no less critical in stopping

54 A town a few miles east of Jerusalem.

the Syrians in the Golan. Aryeh Yitzhaki, in his book *In the Soldiers' Footsteps*, takes a close and interesting look at this issue.

Seeing the fate of Yehuda Arazi's exercise made me all the more worried. If Yehuda, who was considered a fine and experienced battalion commander, had been unable to pull off that exercise, and instead was humiliatingly dismissed, it seemed to me that I had even less chance to succeed.

Two weeks went by, and my battalion was called up for duty. After some preparatory training sessions, we were due for the concluding battalion exercise. Although I am optimistic by nature and usually believe I will succeed, I did not put great hope in this drill after the Yehuda Arazi fiasco, particularly because it was especially difficult.

We began in the daytime in a valley east of Maale Adumim, moving southward. The companies of the battalion started to disperse, and I feared that if I did not bear down and exert tighter control, the whole exercise would fall apart. I put myself in a state of total concentration, scrutinizing each detail and weighing how to deal with it. I took the reins and got control of my units. The movement, and the exercise as a whole, started to go well. At every stage I positioned myself well as commander, both observing the forces and directing them.

Advancing toward our main objective, we moved through a wide gulch while protecting our flanks and overtaking objectives along the way. We reached the main objective about two hours ahead of schedule.

We were supposed to be helped by live fire from the air force before conquering this main objective. But because we had arrived early, the air force's participation was canceled and we took the enemy position by ourselves, without outside help.

We continued moving forward, but Company B under Captain Shmuel's command had trouble crossing one of the ravines. While I was watching, Shmuel told me on the radio that he was crossing it successfully and everything was all right. But that was not true; he was actually stuck. I was very angry. In the case of

General Bren's 162nd Division in the Yom Kippur War, misleadingly optimistic reports by the unit commanders on October 8, 1973, caused faulty decisions at all levels of command, and the result was catastrophic.

After the exercise I told Shmuel that, while he was indeed a good and talented company commander, if he ever gave me an inaccurate report again, I would relieve him of duty.

As the exercise continued, we had to move by night through hilly terrain, leading to an attack at dawn. The drill went well. This time the chief of staff was not present; the senior figure was the head of Central Command, Maj. Gen. Yona Efrat. After we had completed the dawn attack and the exercise itself, he radioed on our battalion's network that our performance was excellent.

I felt wonderful. Not only had the exercise gone well, but I also knew I had a good battalion. If we had to fight, we would do that well, too.

In addition to fine company commanders, I also had a talented deputy commander in Maj. Rami Matan. In the Yom Kippur War he had fought resourcefully and heroically at the Chinese Farm[55] as a company commander in the 79th Battalion under Lt. Col. Amram Mitzna. With his discharge in 1975, Rami joined the police at the rank of superintendent. While he was serving as my deputy in the reserves, he admitted to me that, after finishing his work in the police force, he needed to recover from the chaos that prevailed there, so he worked for a year as a truck driver on the Tel Aviv-Eilat route.

Rami was known as a man of principle, and he adjusted well to his role. He was proficient at his job, and committed to our good working relationship. When I stepped down, Rami replaced me and became battalion commander.

Until I was appointed as battalion commander, I took a tough – even tyrannical to some extent – approach to my commanding

---

[55] The Chinese Farm was an area near the Suez Canal where fierce battles were waged with many Israeli casualties.

196 | Y<small>ES</small>, I<small>T</small>'<small>S</small> P<small>OSSIBLE</small>

roles. That was the style of many of tank commanders I knew. A prime example of this approach in the Armored Corps was Shmulik Gorodish, who constantly kept his soldiers in fear.

This style involves putting consideration and sensitivity aside. Instead you subordinate everything to the goal, and the goal justifies all means, including tyranny. However, when I found myself in the position of battalion commander, I came to the conclusion that it was better to adopt a different approach, friendlier and less harsh.

Of course, quality of performance and devotion to the goal are things that cannot be compromised. But you can take the sensitivities of those who carry out your orders into consideration; you can look at the human being behind each officer or soldier.

One of my models for this more amiable approach was Capt. Shamai Kaplan, who had been my commander when I was a scout. Shamai was pleasant and considerate without sacrificing the effectiveness of his men. As his soldiers, we always strove to do everything as well as possible and live up to his expectations. We liked him and did not merely fear him.

Another example of a more humane approach was that taken by Maj. Gen. Ori Or. He rose through the Armored Corps chain of command, from platoon commander to division commander. He then became head of Central Command, and after that, head of Northern Command. In the Yom Kippur War, under his command, the 679th Reserve Brigade played a key role in stopping the Syrians in the central region of the Golan Heights. Ori's approach was nicely summed up by one of his soldiers after the First Lebanon War (the Peace for Galilee Operation). "Ori's smile gave us the strength for another hour of combat," he said.

These opposing models were similar to the command methods I witnessed during the Yom Kippur War. Arik Sharon's command during the war was severe, but he was also warm and compassionate. The approach of his deputy Jackie Even, however, was more "Prussian," that is, aloof, uptight, haughty, and not very pleasant.

After I had already served for a year as battalion commander, I began to feel that my having avoided taking any courses since the officers' course in 1962 verged on irresponsibility. To be a company commander without having taken a company commanders' course is one thing; to be a battalion commander is something else. I felt I had to take a senior-level course.

I found out about a new, forty-day course for battalion commanders. I signed up for its second run, which was held late in 1976 at the Armored Corps School of the Julis base near the town of Ashkelon. It was a high-level course with good instructors, and I learned a lot. Given my hands-on experience as a battalion commander, I assumed I would be an excellent student. Actually, I was only good, not excellent. I never handled courses well; the pressure and lack of freedom always bothered me. I definitely did not love any of the few courses I took in the army.

One of our more capable instructors was Col. Yehuda Geller. As a battalion commander in the Yom Kippur War, he had fought tenaciously and heroically northeast of where our forces crossed the Suez Canal. Yehuda's battalion had to widen the area where the crossing took place, and for his service Yehuda received a Medal of Courage for showing superb leadership, resolve in executing the mission, and of course, courage. A tall kibbutznik with deep blue eyes, he had solid common sense and extensive knowledge of tank warfare. As well as being a course instructor, he was commander of the 767th Reserve Brigade.

One day during the course, he asked me if I would like to be his deputy commander in that brigade. It would mean spending all my time in its headquarters, located at the Chasah base near Ashkelon. That was where I had served as a scout fourteen years earlier, in the 82nd Battalion under Lt. Col. Haim Deem.

Fed up with wasting my time at the Planning Division of the General Staff, I grabbed the opportunity. I informed the head of the Planning Division, Maj. Gen. Abrasha Tamir, and arranged with the Adjutant Corps to be given the post of deputy brigade commander.

I left the reserve battalion I was commanding and began the new, full-time job of deputy commander of the 767th Brigade.

Now that I had finished my stint as battalion commander, the head of the Armored Corps, Maj. Gen. Mussa Peled, summoned me to a meeting. He said, "While you were a battalion commander, I did not hear good or bad things about you. My conclusion is that you were a passable battalion commander."

I was taken aback. I said, "Your conclusion is mistaken. In my opinion I was a good battalion commander, and I would be happy if you would look into it and then talk with me again."

Mussa never took the trouble to apologize. However, he turned to the acting commander of the brigade, Col. Moshe Verbin, who gave me a special evaluation. Verbin wrote, among other things, that the battalion I commanded had been the most organized and efficient in the brigade, and that I had done an outstanding job of organizing, training, and leading it.

On the first day of my new job as a deputy brigade commander, a reserve battalion that belonged to my brigade was discharged. As that process came to an end, the soldier in charge of ammunition, who was nicknamed Inga'le ("child" in Yiddish), informed me that he suspected eleven grenades had not been returned to him. I told him to look into it and tell me if he was sure beyond a doubt that they were missing. After a few hours, Inga'le came back to me and said the same thing, but he still could not tell me for certain that the grenades were missing. I appointed the supply officer as investigator and asked for clear conclusions by the next day. The supply officer came to me with the same response – he could not say with absolute certainty that they were gone. There were, he explained, about twelve thousand grenades in the storerooms and one could not be totally sure if eleven were missing. I decided to turn to the Investigatory Division of the Military Police.

After few a weeks, the Military Police investigators came to me with their report. It turned out that one of the reserve drivers from the discharged battalion had put together a secret cache of weapons and ammunition in his home. It included rifles, pistols, bullets, and grenades – even a bazooka. I was naïve enough to think I would get compliments for getting to the bottom of the matter, an ammunition and weapons storeroom had been discovered at the driver's home. Usually a cache of that kind is only unearthed after the grenades have already been thrown, or the guns used to settle scores in the underworld.

However, as in so many other cases, the logic and rules of a large bureaucracy work differently. Along with the report from the Military Police came an order to put me on trial. According to military regulations, I was supposed to report on the missing ammunition within twenty-four hours, but had only done so after forty-eight hours. The head of the command had more common sense than the Military Police officer who had signed that order – he threw it in the garbage.

Soon after I started in the new post, I realized that Yehuda Geller, the brigade commander, had deceived me – or, as they say in court, he had told me the truth but not the whole truth. Yehuda had told me I would be deputy brigade commander, but did not tell me that there was already another one, Lt. Col. Bentzi Padan, who as mentioned, had performed superbly with his battalion in the Golan Heights in the Yom Kippur War, playing an important role in blocking the Syrian advance. He was serving as deputy A, while I would serve as deputy B. That meant Bentzi would be responsible for military activity, and I for administration. Bentzi was a good deputy with great knowledge of tanks. Yehuda Geller and Bentzi Padan were both kibbutzniks, and it helped them get along personally as well as professionally.

For my part, my status as deputy B made me an outsider, responsible for seeing that the soldiers' mobilization went smoothly, for the maintenance of the tanks, and for keeping the storerooms in a state of preparedness. It was a role that did not suit me and that I did not like, to say the least. I found nothing interesting about overseeing the paperwork for the reservists, the technical upkeep of the tanks, or maintaining the orderliness of the storerooms. Suddenly I found myself acting like a compulsive homemaker whose life's calling is to keep every item in its place, clean, and working properly. That really is not me.

The staff officers who were at my disposal made me feel even less interested and less fulfilled. Directly in charge of paperwork was Capt. Kirov, who did not understand what was required of him and was mostly busy with his personal problems. The maintenance officer was Capt. Fadida, who to his credit, tried to do his job properly. In charge of our weaponry was Capt. Moishe, who tried to carry out his duties, but was always angry, irritable, and grumbling.

From Fadida and Moishe, though, I learned two different approaches to problem solving. When I told Moishe to get all the tanks in good working order and that I would inspect them at the end of the week, he said in a booming, angry voice, "I don't have enough people and cannot carry out the task."

I said, "It's an order."

At the end of the week, I showed up for the inspection and the tanks were not ready. When I asked Moishe why this was the case, he answered me in his loud, testy, grating voice, "I told you I don't have enough people."

When I came to inspect Fadida's work, the same thing happened; he was never ready. However, he would say, "No problem, I'll have it ready next week. Consider it done." And when I came back the next week, still neither Moishe nor Fadida was ready. But Moishe would give me a hard time, while Fadida reiterated, "No problem, consider it done."

The conclusion is that when given a task that has not yet been carried out, it is better to use the Fadida approach than the Moishe approach. Moishe always tangled with the people around him and left them feeling annoyed. Fadida never fought with anyone and did not stir up antagonism.

Apart from that, I felt confined and discontented in my role as deputy B, and the quality of my work was nothing to brag about. My disappointment reached a peak when it came time for a pared-down, division-level exercise in which my brigade took part. I was on an APC in the main command group, and I saw myself as part of the exercise. But Yehuda, the brigade commander, did not see it that way. He ignored me, ignored my radio contacts, and all but excluded me from the various stages of the exercise. He worked closely and harmoniously with Bentzi Padan, however. It made me realize once and for all that Yehuda had not really appointed me to be deputy brigade commander, but rather the commander of Moishe and Fadida.

Rejection and injustice always disturbed me greatly. In this case, when I had to deal with both, I decided to deal with them my own way.

During the exercise, when I realized I had been relegated to observer status, I ordered my signaler to turn off the radios in the APC, and we parked to take a long lunch break. The APC crew opened cans of battle rations and served me my beloved halvah. My subordinates always knew about my weakness for it. In the War of Attrition, too, my crews would always sort out the halvah cans from the battle rations and bring them to me.

As it turned out, while I was cut off from the world, the brigade commander, Yehuda, had tried to locate me by radio for some nonsense or other. Of course, he was unable to get a hold of me. After we finished the exercise, when it was being evaluated, the brigade commander at that time, Brig. Gen. Nat'ke Nir, harshly criticized me for being inaccessible by radio. If they had known that it was intentional, so I could take a halvah break, they likely would have dismissed me from my post. In any case, that I had resorted to such measures was proof that the situation was hopeless. I was done being the overseer of the storerooms and the commander of Moishe and Fadida.

How to get out of this trap? I had made friends with the commander of the other brigade in the division, Col. Giora Biran. In the Yom Kippur War, Giora had served as a major in the Golan. After the brigade commander was wounded, Giora took command and led fierce tank battles over the next three days. Under Giora's command, the brigade held off the Syrian tanks, destroying about 150 of them. When the brigade commander returned, Giora was given command of a tank battalion. Leading it in a fierce battle, he was wounded and evacuated in critical condition. Giora was given a Medal of Distinguished Service for his valor, leadership, and devotion.

Giora was affable and likable, a talented fellow who always spoke softly and pleasantly. At that time, he did not have a deputy brigade commander, and we agreed between us that I would fill that post. This time I made very sure I would be deputy A, that is, the combat deputy. I enjoyed every moment of it and did my work diligently.

That was well evident in the brigade's concluding exercise, in which I commanded a crew that had to cross a wide trench representing the Jordan River. Afterward, the deputy division commander stated, "The deputy brigade commander (that is, me) did exceptional work here."

The exercise also included a phase where the brigade commander was supposedly wounded, and I had to take his place. About that stage, the commander of the training base, Brig. Gen. Dan Vardi, said, "The deputy brigade commander did good work when he took command."

After the mediocre job I had done as deputy B under Yehuda Geller, it was important to me that I do well as deputy A, both for my ego and for the military record. I proved I could play the role of brigade commander, too. Inwardly, however, I had reached a strategic decision: I no longer desired to fill senior positions in the Armored Corps. I loved the soldiers and the officers in the corps, but I did not love the mentality of some of the senior commanders. I was not interested in continuing to rise through the military ranks, and the end of my term of service was approaching.

At the end of 1977, however, as my discharge drew near, I was again called to a meeting with the Armored Corps commander, Maj. Gen. Mussa Peled. He asked me what my plans were. I said that, back in civilian life, I aimed to get a doctorate or go into private business. The Armored Corps commander replied that if I was headed for the business world he could not help me, but if I was going the academic route he would recommend that the army finance my studies, making me a candidate for promotion to the rank of colonel.

That was an offer I could not refuse: to attend university for two years and get a doctorate on the IDF's tab while not having to work. Those were advantages of a sort that I never had. And getting a higher military rank was also a considerable bonus. The head of the Manpower Administration officially approved my university studies and my promotion. I had an optimistic feeling, and the words came to me: "Thus shall it be done to the man whom the king delighteth to honor" (Esther 6:9). And so I returned once more to academia, to take up the book instead of the sword.

As commander of Battalion 9320, 1976

א. י. 3
לכבוד: בלבד

24/5/77

סמכ"ש/פ,סגל 12
אוגדה 280/ספקד
אוגדה 194/ספקד

הנדון: סא"ל דיספקין אחורי-הערכת פיוחדת
לפי בקשת מלפרגיח של ק.סגל גי"ש

רקע:
1. סא"ל דיספקין שרת תחת פקודי בסב"ד 395/9328 פיום הקפת הגדוד בחודש דצמבר 75 ועד
חודש פברואר 77.

2. בתקופה זו בצע הגדוד הפעילויות העיקריות הבאות:
   א. אימונים
      1) 3 אימוני חפ"ש יחידתיים.
      2) תרגיל ארבתחי גלדי.
      3) תרגיל חטיבתי גלדי פרקטן.
      4) תרגיל חטיבתי גלדי.
   ב. ארגון
      1) הקמת ים"ח בכיח ליד וחעברתו למחנה עופר.
      2) הקמת רשת גירוס.
   ג. בטנניח
      1) ליפנו הפטיפוח האזרפרסיביות וגוהל קרב בגדוד.
      2) בצוע סיורים ותצלג"ים.

הערכת הגדוד
3. גדוד 9328 בפקוד סא"ל דפקין בלא במשך שנה אינטנסיבית זו כגדוד חיומר מיורגן מאורגן ומיומר
   יעיל בחטיבה ואנשיו היו חיומר מעורים בטצרם ובחטי היום של ים"ח של היום הדחמיכה.

4. הסוראל בגדוד, ובעיקר קטרי הגומלין ותרעום בין סגל הפילואים היח חמד גבוה לשוPHנ.

5. עובדות אלה בלשו בקח התרגיל חטיבתי.

הערכת סא"ל דיספקין
6. רצוי להאמר כי סא"ל דיספקין זכח בסב"ד טעולח(רס"ן) רפי מתן)וכך שמבתיבת זריח הראיה
   שלי נטח לדקוף באחריות מלאת את עורת התחגבש לזכרה, של הסב"ד בלבד,זאת מלבד תעובדח
   שהסב"ד ידע לעזור על חרמוניח ורדח צרות ולתמעיל את סגנו ולפרגן את מלחמותיו.

7. רצח המקרה ובשלוית התרגילים הגדודים נכנם הגדוד למצבי לחמבי למד בגין בחזני מדג אויר
   וחקלות אנוש, במצבים אלו בלא יחרונו הגדוד של הסב"ד בכן שבינור רוח ובחפלונה רכה חיל"ץ
   את הגדוד והנהיגו כיאות.

8. לסכום יאמר כי סא"ל דיספקין ארגן,איפן ומנהיב את יחידתו בחצונה רכה ובכשרון.

אלוף ורגין פ/ה

It reads:

Armored Corps/Manpower Administration, March 24, 1977
Division 880/Commander
Division 194/Commander

Re: Lt. Col. Ehud Diskin – Special Evaluation
By telephoned request of the Staff Officer, Armored Corps
Background

1. Lt. Col. Diskin served under my command as a battalion commander of battalion 395/9230 from the day of the battalion's establishment in December 1975 until February 1977.
2. In this period the battalion performed the following main activities:
    a. Training
        1) 3 unit-level initial training sessions.
        2) A basic framework divisional exercise.
        3) A small-scale brigade-level basic framework exercise.
        4) A basic framework brigade-level exercise.
    b. Organization
        1) Setting up the Emergency Supplies Unit of the battalion at Beit Lid and transferring it to the Ofer base.
        2) Setting up a mobilization network.
    c. Preparedness
        1) Learning about the operative tasks and battle procedure of the battalion.
        2) Conducting planning and reconnaissance.

Evaluation of the battalion
3. Battalion 9320 commanded by Lt. Col. Diskin was notable during this intensive year as the most organized and most efficient battalion in the brigade, and its members were the most involved in the routine and daily life of the Emergency Supplies Unit of the battalion and the brigade.
4. The morale in the battalion, and particularly the interactions and comradeship among the reserve staff, were on a high level and well maintained.
5. These facts were well evident during the brigade-level exercise.

Personal evaluation of the battalion commander
6. It is worth noting that Lt. Col. Diskin had an outstanding deputy battalion commander (Major Rami Matan), so that from my perspective it is hard to give credit for the series of achievements to the battalion commander alone, although the battalion commander was able to maintain harmony and team spirit and make use of his deputy and show appreciation for his successes.
7. Incidentally, during the three battalion-level exercises the battalion had to face situations of pressure because of weather conditions and human error, and in these situations the capability of the battalion commander was well evident as he soberly and very shrewdly salvaged the battalion and gave it proper leadership.
8. To sum up, it should be said that Lt. Col. Diskin organized, trained, and led his unit with great acumen and talent.

Col. Moshe Verbin

‫סיכום ההערות‬

1. ‫נוה"ק ברמה החט' תקין. ברמת הגד' לקה בחוסר מחוסר זמן מספיק לתכנון.‬

2. ‫נוה"ק חפוזים תוך מתן פקודות וביצוע תאומים ברמה תקין.‬

3. ‫החיחסות לקרקע ולאוריב תקינה.‬

4. ‫ניצול גד' החי"ר - רצוי היה להקצות לפחות פל' למאמץ החט' השני ולא לרכז את כולו במאמץ אחד.‬

5. ‫עבורה הסמח"ס בשלב שקיבל פיקוד על החט' טובה.‬

6. ‫פה"כ החט' חיפקדה טוב.‬

‫ס.כ.או"ה:‬

א. ‫חט' שנכנסה להרגיל חטיבחי חייכה לבכור את כל הנוהל קרב לפני תחילת האמרן. המערכה היא בזה שחהכ' לא במרה את נרהל הקרב לפני תחילת האמרן.‬

ב. ‫בנוה"ק נפל עומס מיותר על החט' בגלל שלא בבצנו את רבירינו בצורה טובה. יש לחייב אורבה לבוא ולעטות דברים בשטח.‬

ג. ‫יש לחרגל בקשנון כאשר אין אמצעי תאורה, פשרו שאם אין אור, אי אפשר לפגוע נכליל וכאשר ירי עם קטנון פגעו. יש ללמוד זאת כשעור וכתהגולת.‬

ד. ‫נאמרן הזה חייב להתבצע נ.ק.ח.ה, בלילה גדוד אחר לא כצע זאת.‬

ה. ‫מערכת הכבוסה החטיבה למעברי היררן והזרצאתה על בסיס של כוח סמח"ט על כל כל הצאלמנטים של הקטר פבני' דמה מאוד, הסמח"ט עשה כאן פבורה יוצאת מן הכלל, היא עשה זאת בשלדי יום, ובשלדי לילה ברטוב.‬

ו. ‫לא ברורה השכניקה על העעלה ורקמור חח"מ, אם אין למב"ד קשר יטיר לקטנון בושא שלו, אסור לקח.לן להחזיר.‬
   ‫ח"פ נהמן' - אני עבוהי עם הקטנון, אך אין הוא יכיל ליהי יורחחים ועל מ"פ ולא הי"ר לעביר אחו.‬

ז. ‫הפעלת החט' בכניסה עשה ובבני ובהטחלטום עברה יטה.‬

ח. ‫לפי דעתי החדירה של החי"ר ל-גל היתה טובה. ראיתי את הזחל"טים מגיעים ל-3, אך לא הבנתי מדוע הסמח"ב ירד מתנתון הזה, ולא ניסה להפרך את חלקם מזה. לפי רק.י היה אפשר לעשות זאת.‬

ט. ‫אקט של אורליה - באקט של אורליח אני אישית נחתי לסמח"ס את הנהוגים על האוריב. נחתי זאת פם לחץ. נעטתה עבודה יפה של המטה היוטב בנגמ"ש ובבר הסמח"ט נתן הוראה לק.אב"ם להעביר מפיף ידיעות לרטת הגרידית. בכל אופן אהוד הצליח להכנים חטיבה בתנרקת בלתחה בפריסה בשטח הרדי על שני צירים. פעולה זו היתה פערלה מסורבכת של הפעלת 4 יחידות ברמה גדודים בצורה מהראמת ותלקה בכל אופן תופק בשלב זה.‬

י. ‫מבחינת שינוי המטימה לגבי "ארחלו" כמו עמאד המב"ס, הוא קיבל את סינוי .... לאורחים שלא היתה מספיקה.‬

Summary of a brigade-level exercise in which I served as deputy brigade commander, 1977.

It reads:

Summary of Exercise 645 by the commander of the field unit training base, Brig. Gen. Dan Vardi

Main points

1. Battle procedure at the brigade level is proper. At the battalion level, procedure was defective in that inadequate time was allotted for planning.

2. Rapid battle procedure while giving orders and coordinating activity through the network is proper.

3. The approach to ground activity and to the enemy is proper.

4. Use of the infantry battalion – it would have made sense to assign at least a company to the second brigade effort and not to concentrate all of it in one effort.

5. The work of the deputy brigade commander when he received command of the brigade was good.

6. Overall the brigade performed well.

Deputy division commander

a. A brigade that conducts a brigade-level exercise must complete all of the battle procedure before the training session begins. An error was committed in that the brigade did not complete all of the battle procedure before the training session began.

b. During the battle procedure, the brigade was hampered because we did not conduct the activities well. A division must conduct activities in the field.

c. Xenon must be used for an exercise when there is no lighting, because without light it is impossible to hit targets whereas when xenon is used, targets can be hit. This must be learned as a lesson and must be drilled.

d. In this exercise fire, suppressive fire, and assault must be carried out at night, battalion no. 1 did not carry that out.

e. The brigade's entry into the Jordan and successful crossing based on the deputy brigade commander's unit with all the complexities involved went very nicely, the deputy brigade commander did exceptional work here, he did it in the basic-framework format by day, and with live fire in the basic-framework format by night.

f. The technique of using the floodlight is not clear, if the battalion commander has no direct access to xenon through his network, then the lighting must not be done by xenon.

g. The use of the brigade to enter and conquer a built-up area went nicely.

h. In my opinion the infantry's penetration of 3B was good. I saw the half-tracks reach 3B, but I did not understand why the brigade commander did not take this into account, and did not try to draw the lesson. In my opinion it would have been possible to do so.

i. The act of "ORIT" – in this act I personally gave the deputy brigade commander the enemy data, I gave it emphatically. Nice work was done by the staff in the APC and the deputy brigade commander already gave the order to the operations officer to forward the data to the battalions. In any case Ehud managed to keep a brigade moving through hilly terrain along two routes. This operation of moving and coordinating four units simultaneously at a battalion level was complicated, and the lesson was drawn at this stage.

j. As far as changing the operation with regard to "Othello" as the brigade commander said, he agreed to the change.

ספירת ביסות שריון
ש ל י ט ה
07 / 300 / סלי
כא 1 (3) / 1.474
תשל"ח / כסלו
77 / גוב' 30

אוגרת 660/רמ"ח (2)
פיקוד מרכז/אלוף הפיקוד
מנה"ח/ז/רמנה"ט
א פ פרשי
יין 10
1 -
ח.ה.

הנדון: סכום ראיון ו-
471056 מא"ל דיסקין אהרד - חש"נ

1. הנ"ל רואיין ע"י מפקד גי"ש בתאריך 28 נוב' 77.

2. הראיון היה ביוזמת קשל"ג.

3. בראיון הועלו הנושאים הבאים:-

   א. הראיון החקיים בהמשך לראיון הקודם של הקצין עם מפקד גי"ש סיום 18 אוגוסט 77.

   ב. המשך שיבוצו.

4. להלן סכום הראיון:-

   א. מאחר והקצין מבקש לסיים תפקידו ב-1 מרץ 78 סיכם מפקד גי"ש כי. יצא ללמודים אקדמאיים מטעם צה"ל ב-1 מרץ 78 ובתאריך זה יעזוב תפקידו כספח"ס.

   ב. מפקד גי"ש הביע את מלא הערכתו על אופן מלוי תפקידו כספח"ס.

5. אבקשך למסור העתק מסכום זה לידי הקצין.

עא/סל

שאולובן לברס - אל"ם
קצין שריון
כטו: מספק ביסות השריון

ש מ ו ר

Summary of an interview with the Armored Corps commander, 1977.

It reads:

Armored Corps Headquarters
Adjutancy
Manpower 1
November 30, 1977

Division 880/Head of Staff (2)
Central Command/Head of Command

Re: Summary of interview:

Lt. Col. Ehud Diskin ID #471056

1. The above person was interviewed by the Armored Corps Commander on November 26, 1977.

2. The interview was at the initiative of the Battalion Adjutancy Officer.

3. In the interview the following matters were raised:

    a. The interview was a continuation of the officer's previous interview with the Armored Corps Commander on August 10, 1977.

    b. His further assignment.

4. Below is a summary of the interview:

    a. Because the officer is requesting to resign from his position on March 1, 1978, the Armored Corps Commander agreed that he will begin university studies, to be financed by the IDF, on March 1, 1978, and on that date he will leave his position as Deputy Brigade Commander.

    b. The Armored Corps Commander expressed his full appreciation for his fulfillment of his duty as Deputy Brigade Commander.

5. I request that a copy of this summary be sent to the officer.

[signed]

Col. Albert Shaulov

Adjutancy Officer, Armored Corps
In the name of the Armored Corps Commander

Certificate for completing the battalion commanders' course, 1976.

It reads:

Israel Defense Forces
Certificate of Graduation

This certifies that:

Lt. Col. Ehud Diskin 471056 is a graduate of the battalion commanders' course, second session, 1976, at the Armored Corps School.
Lt. Gen. Mordechai Gur, Chief of Staff
Maj. Gen. Moshe Peled, Commander of the Armored Corps
Col. Gideon Avidor, Commander of the Course

October 31, 1976

Chapter 11
· · · · · · · · · · · · · · · · · · ·
RISK AVERSION

I made the most of the offer I could not refuse, but it was not easy. I decided to do my doctorate in Israel's best economics university, the Hebrew University of Jerusalem, where I had also done my bachelor's and master's degrees. For the first time, I applied myself to academic work. I did not crib exercises; I solved them. I did not photocopy other people's classroom notes; I took notes myself.

As for my PhD thesis, I decided it would be in business management. The topic was, "The Approach to Risk in Private and Government Enterprise." I did empirical research using sampling to compare how private firms and government enterprises in similar areas dealt with risk.

While reading literature on the topic, I discovered that Professor Ralph Swalm of Syracuse University in New York had done research on various approaches to risk. I thought it would be worth meeting him, especially since it meant an opportunity to visit the U.S.

I contacted Professor Swalm and went to meet him in Syracuse. The meeting was very helpful. When I told him I wanted to fit a mathematical function to the behavior of company managers and their approach to financial risk, he responded unequivocally, "You won't succeed at that." When I asked why, he explained, "People usually behave inconsistently. For example, someone who has lost out in a deal will tend to take less risk in the next deal, and vice versa."

Back in Israel, I looked seriously into his point about inconsistent behavior. I read books and studies on the psychological aspects of decision making under conditions of uncertainty, including what Amos Tversky and Daniel Kahneman had to say on the topic. Both were then lecturers at Hebrew University. Thirty years later, Professor Kahneman, who meanwhile had moved on to Princeton, was awarded a Nobel Prize for his inquiries. Tversky had died a few years earlier; had he lived, the prize would almost certainly have been given to them jointly.

I assumed that if I could eliminate the factor of psychological inconsistency in my research, I could arrive at the intended goal. I managed to eliminate this factor, and developed a behavioral model that takes into account that the decision-maker's activities are a function of his expectations of the consequential yield, while receiving positive or negative reinforcement as a reward or penalty for the actual yield. Basically I was able to fit a mathematical function to the ways company managers approach financial risk. For readers who know a little about mathematics, I will put it this way: The function was in the form of a fifth-degree polynomial. I was satisfied with my success, especially because of Professor Swalm's warning that I would fail at this task. I recalled the words of the Talmudic sages, "Nothing stands in the way of will." You just have to find a way to convert will into results, and persist at it.

While working on my doctorate, I met with the CEOs of about sixty companies to solidify my findings and compare approaches to risk. Two CEOs in particular made a great impression on me.

One was Maj. Gen. Benny Peled, now retired from the army and the CEO of Elbit Systems, who impressed me with his insight, decisiveness, and analytical ability. During the Yom Kippur War, after the failure of the October 8 counterattack, the top military echelon considered pulling our forces in the Sinai back twenty-five miles. Peled told the senior officers involved in the discussion, "If you keep planning a withdrawal, I will personally come back here with my Uzi and shoot you all." Unfortunately, as I mentioned earlier, despite his military acumen and professionalism, Benny Peled made some faulty decisions before the war broke out, and also in its early stages. His mistakes caused the air force to function below its maximum effectiveness and hampered Israel's early execution of the war. Benny Peled died in 2002.

Another CEO who greatly impressed me was Yaakov Meridor of the Maritime Company for Cargo Transport, a shipping firm that was a world pioneer in transporting bulk cargo. Meridor served briefly as commander of the Irgun, the pre-state underground paramilitary organization. In 1943 he handed the reins to Menachem Begin and became his deputy. Meridor went on to serve as a Likud Member of Knesset and as Minister of Economics from 1981 to 1984. He died in 1995.

In my meeting with Meridor, he told me that his approach to risk was always to reduce it by managing the small details. He gave an interesting example: When he was incarcerated by the British and deported to a detention camp in Eritrea, he decided to escape. That entailed the risk of getting shot by British soldiers, so he and his comrades in the escape reduced this risk by wearing British army uniforms. Meridor figured that if the British guards saw them from afar, they would not shoot since they would fear hitting British soldiers. But once the guards drew nearer, the chances that they would shoot were slim because, for most people with even minimal moral sense, it is hard to shoot someone at close range, especially when you can have eye contact.

My PhD thesis adviser was Professor Yoram Peles, who later became head of the department. He was intelligent, knowledgeable, thorough, and an excellent adviser. He gave me full academic freedom, along with helpful guidance. I got to know various professors. They did not see me as a "typical military person" and were quite welcoming. I would sound them out on academic matters, and they would sound me out on military matters and political views.

Meanwhile I finished my thesis, and it went to a panel of judges composed of two professors. One, Marshall Sarnat, a professor with a great reputation, was full of praise for the paper. The second, someone with a PhD whose name I do not remember, demanded that some parts be revised. The academic administration of the university ruled that Professor Pinhas "Siko" Zusman would serve as an arbiter and would advise me on what needed to be reworked. Here was yet another striking coincidence. I felt that my life kept revolving around the same people. After all, Siko had been my master's thesis adviser, and when I served in the office of the financial adviser to the chief of staff, he had been the Defense Ministry's director general. We had become friends, and as I mentioned earlier, he had also advised me during the Yom Kippur War when he was the commander of Ariel Sharon's command post.

I was lucky enough to encounter and work with a good many intelligent and experienced people, from whom I always tried to learn what I could. Siko was just one of the people my life seemed to revolve around. Another was Haim Erez, who by sheer coincidence was my commander in the army on several different occasions and also played a role in other events of my life. Yet another was Moshe Nativ, who was both my commander in the army and involved in other aspects of my life as well.

I developed good relationships with most of these people who kept popping up in my life; but there was one exception: Amnon Reshef. My experiences with him, strangely enough, were always negative. Our relationship began at the end of the 1960s, when Lt. Col. Reshef was commander of the 189th Reconnaissance Battalion. As an officer with the rank of captain, I was tasked with inspecting his battalion for preparedness. What I found was a mess, and I wrote that in the report I circulated.

Eight years later, by coincidence, it was Brig. Gen. Reshef who commanded the division that arranged the first training exercise of my reserve battalion. As I described earlier, the headquarters of the division, apparently with his approval, planned to avail itself of most of the ammunition allotted for this training exercise and use it for its own purposes. After I got more senior officers involved, the ammunition was returned.

I had other run-ins with him as well. When I finished my studies, he tried to make me a deputy brigade commander in violation of a written agreement that promised me a more appropriate position. Later, when I was a candidate for financial adviser to the chief of staff, Maj. Gen. Reshef acted to block my appointment.

In any case, I did the additional work on my thesis. It was accepted, and I was awarded my PhD. The ceremony was held in the outdoor amphitheater on Hebrew University's Mount Scopus campus. I took my mother to the event, and afterward she said it was the happiest day of her life. No surprise there. What could make a Jewish mother happier than the day her son becomes a doctor?

I was quickly accepted into the world of academia, and even got a post as an adjunct lecturer for master's studies in business management at Hebrew University. Giving these lectures was not my cup of tea, and the students did not impress me. Some of them, instead of listening and learning, tried to show how bright they were by asking provocative, but irrelevant, questions. Realizing there was a limit to how much I could compromise in life, I decided to leave academic teaching and the academic world altogether.

Back in the IDF, I was supposed to be given a position at the rank of colonel in a professional, economic, or planning capacity, while remaining on call for the Armored Corps in case of war. Finding such a position was not easy.

The aforementioned Maj. Gen. Amnon Reshef, who was commander of the Armored Corps at the time, called me to a meeting and told me, "At the moment there's no position open for a colonel, so for the time being you'll serve as a deputy brigade commander." This meant serving at the level of a lieutenant colonel.

I took from my pocket the report of my interview with the head of the Manpower Administration and said, "That goes against what it says here."

Reshef, with a very somber look, replied, "That's an order."

I calmly answered, "Then I'm disobeying your order."

While he sat there stunned, I said, "If we were in Russia (and by that I meant the communist Soviet Union of those days) you could simply draw a pistol and shoot me. But we're in Israel, and in the IDF, the most you can do is file a complaint against me." I added, "I don't think they'll put me in jail for disobeying that order. After all, I'm a lieutenant colonel, and your order contradicts a written commitment."

Reshef, boiling with rage, sent his complaint about me to the chief of staff. Maj. Gen. Moshe Nativ, who was then head of the IDF's Adjutant General Division, and my guardian angel blocked the complaint.

I sometimes wonder how I managed to reach the rank of colonel despite such constant friction with the military brass. The friction stemmed from my insistence on living my life as I wanted to live it, as I had somehow succeeded in doing since the days when I was a private. Meanwhile, late in 1980, as I was waiting for an assignment, Maj. Gen. Moshe Nativ asked me what I thought of serving for the time being as an assistant to Israel Sacharov, chairman of the Libi Fund, a foundation set up that year to promote education in the IDF. I accepted the offer.

האוניברסיטה העברית בירושלים
המשרד לתלמידי-מחקר

 י' בניסן תשמ"א
14 באפריל 1981

אישור זמני

הננו לאשר בזאת כי

מר אהוד דיסקין

הגיש עבודת-מחקר על הנושא:

"הגישה לסיכון בחברות ממשלתיות ופרסיות בישראל"

עבודת-מחקר זאת אושרה מטעם הפקולטה   למדעי-החברה   ועל-ידי הסינט של
האוניברסיטה העברית, והתואר "דוקטור לפילוסופיה" הוענק   למר אהוד דיסקין
ביום   י' ניסן תשמ"א (14 באפריל 1981).

תעודת-הדוקטור תימסר   למר אהוד דיסקין   בטכס חלוקת התעודות
בתום שנת הלימודים.

מזכיר הוועדה לתלמידי-מחקר

Approval of PhD thesis, 1981.

It reads:

Hebrew University of Jerusalem, Office of Graduate Studies   April 14, 1981
Interim certificate

I hereby confirm that
Mr. Ehud Diskin
has submitted a thesis on the topic:
"The Approach to Risk in Government and Private Enterprise in Israel"

This thesis has been approved by the Faculty of Social Sciences and by the Senate of Hebrew University, and the degree of Doctor of Philosophy has been awarded to Mr. Ehud Diskin on the day of April 14, 1981.

The doctoral degree will be presented to Mr. Ehud Diskin at the degree-awarding ceremony at the end of the academic year.

Nitza Slonim
Secretary of the Graduate Studies Committee

האוניברסיטה העברית בירושלים

THE HEBREW UNIVERSITY OF JERUSALEM

THE JERUSALEM SCHOOL OF BUSINESS ADMINISTRATION
Sponsored by The Israel Discount Bank Foundation

בית הספר למינהל עסקים
מיסודה של קרן בנק דיסקונט לישראל

20.5.81

לכבוד
אלו"מ ד"ר אהוד דיסקין
רח' מוריה 38
רמת השרון

אהוד ידידי,

בשמי ובשם ביה"ס למנהל עסקים הנני שמח לברך אותך לסיום לימודיך ולקבלת
התואר דוקטור לפילוסופיה בבית הספר למנהל עסקים של האוניברסיטה העברית
בירושלים.

אין בליבי ספר כי השכלה שרכשת בלימודיך בכלל ובעבודת הדוקטור בפרט,
הספקנות, הכושר האנליטי ויכולת הארגון והביצוע של מחקרים כלכליים,
יעמדו לך הן בעבודתך והן בחיי הרוח שלך בעתיד. הנני מקוה שצה"ל ידע
למצות את יכולתך, כישוריך ומי ומבנותך ויועידך להפקידים חשובים לתועלתו
הוא, לטובת מדינת ישראל וגם לסיפוקך את מעבודתך.

הנני בטוח עתה, לאחר שסיימת את העבודה, יש בליבך סיפוק על כי עמדת במשימה
בכבוד, השקעת מאמץ וזכית לפרי הילולים. נקוה שתמשיך לחקור וליצור גם
בעיסוקיך הבאים. דרך צלחה.

בידידות,

פרופ' יורם פלס
מנהל ביה"ס למנהל עסקים האוניברסית
העברית

*A letter of praise from the director of the School of Business Management,
Professor Yoram Peles, 1981.*

It reads:

May 20, 1981
To: Colonel Dr. Ehud Diskin, 38 Moriah Street, Ramat Hasharon

My friend Ehud,

In my name and in the name of the School of Business Management I am happy to congratulate you on completing your studies and receiving your PhD at the School of Business Management of the Hebrew University of Jerusalem.

I have no doubt that the knowledge you have acquired in your studies in general and in your doctoral work in particular, the critical approach, analytical acumen, and ability to organize and carry out economic research, will benefit you both in your work and your intellectual life in the future. I hope the IDF will make full use of your ability, qualifications, and expertise and will appoint you to important positions, for its own benefit, for the good of the state of Israel, and also for your own fulfillment in your work.

I am sure, now that you have finished this endeavor, that you are inwardly satisfied at having accomplished the task honorably, investing effort and reaping the first fruit. We hope you will continue to both investigate and innovate in your future activities. May your path bring success!

In friendship,
Prof. Yoram Peles, Director of the School of Business Management, Hebrew University

תוכנית יום העיון

3.00—2.30   הרשמה וכיבוד.

3.10—3.00   דברי פתיחה — פרופ׳ **יורם פלס**, ביה״ס למנהל עסקים,
האוניברסיטה העברית.

3.50—3.10   "תפקידי מועצת מנהלים בסקטור הממשלתי והפרטי בישראל"
ד״ר **גדעון שטיאט**, ביה״ס למנהל עסקים, האוניברסיטה
העברית.

4.30—3.50   "גישה לסיכון בחברות פרטיות מול חברות ממשלתיות
בישראל" אל״מ **אהוד דיסקין.**

6.00—5.00   "Private versus Public Enterprise: The Chicago Approach"
George J. Stigler, Charles R. Walgreen Distinguished Service
Professor, Graduate School of Business, University of Chicago

7.00—6.00   ארוחת ערב

8.00—7.00   רב־שיח בהשתתפות :
מר **אפרים ירמנט** — מנהל רשות החברות הממשלתיות.
מר **ישראל סחרוב** — יו"ר מועצת המנהלים, התעשייה־
האווירית.
מר **אריה שחר** — מנכ"ל מפעלי ים־המלח.
פרופ׳ **דוד לבהרי** — האוניברסיטה העברית (מנחה הדיון).

מקום : בית מאירסדורף, הר־הצופים, האוניברסיטה העברית.

תאריך : יום שני, י"ב באדר א׳ תשמ"א (16.2.80).

תשלום : 400 שקל.

My lecture at a conference and a news item (on pages 220–221) on the topic of
approaches to risk, 1980.

The schedule for the conference reads:

Conference schedule

2:30–3:00 Registration and reception

3:00–3:10 Opening remarks – Prof. Yoram Peles, School of Business Management, Hebrew
University.

3:10–3:50 "The Tasks of a Board of Directors in the Government Sector and the Private Sector
in Israel" – Dr. Gideon Shetiyat, School of Business Management, Hebrew University.

3:50–4:30 "The Approach to Risk in Private Companies versus Government Companies in
Israel" – Lieutenant Colonel Ehud Diskin.

5:00–6:00 "Private versus Public Enterprise: The Chicago Approach" – George J. Stigler,
Charles R. Walgreen Distinguished Service Professor, Graduate School of Business,
University of Chicago

6:00–7:00 Dinner

7:00–8:00 Panel discussion with:

Mr. Efraim Yeramnis – Director of the Government Companies Authority

Mr. Israel Sacharov – Chairman of the Board of Directors, Israel Aircraft Industries

Mr. Arieh Sachar – Director-General, Dead Sea Works

Prof. David Levari – Hebrew University (moderator)

Location: Beit Maiersdorf, Mount Scopus, Hebrew University.

Date: Monday, February 16, 1980.

Fee: 400 shekels.

מחקר: המנכ"לים בחברות ממשלתיות – נועזים יותר

לא פלא: חוששים פחות מפיטורין, אין להם חלק בסיכון והמועצה לא מתערבת

מאת אריה דכיא

סופר "הארץ" לעניני כלכלה

הגישה לסיכון בחברות בבעלותית נמצאת יותר מאשר בחברות פרטיות, מתברר ממחקר על הגישה לסיכון בחברות בממשלתיות ופרטיות בישראל שנערך על-ידי אל"מ אהוד דיסקין. המחקר, שנעשה לצורך עבודת דוקטורט ותוגש לסנאט האוני־ ברסיטה העברית, יוצג היום בכנס במלאות ארבע שנים לפטירתו של ישראל ("איזי") גל עד.

מטרת המחקר להשוות את הגישה לסיכון בחברות בממשלתיות מזה ו־ חברות פרטיות מזה, תוך בחינת ה־ הבדלים ביניהן. המחקר מישתמש ב־ גישה חברתיוריסטית (התנהגותית) לגבי הפירמה. גישה זו בוחנת את מקבלי ההחלטות בפירמה, את שי־ קוליהם ואת תהליך קבלת ההחל־ טות.

במסגרת המחקר נפגש כר דיסקין עם 75 מנכ"לים של חברות בממשל־ תיות ופרטיות. עד כה לא נעשתה כל עבודה אצמדית באו"ץ או ב־ חו"ל לבחינת הנושא.

בין הגורמים לנועזות הרבה יותר בחברה הבממשלתית – הסובדה של־ בנכ"ל חברה ממשלתית אין חלק ב־ פירה (אם כי התיפעה קיימת גם בחברות פרטיות), והתערבות מוע־

טה יתר של מועצת המנהלים בנס־ אים כספיים.

בין השאר, התברר כבצנף הח־ רושת יש פער קטן יותר בנועזות של החברה הבממשלתית לעומת ה־ פרטית, ואילו בענף הבנין והגבו־ לות פער זה רב יותר באופן יחסי.

הכדלים נוספים בין חברה בממשל־ תית לחברה פרטית כפי כהתקבלו במחקר של אל"מ דיסקין:

★ בפירבות הבעלתיות שיעור הרווחים מהמחזור נמוך יותר (בין השנים 1976 ו־1978 התבטאו ההב־ דלים במאות אחוזים).

★ מטרת הרווח בחברה הממ־ שלתית מדורגת בדורך־כלל בסגיה במעלה, ואילו בחברות הפרטיות — ראשונה במעלה.

★ בחברה הממשלתית חסרים של המנכ"לים לפיטורים במקרה, כל הפסד. מצטבר שקן יהטות מזה הג־ קיים בחברה פרטית.

★ בעוד שרבית הנועזרבות מוצ־ צת והמנהלים בנרשאים כספיים בחב־ רה הממשלתית פוהונה כזו שבחברה פרטית, הרי התתעלרבות בגישאים — כמו כות אדם והנצאות ראזוה — דבה יותר.

★ ותק המבנכ"לים בחברה הממ־ שלתית הוא בבמוצע 5.5 שנים, בי־ עוד שבחברה הפרטית הערוק מגיע ל־10 שנים בממוצע.

The news item reads:

Study: Managers of Government Companies – More Daring
No Wonder: They Have Less Fear of Being Fired, Have No Stake in the Risk, and the Board
Does Not Interfere

By Ariel Lavi
Haaretz writer on business affairs

The approach to risk in government companies is bolder than in private ones, according to a
study on the approach to risk in government and private companies that was carried out by
Colonel Ehud Diskin. The study, which was conducted for a PhD thesis and submitted to the
Senate of Hebrew University, will be presented today at a conference marking the fortieth
anniversary of the death of Israel ("Izzy") Gal-Ed.

The aim of the study is to compare the approach to risk in government companies on one hand
and in private ones on the other, examining the differences between these approaches. The study
uses a behavioristic approach to a company. This approach focuses on the decision-makers in the
firm, their considerations, and the decision-making process.

As part of the study, Mr. Diskin met with 75 managers of government and private firms. So far,
no empirical work has been done on this topic in Israel or abroad.

Among the reasons for greater boldness in a government company is the fact that the manager
of a government company plays no role in the firm (though the phenomenon also exists among
private companies), and there is less involvement of the board of directors in financial matters.

Among other findings, it emerged that in the industrial sector there is a smaller disparity in the
boldness of government companies as opposed to private ones, while in the construction and
transportation sector the disparity is relatively larger.

Additional differences between government and private companies, as revealed in the study by
Colonel Diskin:

- In the government firms, the amount of profit from turnover is lower (from 1976 to 1978 the
  gap amounted to hundreds of percentage points).

- In a government company the profit goal is usually ranked second in importance, while in
  private firms it is ranked first.

- In a government company the manager's fear of being fired in case of accumulated loss is
  relatively smaller than in a private company.

- While the board of directors is less involved in financial matters in a government company
  than in a private company, involvement in matters such as manpower and demonstration costs
  is greater.

- The seniority of the managers in a government company is 5.5 years on average, while in a
  private company it amounts to 10 years on average.

ישראל סחרוב
שד' דוד המלך 30, ת"א.

27 באפריל 1981

לכבוד
אל"מ אהוד דיסקין,
רח' מוריה 38,
רמת השרון.

אהוד יקירי,

אני שמח לברכך מקרב לב על קבלתך את התואר "דוקטור לפילוסופיה" מטעם
הפקולטה למדעי החברה של האוניברסיטה העברית בירושלים.

אני חושב שתוספת ההשכלה שרכשת בלימודים אלה יאפשרו לצה"ל להועיד אותך
לתפקידים חשובים אשר יתנו לך הזדמנות לנצל את מלוא יכולתך, השכלתך וכישוריך.

עוד עתיד גדול נכון לך.

ברגשי ידידות,

ישראל סחרוב

A letter of congratulations and praise from Israel Sacharov (chairman of the board of the Libi Fund), on receipt of my PhD, 1981.

It reads: April 27, 1981
To: Colonel Ehud Diskin
38 Moriah Street, Ramat Hasharon

Dear Ehud,
I am happy to give you my heartfelt congratulations on receiving your PhD from the Faculty of Social Sciences at Hebrew University of Jerusalem.

I think the enhanced education you have acquired in these studies will enable the IDF to appoint you to important positions that will afford you the opportunity to use the full range of your ability, education, and qualifications.

A great future awaits you.

Warmly,
Israel Sacharov

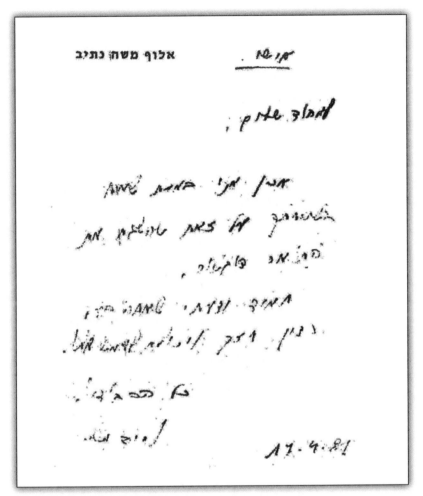

A letter of congratulations from General Moshe Nativ upon receiving my PhD, 1981.

It reads:

Personal
Maj. Gen. Moshe Nativ

Dear Ehud,

I rejoice in your happiness on having attained your PhD.

I always knew that you have a strong will and the ability to execute whatever you take on.

Well done!

Moshe Nativ April 17, 1981

Chapter 12
TEACH THY SOLDIERS

When I proposed that I take charge of the Libi Fund's public relations, Yitzhak Avinoam gave me a fixed, penetrating look and said sternly, "You are irresponsible, and in the end you're going to fail."

This was in 1980, about a year after Prime Minister Menachem Begin and chief of staff Lt. Gen. Rafael "Raful" Eitan had established a fund to provide educational programming for soldiers. The goal of the fund was to obtain donations from sources outside the IDF for the remedial education of soldiers who had not finished school.

Raising more money than what was allocated in the defense budget, Raful believed, would get more people in Israel involved in volunteering and contributing in general. Prime Minister Begin, for his part, strongly backed both Raful's approach and the fund itself. And then, as so often happens, the Israeli public split into two camps: Right-wingers supported the fund, while left-wingers did not.

The media opposed the fund and dubbed it the "Raful Fund" or the "Begin Fund." The Histadrut[56] Labor Federation, then headed by Yeruham Meshel, associated the fund with the right-wing Begin government and came out against it as well. The fund was constantly in the headlines because of its novelty and the right-left dispute it sparked. Over the years, though, both its uniqueness and

---

[56] The Workers' Union, an organization of employees that represents and amalgamates the workers in Israel.

its popularity declined, as it became another run-of-the-mill fund-raising operation.

Hostility was not the only problem to beset the Libi Fund. Its leadership was not formed in a practical way. Initially, a public committee was appointed that included well-respected figures like Chief Rabbi Gen. (ret.) Shlomo Goren, Yitzhak Avinoam,[57] and others, but their organizational and practical input was negligible.

Israel Sacharov was recruited to lift the fund from the morass into which the Israeli left had plunged it. Sacharov, in contrast to the original committee members, was an effective, intelligent person skilled in the intricacies of politics and a successful businessman. Sacharov had fought as an officer for the British army during the World War II. In Israel he became a member of the General Zionist Party, which later morphed into the Liberal Party. He was sixty-seven years old when he took the reins of the Libi Fund, and he soon began interviewing a string of army officers looking to find someone who could help him manage the operation. At the end of a meeting with him in his apartment in Tel Aviv, he offered me the post, and I accepted it.

We worked together to repair the dysfunctional fund. We gave it the name Libi, which means "my heart" in Hebrew and is also an acronym of "For Israel's Security." First, we had to counteract all those who held honorary positions in Libi but hindered the kind of work that could actually get something done. Israel Sacharov, who was a political whiz, maneuvered successfully to get rid of all the excess baggage. As the political protégé of Simcha Erlich,[58] he

---

[57] Yitzhak Avinoam was the commander of the Irgun in Jerusalem during the British Mandate. At that time the Irgun carried out daring strikes against British rule, including an attack on the British Intelligence offices, the bombing of the King David Hotel in Jerusalem, an attack on the British Officers' Club, and an attack on the Schneller military base. In March 1947, Avinoam was arrested by the British and sent to a prison camp in Africa. After the establishment of the state he was released, and he returned to Israel.

[58] An Israeli politician who died in 1983. Erlich guided the Liberal Party for many years. With the formation of the first Begin government in 1977, he was appointed deputy prime minister and finance minister.

adopted his mentor's rule: Instead of killing flies with vinegar, one can drown them in honey – the result is the same but less bitter. So Sacharov displayed great deference and courtesy toward all those distinguished personages who were, in his view, extraneous. He never berated them, but acted behind the scenes to free them for other endeavors where they would have more to offer.

Israel Sacharov generally operated behind the scenes of Israeli politics. Thanks to his experience and shrewdness, not to mention his political connections, he was very much in demand as a chairman or board member for many companies. Among other posts, he served at various times as chairman of the board of Israel Aircraft Industries, chairman of Israel Chemicals, chairman of Bank Leumi, chairman of the Bezeq Telecommunications Company, and he was also put in charge of the privatization and sale of government companies. These positions of economic power made him even stronger politically.

His many roles did not leave him much time for the Libi Fund. As our working relationship developed, he showed full confidence in me, and I became the de facto director of the fund.

After a few months on the job, I reached the conclusion that unless we could get the Israeli public to view the Libi Fund as a positive force, it would collapse. I proposed to Sacharov that he let me deal with public relations, which until then was in the hands of the spokesman for the Ministry of Trade and Industry. This displeased Yitzhak Avinoam and prompted his nasty remark about my irresponsibility. He doubted my public relations skills. I told Avinoam that, while I indeed lacked knowledge and experience in the field, I had already proved myself to be a good organization man. I added that if I could get some capable professionals on my staff and organize them properly, I could achieve good results. Sacharov did not share Avinoam's opposition to my taking on the public relations responsibilities, and I began executing my plans.

The academic world sometimes tries to simplify life by using mathematical and behavioral models. As for myself, I applied a model of mountainous-terrain combat to my work at the Libi Fund, combining the academic approach with my military experience. In mountainous terrain you have to restrict movement and combat activity to a limited number of paths. You have to make the most of these, and if you find one avenue more promising or available than the rest, you apply all your focus there. Years later, when I entered the business world, I sometimes applied this same model to my work, since it proved itself.

For the Libi Fund's public relations campaign, I decided to aggressively recruit media outlets to our cause, and even try to gain the support of those outfits that opposed Libi, most of all the Histadrut. Through the IDF spokesman, I mobilized key journalists to do reserve duty for the Libi Fund. My basic assumption was that since the Libi Fund's main focus was education, creating public awareness of its successful programs would turn public opinion in its favor.

I recruited journalists from the three main Israeli newspapers, *Haaretz*, *Maariv*, and *Yedioth Ahronot*, and soon sympathetic articles started turning up in their pages. Of all the journalists who did reserve duty for Libi, I was most impressed by Shlomo Nakdimon. He had been the media adviser to Prime Minister Begin and seemed especially talented. Nakdimon was a Zionist, tireless and devoted, and had political connections. Since it was for a great cause, rather than his personal advancement, he applied himself unstintingly. It was through him that I met the politician Moshe Shahal, who was then part of the group lobbying on behalf of the city of Haifa. I also met Ehud Olmert, the future prime minister, who was then part of the Jerusalem lobby.

Shlomo Nakdimon also organized a meeting with the Dankner family of Haifa, one of Israel's richest families. Mrs. Janet Dankner made us feel at home and served us delicious cakes, though ultimately we did not raise any money through her.

I also turned to the radio and TV worlds, and got them to feature us, sometimes close to the hourly news reports. Here I was helped by Yosef "Tommy" Lapid, then director general of the Broadcasting Authority. Tommy was a controversial person, a Hungarian holocaust survivor who became a very active political figure in Israel. Today his son, Yair Lapid, is the Finance Minister in Israel. I met with Tommy a few times, told him about Libi, and was impressed by his personality. He was warmhearted and supported the kind of nonprofit work our fund represented. He joined our cause enthusiastically, pulling his weight with all the key radio and TV people who could help improve our public image. It was indeed thanks to his backing that I gained greater and more effective access to the radio and TV networks.

This was a war in which I had to painstakingly conquer one hill after another, and slowly but surely our efforts gained momentum. Soon, I decided to approach a key target: Yeruham Meshel, secretary-general of the Histadrut.

Through contacts, I organized a visit for Meshel to a course where female soldiers taught Hebrew to IDF soldiers who had trouble with the language. I had discovered, to my amazement, that there are native Israeli soldiers in the IDF who can barely read or write Hebrew.

I planned it so that, as Meshel was winding up his visit, he found himself facing a battery of journalists and photographers from "my forces." One of them asked, "What do you think of what you've seen?"

Of course, he said that what he had seen was great. Did he have a choice?

The next day there were reports in the papers – even on the front page of one daily – with photos of Meshel as he declared his support for Libi.

That was the turning point. From there the Libi Fund's fortunes began to rise. Public opposition petered out. We could now appeal to any organization connected to the Histadrut, which was then competing for power with the government, and get that organization's support and funding.

Whereas only a year earlier the Libi Fund had been largely rejected by the public, it was now sought after. It was considered an honor to donate to it, and to gain publicity for having done so. When necessary, I recruited Raful and Begin for photo ops with large-scale donors, and I made sure the press would publish their pictures and the sums they had provided. From these interactions, I learned to respect Menachem Begin as an intelligent person and true gentleman.

Looking back, promoting the Libi Fund was one of my most complicated and daunting tasks, and the crowning glory was a 180-degree change in Israeli public opinion. I achieved that with the help of partners who saw our work as a national mission.

Similar to Yitzhak Avinoam's questioning of my qualifications for public relations, I have had doubt cast upon my abilities on many other occasions, particularly when I entered the business world. Such pronouncements, usually made disdainfully, often had me wondering why people were so sure I would not succeed. Was it because I do not make the right sort of impression? Or maybe because the task appeared impossible in the first place? Or maybe it was a combination of the two.

In any case, the Libi Fund began to blossom, and large donations started arriving, which we channeled into soldiers' educations.

For my part, I became something of a celebrity. My picture began to turn up in the papers, I was invited to kick the first ball at soccer games, and I was asked to lecture to various groups.

One of the lectures I gave was to the Women's International Zionist Organization (WIZO). The WIZO treasurer, Dr. Genia Kanovich, had invited me to speak at one of its events. While I was still in the waiting room, a very old woman came up to me, hugged me, and gave me a kiss. When Kanovich asked her, "What do you want from him?" she answered, "What do you mean? I'm his aunt!" Up to this day, I do not know who she was.

In the hall were about three hundred women, and each looked to be about ninety years old. As I went up on the stage,

Dr. Kanovich introduced me, but before I could begin, one of the women turned toward me and asked, "Which Diskin is that? Is that the Diskin from the wine world?"

I informed her that he was a distant relative of mine, and tried to begin the lecture. Then another woman broke in, "Is that Diskin the contractor?"

I told her that Diskin the contractor was my father's cousin. For about fifteen minutes, to satisfy their curiosity, I outlined my family connections. I soon realized that they were more interested in my family tree than the topic. A few minutes after I finally began the speech, most of the women lost interest – some even took a nap.

Working with Sacharov, I saw well-known public figures come to him for help or advice. I saw his ability to get things done, like the time we managed to get laws passed in the Knesset[59] that gave major tax benefits to donors to the fund, a move that definitely helped Libi financially.

Sacharov was a talented businessman. Years earlier, after he had done very well in a series of deals – some of them involving two concerns he helped set up: the Sahar Insurance Company and United Wood Industries – he decided to go into public service on a pro bono basis, which was how he ended up as chairman of the Libi Fund. As for me, still quite new to the political and business worlds, Israel Sacharov taught me how to get results. I won his trust, and he would share discreet political matters with me. He complained to me regularly about the hypocrisy and dishonesty of politicians, and I learned from our long talks which public figures were truly decent.

Sacharov, who learned British decorum while serving as a British army officer, always made sure to introduce me as a colonel and a doctor.

I did not always agree with his approach to people. One day when he criticized my friend Maj. Gen. Shmulik Gorodish, I told

[59] The Israeli parliament.

him, "I'm sorry, but Gorodish is my friend, and I'm not prepared to hear something negative about him."

Sacharov replied, "Friends! I don't believe in friendship! My best friends did the worst things to me."

Sacharov had very good relations with his brother-in-law, his wife's twin brother Lova Eliav,[60] even though Lova was politically left wing. I saw Lova Eliav's admirable public activity firsthand. He was an idealist and a kind person. He served as secretary-general of the Labor Party, then left the party, and while in the political wilderness, he helped young people in distress and devoted his time to the Nitzana Educational Youth Village in the Negev desert.

Israel Sacharov was one of two people from whom I learned a lot in my life. The other was Shmulik Gorodish. Although they worked in different fields, they were both intelligent and experienced. Each of them, like all of us, had his failings, but even from their failings I learned important lessons.

Sacharov, despite his power and status, had an intense concern, perhaps overly so, for his good name. One morning he showed me a letter he received from the finance minister. It was an offer to be appointed commissioner of the Bank of Israel. I said the job was tailor-made for him. But he said he would reject the offer because the post did not bolster the reputations of those who held it.

A few weeks later Sacharov showed me a letter from Prime Minister Menachem Begin – this time an offer for him to serve as finance minister. In this case, too, Sacharov told me he intended to turn it down. The job sullied the name of those who held it, and he aspired to leave a good impression on the public in general, and on his family and grandchildren in particular.

Sacharov would show me every letter of appreciation he received, and he would always repeat the same refrain, "I'll leave it in safekeeping for my grandchildren, and they'll read it and be impressed by all this praise that I received."

---

[60] An Israeli politician and activist who died in 2010.

I hope that after he died, some twenty years later, all those documents and letters were kept and not just discarded. As we get older, we sometimes entertain illusions about how much interest our children and grandchildren will have in us after we are gone. And maybe it's a good thing to harbor such hopes.

As always, I made sure I was on call for reserve duty in case of war. My emergency appointment was in a field unit of the Intelligence Corps, at the rank of colonel. And though I had originally planned to work at Libi for only a few months, I ended up staying there for almost two years.

After a while, an opening for the position of financial adviser to the chief of staff became available, at the rank of brigadier general. It was a position I very much wanted. I thought my experience could be of considerable help when it came to efficiently organizing and managing the defense budget. I had, of course, already gained hands-on experience at the Financial Adviser's Office and in organizational and command roles in the field. And my academic background, with my specialization in budgeting issues, nicely rounded out these qualifications.

On my own initiative I met with the chief of staff, Raful, who told me officially that I was a candidate for the job. Although the chief of staff ultimately decides who gets this post, the issue is first discussed by a group of IDF generals and the Defense Ministry's director general, as the financial adviser to the chief of staff also serves as head of the Budget Division of the Defense Ministry.

I met with Avraham Ben-Yosef. He was considered as one of the Defense Ministry's power brokers and held senior posts in the defense establishment from 1955 to the end of the 1980s, including director general of the ministry under Defense Minister Ariel Sharon. Avraham told me that the ministry would back my candidacy. Raful did not favor it because he saw me as too much a learned highbrow, a trait he considered a hindrance rather than an advantage. And the one who apparently drove the nail further into the coffin of my candidacy was Maj. Gen. Amnon Reshef, who had his fill of me from our past run-ins. I was informed that when my name came up for discussion, Reshef poured fire and brimstone on me as a candidate. His words found an attentive ear in Raful, who believed too much academic background or intelligence was a drawback.

In the end, Raful's choice for the financial adviser's position was Reuven Hershko, a product of the Financial Adviser's Office who had risen there in rank from lieutenant to colonel.

Once that was determined, I was fed up and declared I wanted to be discharged from the IDF. They tried to convince me to be patient and wait for my promotion; I had been a colonel for less than two years and was not yet thirty-eight years old. The head of the Manpower Division, Maj. Gen. Moshe Nativ, suggested I serve three years as deputy financial adviser, and then I could fill his shoes. I rejected the offer and decided to leave the army.

It was also at that time that I separated from my wife, Nili, and a few months later, met my next wife, Rita. We were introduced by Capt. Miri Shomron, my assistant at the Libi Fund and the former wife of Dan Shomron, who later served as chief of staff. Miri Shomron handled our contacts with potential large donors. One day Miri told me she knew a young American woman named Rita who was living in Israel and could be of great help to Libi. I discovered that Rita's father was one of the wealthiest Jews in California. Miri set up a meeting with her, during which we tried to recruit her to help Libi, but she said that Libi's money should come to the IDF from the defense budget, not from donors.

So my initial aim in meeting Rita did not succeed. However, I was quite taken with her on a personal level, and at the end of the meeting I even drove her in my military vehicle to the hotel where she was staying.

I fell in love with Rita, she became my girlfriend, and after that we got married.

I have been asked why I got married a few times, and I have always answered that the number of cases where I rejected women's marriage proposals is four times greater than the number of times I got married. I suppose being a romantic type had to do a lot with this. True, in my career, and in the business world that I entered later, I was quite practical, but not necessarily in my personal life, where I made decisions on emotion rather than logic. Of course, I sometimes paid for this when I had to deal with reality.

Before we were married, Rita's father told me I should not take a salaried position, and suggested I should be an independent businessman instead. He promised to get me started with $1 million if I found a worthwhile investment.

Israel Sacharov, however, advised me against private business. He suggested that I become a well-paid CEO with good perks like a company car, a secretary, and so on. Sacharov could easily have worked out such a job for me. He further claimed that as a CEO I would deal with truly weighty concerns, instead of the minor matters that would occupy me as a businessman. And who, he asked, could guarantee that I would succeed in my deals? As he saw it, there was a high chance of failure. And yet, I told him I had decided to go into private business.

Maj. Gen. (ret.) Dan Tolkovsky, a former air force commander, was then director general of the large IDB investment firm, a creation of the Recanati family who were the owners of Bank Discount. Tolkovsky set up a meeting with me and asked if I was interested in joining IDB. We were not acquainted, but he had heard about me, and his offer was very flattering. But, again, I said I was looking to go into private business instead of taking a salaried position.

And so, having been in the military and in academia, I now ventured into a new world and a new stage of my life.

A meeting of the public committee of the Libi Fund, 1981. Back to the camera, from left: Israel Sacharov, Chief Rabbi Shlomo Goren. Opposite: me, second from left (photo: Israel San, courtesy of the IDF Spokesperson's Unit).

With Menachem Begin, 1981 (courtesy of the IDF Spokesperson's Unit)

A lecture I gave in the town of Kiryat Malachi, 1981. At the center stands the head of the town council, Moshe Katzav (later a cabinet minister and president of Israel); I am sitting beside him to the right (courtesy of the IDF Spokesperson's Unit).

With the chief of staff, Lt. Gen. Rafael ("Raful") Eitan during a radio interview, 1981 (photo: Aharon Yoslovich, courtesy of the IDF Spokesperson's Unit)

Right, *Menachem Begin;* left, *Israel Sacharov; I am second from the left.*
Sacharov is telling Begin that I have received my doctorate, and Begin shakes my
hand, 1981. After some time he sent me a copy of this picture with a dedication
(courtesy of the IDF Spokesperson's Unit).

A conversation with Ariel Sharon, 1981

With Lily Sharon, 1981

With Ehud Olmert (who served as prime minister 2006–2009) and his wife Aliza, 1982 (courtesy of the IDF Spokesperson's Unit)

A ceremony at RAFAEL Advanced Defense Systems Ltd., 1982. From right: *Dr. Ben-Zion Naveh, director-general of RAFAEL; Brig. Gen. (ret.) Yosef Maayan, director general of the Defense Ministry; I am standing on the left (courtesy of the IDF Spokesperson's Unit).*

With the chief of staff, Lt. Gen. Rafael ("Raful") Eitan, 1981 (courtesy of the IDF Spokesperson's Unit)

From left: *me, the navy commander;* last on right: *businessman Yuli Ofer; with his back to the camera is Lt. Gen. Rafael ("Raful") Eitan (courtesy of the IDF Spokesperson's Unit)*

Left to right: *Prime Minister Menachem Begin, Israel Sacharov, me, and the donor Zvi Zinkin (courtesy of the IDF Spokesperson's Unit)*

*With Lt. Gen. (ret.) Mordechai ("Motta") Gur (left), 1982
(courtesy of the IDF Spokesperson's Unit)*

תן לבך ללבי
תרום לקרן-למען
בטחון ישראל

*Opening ceremony for a soccer game of the team Hapoel Tel Aviv, which
contributed to the Libi Fund, 1981. The sign reads: Give your heart to Libi.
Contribute to the Fund for Israel's Security (photo: Aryeh Kanfer).*

A certificate of appreciation from the Lions organization for a lecture I gave to them, 1981

Chapter 13
WHO IS RICH? HE WHO IS HAPPY WITH HIS LOT

Making my way into the business world, I was naive enough to see myself as a sort of superman who could do anything. This was right after my work at Libi, which put me in the headlines and inflated my ego. Here I am, I thought to myself, a colonel with a great deal of organizational experience, and a PhD in business management.

But I realized very quickly that I was basically an ignoramus in business matters. The business world bears little resemblance to academic economic theory, and has nothing in common with the military world.

I always tried to be honest with myself, and I had to admit that when it came to business, I was nothing but a novice. But I was not discouraged. I stepped into the business world anyway and made a serious effort to learn the ropes. Today, after many years in business, I have come to the conclusion that what is most important is the school of life, that is, experience over theory, which at best can only simplify a thought process and sometimes help with decision making.

I searched intensively for a business that needed an investment of $1 million, so that I could pitch it to my father-in-law. At that time, insurance companies were good businesses, and there were only a few of them in Israel. To set up an insurance company, you had to get a license from the Finance Ministry, and of course, bring in customers.

To that end, I took the approach of a funny story called "Matchmaking with Rothschild's Daughter." It originally appeared in the *Book of Jokes and Wit*, published by the writer and Zionist leader Alter Druyanov in 1922. This story later became associated with Henry Kissinger, the American Jewish statesman, who was known for his shrewdness.

In the story, Kissinger had an uncle who was sixty years old and never been married. The family pressed Kissinger to get the uncle to marry someone. Kissinger went to him and said, "Uncle, the time has come for you to get married."

The uncle replied, "I'm already used to bachelorhood."

Kissinger said, "And what if your wife-to-be was the daughter of Rothschild?"

His uncle answered, "If we're talking about Rothschild's daughter, that's a different story."

Kissinger went to Rothschild and said, "Rothschild, I have a wonderful match for your daughter."

"Who might that be?" asked Rothschild.

"My uncle," Kissinger replied.

"How old is your uncle?" asked Rothschild.

"Sixty," said Kissinger.

"What kind of joke is this," Rothschild said angrily, "my daughter is thirty-five."

"And what would you say if my uncle is chairman of the board of Chase Bank?" said Kissinger.

"If that's the case," said Rothschild, "then it's a different story."

Now Kissinger went to Chase Bank and told them, "I have an excellent chairman of the board for you."

"But we have a chairman," they replied.

"But the chairman I am offering you is the son-in-law of Rothschild!" said Kissinger.

"If the new chairman is the son-in-law of Rothschild, then that is a different story," said the heads of the bank. And in this way Kissinger arranged a marriage for his elderly uncle.

In similar fashion, I persuaded Bank Otsar Ha-Hayal[61] to become a partner in the insurance company I was planning. That meant many of the bank's customers would be my customers as well. At that time, Professor Ezra Sadan was the director general of the Finance Ministry; we had met a few years earlier when he was an economics lecturer at the Rehovot branch of Hebrew University. We held each other in high regard, and were also friends. Sadan was intelligent, professional, and amiable. He was the right person to issue a license for my new insurance company, which would be built upon Otsar Ha-Hayal customers. But when I proposed this scheme to my father-in-law, Abe, he shot it down, saying it was too risky. And so a promising idea collapsed before it even began to take shape.

My great friendship with Israel Sacharov continued, and we would meet often for lunch or dinner. As the official in charge of privatizing government companies, Sacharov suggested Hachsharat Hayishuv, a company that was involved in land settlement and real estate. He explained this would be a promising acquisition because the company, which was established by the World Zionist Organization at the beginning of the twentieth century, owned a great deal of valuable land – much of it unbeknownst even to the company's managers. I brought this proposal to my father-in-law, and he rejected it as well. Eventually, the businessman Yaakov Nimrodi acquired Hachsharat Hayishuv, and it yielded him many millions of shekels.

The lawyer Moshe Shahal, a former Labor Party leader who was then in private business, also made me offer, and it met the same fate with my father-in-law.

I respected Rita's brother, Tom. He was a friendly, straightforward gentleman, and I got along well with him. He told me bluntly, "Do not believe my father's promises; he is a liar, and he's lying." I came to the conclusion that Abe actually had no intention

---

[61] An Israeli bank. The name literally means "Bank of the Soldier Treasury." Originally only for soldiers, in 1972 it opened to the general public.

of keeping his word. I told him I had no more need for his promises, and decided to make my way in the business world by myself, even though it meant creating something out of nothing.

We got married in pomp and splendor. Abe, the dominant figure in the family, decided that the ceremony would be held at the King David Hotel in Jerusalem. Abe was a donor to Yad Vashem,[62] Beit Hatfutsot,[63] and Bar-Ilan University. He also made a point of getting chummy with Israeli decision-makers, and making large donations to individuals, parties, institutions, and organizations.

As a result of his donations and promises, everyone was beholden to him. Abe had his own methods of getting well-known figures, both in the United States and Israel, to feel personally indebted to him when he needed a favor. Abe would buy Israel bonds[64] in annual sums of over $100,000, making him part of an exclusive club of large donors. He would redeem some of these bonds through relatives, or donate them. One day, I brought a sizable donation from Abe to the home of Yitzhak and Leah Rabin in Tel Aviv for ALUT, the Israeli Society for Autistic Children, of which Leah Rabin was the director. When Mrs. Rabin opened the large manila envelope with the donation in it, her face clouded over. The donation was in the form of Israel bonds. Being a very forthright person, she turned to me and said, "What is the point of this? Why is he giving me bonds that I have to redeem?" I suggested that she hold onto the bonds, and I would talk with Abe. I did, but I do not know whether the problem was solved.

Present at our wedding were public figures like then Prime Minister Menachem Begin, Yitzhak Rabin, Arik Sharon, Shlomo Lahat,[65] Zevulun Hammer,[66] and many others.

---

[62] The Holocaust Museum

[63] The Museum of the Jewish People in Tel Aviv.

[64] Debt instruments issued by the company Israel Bonds.

[65] A mayor of Tel Aviv for almost two decades.

[66] A politician who died in 1998.

Begin sat at our table throughout the reception. I was well aware why we were given this honor; Abe told me he had donated large sums to the Tel Hai Fund[67] to help rescue it from a humiliating bankruptcy. In the 1960s and 1970s the manager of the fund took out loans in the gray market at punishing interest rates, and by 1975 the fund was on the verge of collapse. Begin, who until then had hardly dealt with financial matters, came to the fund's rescue by soliciting donations from wealthy individuals in Israel and abroad. His efforts succeeded, the fund was allowed to restructure its debt, and bankruptcy was averted. My father-in-law said Begin felt deep gratitude toward him as one of the donors.

I empathized with Begin's plight as people constantly asked to take photographs with him during the reception. Polish gentleman that he was, he complied graciously with every request. A few weeks earlier, when Rita and I came to pay him a courtesy call at his office, he asked Rita, "How do you know Hebrew so well?"

She answered with a smile, "You always ask me the same question."

Begin kept his cool and, also with a smile, replied, "That's because I always love to hear the answer."

Rita had immigrated to Israel by herself ten years earlier, and she had integrated well. Our first son, Barak, was born in 1984. Barak's *brit milah* was performed in a lavish setting at the Dan Hotel in Tel Aviv. Here too, all the distinguished figures were present. Yitzhak Rabin served as the *sandak*,[68] cabinet minister Eliezer Shostak as the *kvater*.[69] I saw his hands shaking as he carried Barak, and I was ready to jump over and catch him if he was dropped.

After Barak was born, his grandfather Abe wanted us to come and live in the U.S. Family values were important to him, and he

---

[67] The main financial tool of the right-wing Revisionist movement, led by Ze'ev Jabotinsky in the pre-state period, and of its successor, the Herut movement led by Begin after statehood.

[68] The person who holds the baby in his lap during the brit milah.

[69] The person designated to hand the baby to the sandak.

wanted his daughter and grandson to be near him. To his credit, he turned out to be a warm and loving grandfather to his grand-children. Abe gave Rita an ultimatum, "If you don't come back to America, I'll put all your assets in an irrevocable trust, and you won't have any control over them."

He claimed the Israeli government was scheming to confis-cate the foreign holdings of Israeli residents and would nationalize Rita's assets, too. This was a hollow pretext, but the ultimatum was serious, and Rita wanted to return to the U.S. I was inwardly divided. On the one hand, the idea of spending a few years in the States appealed to me, but on the other, I had children in Israel. When I told Rita I was undecided, she said unequivocally, "You have to think about me too."

We decided to make our home in New York, since Rita did not want to live too close to her family. New York is a wonderful city, and I loved it, but our lives were not easy. Meanwhile our second son, Ron, was born. So we now had two babies on our hands. I kept trying to make deals in the business world, since it was emo-tionally rough for me to be supported by Rita – or more accurately, by her father – who sent her funds that always had strings attached. I put all my severance pay from the IDF into our common expens-es, investing in our shared life, but it was a drop in the bucket. Under all this emotional stress, I started to fall apart physically. I came down with cholestatic liver disease, thyroid problems, and a host of other issues. Although I may seem tough on the outside, inwardly I am as sensitive as they come.

We lived in a plush apartment on Manhattan's East Side. We had maids and nannies that worked around the clock. We also spent huge sums on travel. Rita always wanted to fly first class, since that was what she was used to, but I preferred economy class, not wanting her father's money to foot any unnecessary expense for me. In the end, we compromised on business class.

Despite our high standard of living, those were the most dif-ficult, and indeed the worst, days of my life. More difficult than the

War of Attrition and the Yom Kippur War, worse than anything I had previously experienced.

At the end 1985, I took a trip to Israel, and when I returned to New York, I was shocked to find an empty apartment. Rita had taken the children and moved to Los Angeles without any advance notice, discussion, or warning. The trading company I had set up was yielding little profit, and I had to cut back. I moved to a smaller, less expensive apartment and drastically scaled back my expenses.

I would visit the children in Los Angeles, and on one of those visits Rita and I decided to get a divorce. We agreed to do it in a reasonable fashion, but instead, I found myself being served with legal papers. I was accused of planning to kidnap our children and take them to Israel. When I went to Rita's house to see Barak and Ron, security guards were on hand to prevent me from taking them off the premises. I could hardly believe what was happening to me. It turned out to be the California approach: Slam the other person as hard as you can, then make a deal with him when you have the upper hand. In charge of Rita's affairs, as always, was the person who ran the whole family, her father.

I was facing a well-oiled machine, ready to spend unlimited funds to defeat me. Rita and her father hired a famous divorce lawyer named Dennis Wasser, whose clients included Clint Eastwood, Tom Cruise, Steven Spielberg, and Jennifer Lopez. I had two options: fight or give in. Despite my limited resources, I decided to fight.

My lawyers took me for every cent. The name of the game for lawyers is, "milk the client as much as you can." It got to the point where I had trouble paying my bills. Making support payments for my children in Israel was always a top priority. But now, not only did I have difficulty making those payments, but also paying my rent, electricity, and water bills was an issue.

Salvation came from an unexpected source. I turned out to be an outstanding blackjack player.

I got good at the game by studying it. In blackjack, unlike other casino games, the gambler's knowledge plays an important role. In other games, there is no way to calculate the probabilities based on what has already happened. In roulette, for example, even if the ball lands on red three times in a row, the chances that it will do so with the next turn of the wheel do not depend on, and are not affected by, what has happened so far. In blackjack, however, the cards are dealt from a set of decks called the "shoe," and a card that is played will not return to the game until the shoe is depleted. Therefore, counting the cards that have already been dealt can give the gambler a considerable advantage over the casino.

I was blessed with a good visual memory, and it helped me track which cards had already been dealt and predict which had a high chance of turning up in the future. In particular, I would estimate the chances of high or low cards appearing in the deck. But I also realized some luck was involved. So before sitting down at any gambling table, I would walk around the room and watch the faces of the dealers, trying to figure out what sort of luck they were having. I would try to play at tables with loser dealers, not at those of winners. If I realized I had made a mistake, I would get up and move to a different table.

I would play in the late hours of the night, when the dealers would be tired and the casino less crowded. I would also play two or three hands simultaneously, and would change the number of hands I played, so the dealer would get poor cards and I would get good ones. It is also very important to know when to get up and leave, whether you are losing or winning at that moment. On average, four out of every six times I gambled, I came out a winner.

I would often make my way to Atlantic City, about two and a half hours from Manhattan, and won sums that helped cover my living expenses. In Atlantic City, I would also enjoy the free meals that the casinos provided to their more serious gamblers. People watching me play would often ask why I did not become a professional gambler. I told them I never saw it as the right sort of life for me.

Around that time, I was reminded of my friend Israel Sacharov's warning not to go into business for myself, but to become a salaried CEO instead. I wondered if he was right after all. I was close to the breaking point, alone in a foreign country, and locked in a legal battle with my father-in-law. My lawyers said they had learned through Rita's lawyers that Abe was prepared to spend $5 million to destroy me. A detective agency from New Jersey was hired to keep tabs on me and harass me. I kept weighing whether it would be better to take a salaried position, such as a limousine driver or a sales representative, even though these sorts of jobs were far below my expectations for myself.

I was reminded of a story about Yitzhak Rabin when he commanded the Harel Brigade of the Palmach, in the battle of San Simon, in Jerusalem during the War of Independence. He quoted a saying of Palmach commander Yitzhak Sadeh, which apparently originated with a Russian general, "Remember that when it rains, the enemy gets wet, too; the winner is the one who holds out a moment longer than his adversary." The Palmach fighters were on the verge of collapse, but Rabin assumed the enemy was also having a hard time and about to break. The battle continued until the enemy actually did break.

I did not give in, and did not break, even though I was close to it. I took some unconventional legal measures to give me both breathing space and some advantage in the situation. One of the better lawyers in Los Angeles, who turned me down when I tried to hire him, told me, "You're like a monkey fighting an elephant."

At least there was progress on the business side of things. I made my first large deal by representing a New York-based American firm that sold bulletproof vests to the Israel Defense Ministry delegation in New York. The American company was called Point Blank. Its president was Richard Stone, a warm and very loyal Jew. When his company won a large tender to sell bulletproof vests to the Pakistani army, he was supposed to sign a document saying he would comply with the Arab boycott of Israel. Instead he returned the document without approval of the boycott clauses, but with a letter attached that said he was a devoted Jew who loved Israel, and if that meant Pakistan refused to buy his merchandise, so be it. In the end, Richard got the Pakistani order even though he would not go along with the boycott.

The deal revealed to me the differences in approach between Israeli and American businesses. A year earlier I had represented an Israeli firm in the United States called Hagor, which produced combat equipment for soldiers. I arranged a meeting for them with Richard Stone at Point Blank. A few months later, Hagor failed to fill an American order that I obtained for them, and I stopped representing them.

Now, a year later, Richard called me and said Hagor had proposed a joint project to him and he had asked, "What about Ehud Diskin?" When they told him I no longer represented them, Richard called to make sure that was true. I said it was, and gave him the green light to work with them directly. I was impressed by the high moral standards of this American businessman. I had met him only once, but he wanted to be certain it would be all right for him to work directly with Hagor. They did not bother contacting me at all, despite having certain moral obligations toward me.

Two weeks later, Richard called and said he wanted me to represent him. I told him that he would have to pay me a commission. He not only agreed, but also said that if I did not represent him, he would not go through with the deal. I sent him a contract with a clause about the commission, and he signed it right away without any revisions.

This deal was in the range of $2 million. At that time, Hagor was part of a cartel of heavy-textile manufacturers in Israel that had an agreement saying the Eagle Company, a member of the group, would get this tender. Hagor told Richard, who was the chief contractor for this deal, to submit an offer of $400 per bulletproof vest, so the Eagle Company would win. I advised him to offer $300, since the product would then be competitive. We won the tender and broke the Israeli cartel. The Defense Ministry, who in the past had paid excessive sums for bulletproof vests, was very pleased about that.

I encountered a further example of the differences in approach to business between the United States and Israel when we convened for a business meeting in Manhattan. The meeting included Natan Zomer (then director general of Hagor), Point Blank's president Richard Stone, and me. Natan declared, "Ehud Diskin is getting too much money here, and I would like him, on his own initiative, to lower his commission." I did not reply because I was representing the American company, not the Israeli one. But Richard responded at length, describing me as his best worker. He said, even though he was not paying me a salary, I brought him a great deal and it was paying off handsomely for him. Richard added that if he did not compensate me generously, or if I was not satisfied, I would not bring him more deals, and so he rejected the request to lower my commission. To Natan's credit, he responded with, "Maybe I've learned something here."

A few years later, Richard Stone sold his successful company at a profit, pocketing more than $10 million. Hagor ceased to be a significant factor in the Israeli market and was acquired by Eagle, under the ownership of Avraham Zilberschatz.

I enjoyed my social life in New York and was content with my circumstances. I realized that money is not a necessary condition for happiness. As our sages said, "Who is *rich? He* who is happy with his lot" (Avot 4:1). Yet at the beginning of 1988, after another two years in New York, I decided I needed to move to Los Angeles. My children were there, and they needed me.

I had no choice but to take on first-rate lawyers to fight those Rita's father was employing, and they were squeezing me for all I was worth. In light of Abe's connections and his influence over decision-makers in California in general, and in Los Angeles in particular, my lawyers were worried that the ruling would be biased against me, and I would not obtain justice no matter what I did. Abe was known to be close to Tom Bradley, the mayor of Los Angeles at the time.

I could sense what my lawyers were referring to when I found out that, when Rita moved from New York to Los Angeles, the judge immediately decided that she qualified as a resident of Los Angeles, which meant a Los Angeles court could hear our case. I presented clear evidence that Rita had spent ten of the last eleven years in Israel, followed by another year in New York. The judge ignored that, just as he ignored the fact that the court could only hear her case if she had resided in Los Angeles for the past six months, which, of course, she had not. I wanted the case to be decided in New York, our place of residence for about two months before the claim was filed. I assumed that Rita's father did not carry any weight in the New York legal system.

After I moved to Los Angeles, I lived in a rundown one-bedroom apartment in West Hollywood. I owed $60,000 in credit cards debts.

One summer morning, I left my apartment to take a walk. I wanted to fly to Israel and visit my children there. I wanted to buy them presents, but I did not have the money for it. That morning I decided to make a tactical retreat. I would work out a compromise agreement with Rita until I had enough money to again petition the court and improve the situation.

Rita and her father were restricting my contact with the boys, claiming that I intended to kidnap them. I agreed to the restricted visits, during which I could not take Barak and Ron out of Rita's house and had to spend time with them in the presence of a security guard. In return, they gave me enough money to cover my debts, my legal expenses, and a little extra.

It was Rita's father who paid this money, which came out of one of the trusts he had opened for her. I saw it as compensation for his deceit regarding the business investment he had promised to give me and never did, while constantly telling me not to accept a position in the Israeli private sector. Rita and her father saw these payments as hush money, and they made sure it was in installments, in case I violated the terms of my visitations. I was not proud of myself for making this agreement; indeed, I was angry with myself. Furthermore, the agreement, which was ratified by a court, included a clause that only the courts in California could rule on any future claim. But I felt I had no choice because all the other options were worse. I assumed the agreement would last only until I had enough money to find a court that would rule fairly on the case.

This unjust arrangement of me having to see the kids only at Rita's house depressed me. It was galling to visit and see their over-the-top privileged and indulgent life style, the worship of money, and the fact that the boys were usually under the "care" of nannies and male caretakers. During the first three years the boys were in Los Angeles, they had no fewer than fifty such nannies and caretakers, who were usually replaced after a short time on the job. I did not have the financial means to fight Rita and her father legally, and I had no desire to confront them any other way. Abe feared I would take physical revenge and employed a twenty-four-hour bodyguard.

To change the nature of the visitation, I offered to deposit my passport with a lawyer, to no avail. The boys and I were being punished for nothing, with no way of developing normal father-son relationships.

I felt like Samson, whose eyes were gouged out in the Philistine temple. It was the only time in my life that, in a state of desperation, I made a request of God. "They're stronger than me because of all their wealth," I said. "I can do no more. Please damage them financially so I can turn the tables." I do not know if God listened to my prayer, or if it was the hand of fate, but Abe's bank went out of business. It had purchased a huge quantity of junk bonds that offered high yields, but also entailed great risk.

The bonds had been bought with funds from savings that customers deposited in the bank, and their value declined drastically, far below the level of the original deposits. The authorities were not pleased with these transactions and took over the bank. Abe, for his part, went from being a billionaire to a millionaire with much less clout.

Some time later, a reporter from the *Los Angeles Times* named Judy, got in touch with me, looking for dirt on Abe. But even though I did have some interesting information, and despite all my outrage at what he had done to me, I decided not to tell her anything. In the end, he was my children's grandfather. However, during our conversations, Judy told me about Abe's strong sway over Mayor Tom Bradley, and about the ways in which he had made his money.

Just as Shmulik Gorodish had gone to Africa to mine for diamonds so he could put together enough money to fight the conclusions of the Agranat Commission and clear his name, I too, worked hard to make enough money to change the legal arrangement, so the boys and I could develop normal father-son relationships. Once I started to earn more, I petitioned the court to end the supervised visits at Rita's house and instead grant joint physical custody over the boys. Since it seemed to me that Abe had lost his influence, I thought I would get a fair ruling this time. I hired a good, expensive lawyer named Don Eisenberg, and we filed a motion.

Rita, through her lawyer, came up with the imaginary claim about me wanting to abduct the kids to Israel, from where they would not return to Los Angeles. She completely ignored the legal aspects of our case and our previous ruling. She ignored the fact that, to mollify her, we had, by agreement, obtained a ruling by an Israeli court and by a California court that the Israeli judicial system would have no authority over the case, and that the California legal system and only California courts have jurisdiction over this matter. Rita also ignored the fact that there is a ruling of the Hague Tribunal, to which both Israel and the United States are signatories, that in a case of kidnapping, the children have to be returned immediately to the country from which they were taken. In short, there were no grounds for her claim.

I told my lawyer that I wanted to bring a lawyer from Israel who could testify that all of Rita's claims were without merit. Eisenberg rejected the request, but I insisted. I told him it was my money, it was my case, and it was my decision. On legal issues, too, I always forged my own path. I see lawyers as technical assistants who are well grounded in the law and know how to formulate and present the arguments. However, they do not have the drive or the emotional involvement necessary to persevere in individual cases. They do not grasp the fine details and nuances of the events in question, and they are often less intelligent than their clients.

In Israel, I hired Yaakov Cohen, a young, energetic, intelligent, and knowledgeable lawyer. I paid for his flight so he could appear at the first hearing of the court in Los Angeles.

From that point onward, things evolved as in a Hollywood movie. As the hearing started, I was taken aback to see that Rita's defense team included the lawyer and professor Ariel Rosen-Zvi, then head of the Faculty of Law at Tel Aviv University. Rosen-Zvi was considered an almost sure bet to become an Israeli Supreme Court justice. At that moment, I was glad that I too had decided to bring a lawyer from Israel, despite my lawyer's objections.

Before testifying, Rosen-Zvi was introduced to the judge with all his credentials, which were extremely impressive. My stress mounted, as Cohen still had not arrived from the airport. But with cinematic timing, right after Rosen-Zvi was introduced to the judge, Cohen and Miri entered the room. My lawyer chimed in immediately, "We too have brought an expert lawyer from Israel, now entering the courtroom."

Rosen-Zvi's testimony put me in a state of shock. He implied that Israel was like Iran. He claimed that the rabbinical courts controlled the legal system in Israel, and if I were to kidnap the boys and take them there, these courts would rule that they not be returned to the U.S. He downplayed the fact that Rita and I had obtained a ruling, by agreement, from an Israeli court stating that only the American courts could decide on custodial rights. Rosen-Zvi asserted that the legal system and the Supreme Court in Israel had no standing against the rabbinical system, and an Israeli Supreme Court verdict was nothing but a "rubber stamp."

Cohen demolished Rosen-Zvi's assertions one by one. He brought legal evidence and precedential rulings to the contrary, making clear that Israeli courts are fair, and showing that, even though the whole kidnapping claim was a fabrication, in the hypothetical case of abduction, the boys would be immediately returned to the U.S. When the judge made his ruling, he explicitly noted that he accepted and agreed with the findings of Attorney Cohen, and not with the claims of Rosen-Zvi.

Later on, my lawyer asked Rita what evidence she had that I was planning to kidnap the boys. Rita answered that a car had once parked beside her house and stayed there for some time. When Eisenberg asked if she had identified who was in the car, she replied in the negative. The judge reacted to this exchange by saying, "Enough is enough," and added that Rita would not be happy with his ruling. Indeed, he lifted all restrictions on my visits and granted me joint physical custody of the boys. Finally, I could develop a normal bond with Barak and Ron, something that helped them a great deal over the years.

Rosen-Zvi's testimony, with its distortions and falsehoods, and its depiction of Israel's legal system as morally compromised and submissive to the rabbinate, angered me immensely. I was not looking for revenge, but I thought it unacceptable that a person who would give such distorted testimony should serve as an Israeli Supreme Court justice. It was made all the worse by the fact that Rosen-Zvi wore a yarmulke and apparently was an observant Jew – false testimony is a serious offense in Judaism.

So I sent letters to the Israeli Justice Minister, the director general of the Justice Ministry, and the president of the Supreme Court. To ensure they would not toss it in the trash without reading it, I made clear at the outset that I was a colonel in the reserves and held a PhD. I then presented choice quotes from Rosen-Zvi's testimony, such as, "The Israeli Supreme Court is a rubber stamp." And I attached the full, official, recorded minutes, noting that the recipient could listen to Rosen-Zvi's testimony word for word to verify the letter.

Some of the addressees sent me a confirmation of receipt. And ultimately, Rosen-Zvi was not appointed to the Supreme Court. Years later I told the story to my friend, the journalist and writer Shlomo Nakdimon. He told me he had been surprised when Rosen-Zvi did not get the appointment, since it had already been decided and agreed upon.

I chose not to send the letter to Tel Aviv University, where Rosen-Zvi was head of the Faculty of Law. I did not want to go too far and destroy his livelihood. But I did send the letter to the Israel Bar Association, since I did not think such a person should have a place in the legal system. Two days before the Bar Association was to hold a hearing on the matter, Rita asked me to withdraw my complaint, almost certainly at Rosen-Zvi's request. I complied and wrote to the association that, while not retracting its content, I was withdrawing the complaint itself. The result was that the hearing was never held. Professor Rosen-Zvi died a few years later from a severe illness.

It was with great disappointment that I saw how much clout money wields. Rosen-Zvi was never my friend, but Rita and I did have friends in common who were obsessed with money, twisted the truth, and wronged me. Fortunately for me, I had four decent, principled people on my side. Shlomo Nakdimon and his charming wife Zehava received an ultimatum from Rita to break off contact with me, and refused. She reacted by cutting all ties with them. An American Jewish psychologist living in Israel, who was a friend of Rita's, was incensed by what was being done to me, particularly regarding the boys, and said to me, "Don't give in to them. Fight!" My friend from Venezuela, Geza Kahan, who was a friend of Abe's for many years and helped him with a big loan to get him started in business, was also warned by Rita and Abe to cut ties with me, but told Abe that he liked me and would keep being my friend. He too was cut off.

A short time after I moved from New York to Los Angeles, I met Miri, a woman who became my wife. Whereas I enjoyed New York, at first, right after moving to Los Angeles, it depressed me. At a dinner with friends, after mentioning that I needed a morale boost, a woman who worked at a skin-care salon suggested I have a massage there. A few days later, while I was chatting with the masseuse before the massage, a stunningly beautiful blond woman caught my gaze. It turned out she was the owner of the place, an Israeli named Miri. I was captivated by her beauty and personality, and I fell in love with her like a kid.

Miri was a divorcee with two young daughters, and she had a boyfriend of four years. Her relationship with Rafi was serious, but at a standstill. And while Rafi was wealthy, I was poor as a church mouse.

Miri wanted to end her relationship with Rafi, and so we became involved. After a couple weeks Rafi came back to Miri saying he had made a mistake and that he wanted to marry her, would buy them a house, and so on. Miri had a tough time deciding between the two of us. So I found myself in an insane triangle as Miri vacillated back and forth over the course of a year. Finally the church mouse prevailed. We have been together ever since, now more than twenty-seven years.

Chapter 14
. . . .
THE TURBULENT ROAD TO PROSPERITY

"From profound darkness to bright light".
The Passover Haggadah

I had almost no business activity in Los Angeles and again had to start from scratch. I was living in a small, one-bedroom, rented apartment in West Hollywood, which I entered through a sliding glass door. A wardrobe with sliding doors served as my office. In it I put two typewriters I brought from Israel, one in Hebrew and the other in English. To use them I needed a transformer, and anyone who was not careful and touched it by mistake got an electric shock. Since I did not know how to type, I had to ask Miri for help or find affordable part-time typists.

My neighbors on the floor were a lesbian couple who had constant loud fights over who should wash the dishes. Below me lived a couple with two children. Even though their apartment was small and old like mine, the husband drove a brand-new Mercedes sports car. After all, this was Los Angeles. The rule in L.A. is, even if you are destitute, you have to impress the people around you, and maybe also yourself.

One sunny L.A. morning, I left my apartment for my regular morning jog. As I was jogging, I saw a sign that read A-1 Office Supplies. While living in New York, I made contacts with companies that manufactured office supplies. Wearing shorts, I went into A-1 and found my way to the owner. In a polite California-style preliminary chat, he said very graciously, that his company was small, and if I wanted to sell in bulk quantities I should approach his supplier. He told me how to get in touch with the supplier, and I set up a meeting.

I told the owner of the supply company that I had numerous connections on the East Coast in the office-supply field, and asked which products he was interested in. Apparently I made a good impression because he gave me a detailed list of the products he usually purchased, including the price he paid for each of them. It appeared to me that I held an advantage on manila envelopes. He said he regularly bought large quantities of these – three containers per month. Despite the cost of transport from the East Coast, I figured I could offer him the product at a price 10 percent below what he had been paying. My profit on this deal also came to 10 percent of its full value.

Although I did not have the funds to buy the merchandise, I convinced the owner of the company to extend me a letter of credit, which ordered his bank to pay me in return for documents showing that the merchandise had been shipped to him. As for the money I received via this letter of credit, after deducting the transportation expenses and my profit, I transferred it to the producer of the envelopes on the East Coast.

When I started my business in Los Angeles, I realized that in California, people often do not say what they mean and do not mean what they say. And they usually do not say no, instead they give an evasive answer like, "Let me think about it."

For example, I contacted another potential envelope customer, and after doing my homework, I offered him envelopes at a price 10 percent lower than what he had been paying as well. He eagerly replied, "That's a great price. I'd be interested in ordering two containers per month." When I asked if he wanted to place an order right then, he said, "First give me two weeks to check my inventory." After two weeks, I called, but he still had not checked his inventory. After two months, he still had not gotten around to it. After three months, I realized he was never going to check his inventory.

After moving from New York, I had to get used to the California mentality. In New York they would have simply said, "We don't have any need for your envelopes." Here is the difference between New York and Los Angeles: In New York, if someone dies in the street, no one will stop and no one will care. In Los Angeles no one will care either, but people will stop and say, "What a wonderful way to die." People always tell you everything is wonderful and promising. They call you "honey" and ask how your weekend went, even though it interests them about as much as last year's snow. I once asked one of my Los Angeles friends, a woman named Carol, how she was doing. She replied, "Wonderful," but I could see her face was gloomy. So I said again, "Really, how are you doing?" She then replied, "Awful."

In America, and in Israel too, like everywhere else, a great deal of social chitchat goes on, but there is no place like California. People do not ask themselves if their long-winded stories actually interest their listeners. I suffer from impatience in that regard. I have never understood people who subject their listeners to dull, interminable stories. If someone reads a book that is not interesting, he can stop and toss it in the trash. If someone watches a boring TV show, he can turn off the TV or change the channel. But if you talk to someone who goes on and on about something of interest only to him, you have to suffer until he has said his fill.

I preferred the New York mentality, and I would seize every opportunity my work afforded me to visit, whether for envelope deals or meetings with the Israeli Defense Ministry delegation to get other deals going.

During one such trip, on a wintry Sunday evening in New York, I took a walk on the western side of midtown Manhattan. The street was totally empty. Suddenly, from a building entrance, a big, tall, dark man came charging at me. He held a knife over my head and commanded, "The money!" Logic said to give him my wallet and run while I still could, but my military instinct kicked in.

Twenty years earlier I had taken a judo course, and now I had a chance to use it. With my left hand I blocked the hand holding the raised knife, and with my right hand, which was in a leather glove, I gripped the blade and twisted it from side to side. Basic judo tells you to grip the palm of the assailant's hand and turn it so that the knife drops. Since I was wearing thick leather gloves, I grabbed the blade itself and twisted it back and forth to break it or get it out of the attacker's hand. It was a sharp kitchen knife, but I was able to break the blade. At the same time, I shoved my knee into his groin. I managed to knock him over and, in a fury, began kicking him with the army boots I was wearing, mainly around his ribs. The would-be attacker started sobbing and begged, "Let me go, leave me alone." How pathetic. Just a moment earlier he was threatening me, and I was the helpless victim, now he was the crybaby. I did not call the police because I feared it would be me who was charged with assault, and the guy would sue me over his broken ribs. Instead, I left him there and went on my way. I still have the blade as a souvenir.

I thought things on the business side were going well. I had a few office-supply customers and could live comfortably by selling two containers of envelopes per month. But business is dynamic, and suddenly chain stores like Office Depot started popping up. My customers, the office-supply wholesalers, went bankrupt, and I was left without envelope deals. But thanks to fate or good sense, I had developed other lines of business. Through the Defense Ministry delegation in New York, I learned the IDF was looking to buy new American tents for its soldiers. I thought, what if instead of the IDF buying a new tent, it could buy a reconditioned tent for a quarter of the price?

At a business fair in Las Vegas, I met a fellow named Leon Zalben who owned a tent-reconditioning company in Los Angeles. His competitors considered him a tough businessman, but we got along well and, even though he was about thirty years older than I was, we became friends. Over a breakfast of lox and bagels at his house in Beverly Hills, we agreed that his company, American Canvas, would recondition tents for me.

Meanwhile, I contacted the Israeli army and the Defense Ministry and tried to talk them into buying reconditioned tents instead of new ones. Some of the decision-makers in Israel were dead set against the idea. Once again, I was told I had a lot of audacity to come up with such ideas, especially when I knew nothing about textiles or tents. One of the army's technical officers discovered that reconditioned tents tend to shrink over the years, and eventually the ceiling poles no longer fit. So my suggestion that the Israeli army buy reconditioned tents was rejected out of hand.

About that time I got a phone call from Leon Zalben's son Norman, telling me that his father had a heart attack and was in the hospital. Norman said his father wrote me a note saying he was sorry, but because of his medical condition, he could not provide me with the tents he had promised. I was left with no customer and no supplier, but with a good idea. And where there is a will, there is a way. I decided I would persevere and reach my goal.

I solved the shrinking problem by extending the tent's ceiling material, adding a strip of cloth that was the same width as the piece that was missing when the tent would shrink. When I showed this solution to the army's technical officers, they approved it. The deputy head of the Quartermaster Division, Brig. Gen. Yossi Snir, a talented man with a long-term outlook, saw great potential for saving money and pushed for the purchase. I urged Norman to fill the order in place of his father, and he agreed.

So I began supplying the IDF with reconditioned tents at one-fourth the price they had been paying. The steady supply led everyone to cancel their objections, and they all became ardent supporters of reconditioned tents. I also began to supply internal tent liners, tent poles, and other tent-related items. I made decent profits and the IDF saved millions of dollars.

Meanwhile, Leon Zalben had died and Norman took over. Norman claimed he lost money on the deal and had no more interest in supplying reconditioned tents. Another subcontractor I found failed to supply the tents on time. Meanwhile the IDF was demanding the full quantity of tents they had purchased from me. For lack of any other option, I set up a company that would buy used tents from the U.S. government, as well as repair and recondition them. I rented a storage facility in downtown Los Angeles, hired seamstresses, and bought sewing machines. At the same time, I started buying other surplus material from the U.S. army, such as clothing and field gear, which I sold on the local market.

Basically, I took over the tent-reconditioning business in the U.S. and bought the stock of several competing companies, including the Zalben family's tents. I became the largest supplier of reconditioned tents in America. Along with my successful purchases of surplus equipment from the U.S. government, I bought with two partners the entire stock of an American tent manufacturer that the government was boycotting.

I did not know the reasons for the boycott at the time, but eventually I learned that the tent manufacturer had not complied with the terms of the government's order. The government had then canceled the order and boycotted the company's stock of raw materials, having already made a down payment. Next, the government published an official tender for the sale of the stock, which my competitor, Kenny Shifran of Los Angeles, and I both saw. He suggested that the two of us, along with another partner, make a joint offer for the tender. I agreed, since that would reduce competition. We agreed that Kenny would deal with the purchase and I with the sale, if and when we were awarded the tender.

Kenny was a native Californian who spoke fluent Hebrew. When I asked him about it, he told me his parents, fearing he would be drafted by the U.S. army and sent to Vietnam, had sent him to Israel. There he was soon drafted into the IDF, and in the Yom Kippur War found himself in the Golan Heights facing a Syrian offensive. This Jewish fellow, whose parents had rescued him from the Vietnam War, could have been killed or taken prisoner by the Syrians. As the prophet Amos said, "As if a man did flee from a lion, and a bear met him; or went into the house, and leaned his hand on the wall, and a serpent bit him" (Amos 5:19).

We were awarded the tender to buy the tents because Kenny knew how to submit a proposal. The merchandise we purchased was stored at a military base in Corpus Christi, Texas. We moved it from there and rented our own storage space for it.

Corpus Christi is on the coast and has great seafood, which I really enjoyed. The city is also known for dog racing. After an exhausting day of work, our local representative suggested we go see the races. We arrived at the stadium in the evening, with two events still to go. I bought a betting ticket for two dollars, but my prediction didn't work out.

I bought another ticket, but this time I went to have a close look at the twelve dogs slated for the race. Each sat in its cage; the race would begin the moment the cage doors opened. I do not know what I was thinking. I scrutinized the canines, particularly their eyes, and predicted which ones would come in first, second, and third.

On that basis I wrote down the dogs' numbers and filled out the form. "My" three dogs came in first, second, and third, and I won $800. But I found out that, because I did not know the betting rules, I had passed up a much bigger prize. I guessed correctly who would come in first, second, and third, but due to my lack of knowledge and experience, I did not include those details on the form. If I had specified the order of the winners, I would have won $10,000!

After we won the tender for the tents, I had to carry out my part of the deal and sell the merchandise. I searched and found a potential buyer, the Greenbrier Company, a supplier of tents, uniforms, and field gear to the U.S. government.

The owner of Greenbrier was Avraham Zilberschatz, who also owned the Eagle Company in Israel, which had supplied those same products to the Israeli Defense Ministry. Even though I had competed with Eagle over the bulletproof-vest deal, for which Point Blank won the tender, I got along with Zilberschatz and sold his company most of the merchandise we had acquired. Because I did not have confidence in Greenbrier's economic stability or commitment to making payments, I collected 50 percent of the cost up front and received the rest in the form of three promissory notes. The first two notes were redeemed, but I never cashed in the third because Greenbrier went bankrupt. Still, I made a good deal of profit on the sale.

Then, with Greenbrier bankrupt, I decided to buy back the same stock once again, through the lawyers who were appointed the official receivers for the company. I flew from Los Angeles to New York and drove to the office in New Jersey in heavy snow. The lawyers asked me how much I was willing to pay. I answered, "I'll pay the same price I paid the U.S. government when I bought the merchandise in the first place." I produced the government purchase contract, which I had kept at the ready, and showed it to them.

Their jaws dropped and they said, "We're surprised that you bought so low and sold at such a high price."

I replied, "Did I break the law in any way?"

They immediately answered as one, "No, we're simply amazed at the profit you made." They tried to find a different buyer who would pay more, but to no avail. So I bought the merchandise a second time, at the same price I had paid the U.S. government for it. I sold the merchandise again at a profit, though smaller this time.

I had discovered that groups of companies in Israel, like Zilberschatz's Eagle Company, would sell their products to the Defense Ministry at relatively high prices. That meant I could sell the same products at lower prices, which I did. The Defense Ministry ended up saving a lot of money buying from me.

The Defense Ministry asked me to find a U.S. boot manufacturer to compete with the three Israeli companies that produced boots for the IDF. This was a difficult project because Israeli military specifications for boots were, for some reason, extremely complicated, and finding an American firm that could meet them was a challenge.

After an exhaustive search I came up with the McRae Footwear Company of North Carolina. The CEO, an American of Lebanese descent named Victor Karam, agreed to abide by the specifications. Despite many difficulties, and with minimal cooperation from the Israeli army's technical staff, we managed to produce boots that met the requirements. After showing that we could come through, we started to supply the entire quantity of high, heavy boots that the army needed. It worked out well for everybody: me, the McRae Company, and the IDF, which now bought boots at lower prices than before.

Over time, Victor Karam became a supporter and a donor to Israel. The McRae Company donated to the Association for the Wellbeing of Israel's Soldiers and to the Armored Corps Museum in Latrun. My former commander and friend until today, Maj. Gen. (ret.) Haim Erez, who was discharged from the IDF in 1988 and served as director general of Israel Chemicals and then as CEO of several companies, was appointed chairman of the Armored Corps Association at Latrun. At various conferences Haim mentioned his appreciation that a U.S. CEO of Lebanese descent was making contributions to his association.

I then ventured into the leather field. For more than forty years, the Defense Ministry had bought leather products from three Israeli tanneries at high prices because the IDF specifications were complicated and written in a way that screened out new suppliers.

With the help of professionals, I mastered the intricacies of IDF leather requirements. Here, too, I was told repeatedly, "What are you doing in the leather business? You don't know a thing about it."

Although, from a technical standpoint, it was almost mission impossible to make the leather as specified, it was easy to win the

Defense Ministry's tender, since for years the leather tanneries had sold their wares at the same relatively high prices. The annual size of the deal had been about $2 million. I offered a price 10 percent lower, and of course I was awarded the tender. In a meeting at the Defense Ministry, I was told I would get an order for only half the total quantity, but if I provided a further discount of 5 percent, I could get the rest as well. I indeed dropped my price another 5 percent, but unfortunately the ministry did not keep its word, and I received an order for only half the quantity.

The order was filled to the army's full satisfaction, but naturally I raised the hackles of the local industrialists, and my competitors tried to defame me. The journalist Amnon Barzilai started digging up information on me for an article in the daily newspaper *Haaretz* that would accuse me of destroying the local industry. He did not heed my protestations that, thanks to me, the Defense Ministry had saved millions of shekels. A firm that the competitors hired to investigate me left no stone unturned in digging up my entire life history.

Barzilai asked to meet with me and wanted to bring a photographer to the meeting. In a phone conversation he tried to make clear that he knew everything about me. Among other things, he told me that the journalist and writer Amnon Dankner, who had grown up in Jerusalem and was two years younger than I, told him I was the only one who had managed to become the boyfriend of Rina Oster, considered one of Jerusalem's great beauties at that time. (Dankner even named his short-story collection *The Summer of Rina Oster*.) It was not true; I had been friends with Rina but never her boyfriend.

In 2009, I met with Amnon Dankner for lunch at Taami, a Jerusalem restaurant, after the publication of his best-selling novel *Aunt Eva, His Nights and Days*, which deals with Jerusalem during the era in which I grew up. When I asked him if he had really told Amnon Barzilai that I was Rina Oster's boyfriend, Dankner denied it. We talked of how we missed Jerusalem of the 1950s and

1960s, sharing memories of the high school we had both attended, and I was struck by his phenomenal memory for events and people's names. He also gave me a copy of his book with a personal dedication.

Years later, as I was writing this book, Dankner helped me out. I had forgotten the first name of the English teacher at the Maaleh high school, though I remembered that her last name was Sar-Shalom. Dankner had no trouble recalling the name Sheila immediately from his archival memory. When I was in the latter stages of writing this book, I was sorry to hear of Amnon Dankner's untimely death.

In the end, the defamatory article was not published. My friend Miki Stark told me that he knew Amnon Barzilai well, and that he talked him out of printing it. In hindsight, it could be that Barzilai never actually intended to publish it but just wanted to pressure me.

Through the years, I had maintained my close friendship with Miki.

On one of my visits to Israel, while I was packing for my flight back to the U.S., my cell phone rang. A woman told me she was calling from "Line 058" and had a readout in her hand saying I owed them money. When I asked what Line 058 was, she said it was the sex-talk line I had used. When I told her I had done no such thing and asked her not to bother me, she said I had to talk with the manager and transferred me. The "manager" turned out to be Miki, and the woman on the phone was his daughter Irit. I was annoyed at this practical joke, which came while I was busy packing, and promised myself that I would get even with Miki on my next visit.

Miki was then the medical director of the Misgav Ladach hospital in Jerusalem. My next visit was in 1996, around the time a new government had been formed following the elections. I was with Miri in our apartment in Tel Aviv, along with a neighbor named Sharon. I asked Sharon to call Misgav Ladach, introduce herself as a secretary in the office of the health minister, ask to speak with the director, Dr. Michael Stark, and tell him he was invited, along with the other hospital directors in the country, to a meeting on Israel's health policy for the next four years. Sharon complied. After a few minutes, I asked her to call Miki again and tell him that, unfortunately, there had been a mistake; they were inviting only the directors of the large hospitals to the meeting, and since Misgav Ladach did not fall into that category, his invitation was canceled. Miki, quite miffed, started arguing with Sharon and asked her who was the head of the minister's office, demanding to have a word with him. Knowing Miki as I did, I anticipated what he would do and told Sharon how to react. She informed him that the head of the minister's office was one Moshe Rabinovich, and gave him the phone number of our apartment, which Miki no longer recognized.

When Miki called the number about a minute later, Miri answered and said, "Hello, minister's office." Miki asked to speak with Moshe Rabinovich. "Who wants to speak with him?" Miri asked, and not surprisingly was answered, "Doctor Michael Stark." Miri handed me the phone, and I asked Miki how I could help him. Usually when I play pranks with Miki I change my voice, but he knows who I am immediately. In this case I used my regular voice, but for some reason he did not realize it was me. He was, after all, expecting "Moshe Rabinovich."

He started complaining to me and said, "You people always give us a hard time." I said I was sorry, but the minister had decided to meet only with the directors of the large hospitals, who were more experienced and hence in a better position to advise him. Miki did not give in, trying to create a personal connection with me, that is, Rabinovich. He asked if we knew each other from somewhere, and I said yes. "From where?" he asked. I replied, "From the lemons" (the two of us had some inside jokes about lemons).

But even then he did not realize who it was. By now I felt sorry for him and confessed. But the big joke occurred weeks later when the health minister's office really did call Miki to invite him to a meeting; he told the secretary he was sick of Ehud's pranks and hung up on her.

I would visit Israel about four times a year and use those opportunities to meet up with friends. Even though I lived in the U.S., I felt I was part of Israel. One of the people I would meet with was Maj. Gen. (ret.) Moshe Nativ, who was appointed director general of the Jewish Agency in 1989 and served in that post during the large-scale immigration from Russia in the early 1990s. Once, in 2000, I had lunch with Nativ at the Olympia restaurant in Tel Aviv. It was during the time of the IDF's withdrawal from the security zone in southern Lebanon. I told him that, in my view, Israel should not be leaving southern Lebanon; it was better for the army to deal with Hizbullah than for civilians to have to deal with it. Nativ disagreed and invoked someone who had been his friend, Yitzhak Rabin. He told me Rabin had once said that he felt obligated to make peace and prevent war. The reason was that future generations in Israel were not the generation of Rabin and of Nativ, they were not the generation of the Palmach, and they could not endure constant conflict with the Arabs.

In those days I flew a lot and had quite a few experiences, some pleasant and some less so. Friends would tell me about nice women they had met on flights. During my time as a single man I had only two such encounters.

Once, while I was living in New York, on a flight to Israel, I met a nice, attractive woman from Mexico City who sat next to me, and we exchanged telephone numbers. She sent me a fax for Valentine's Day with the news that she was coming to New York. A few days later she called and said she was in New York at the Hilton, and wanted to get together with me. I took her out for dinner in Greenwich Village. As we chatted, I wondered what had brought her to New York. I asked if she had business in the city

274 | Yes, It's Possible

and she said no. She had no relatives or friends there either. When she started telling me how rich she was, and praising the Jewish women in Mexico, I began to suspect that she had come to New York to see me. That suspicion was confirmed when I heard her say she was divorced, something she had not bothered to tell me on the flight.

I had no interest in starting anything with her beyond our casual encounter on the flight, and the longer the evening progressed the less and less she appealed to me. By chance, I told her a certain food was not healthy. She responded by saying I should not be like other Americans, who talk constantly about what is healthy and what is not. That gave me an idea of how to get rid of her without offending her. I kept talking about issues of health and healthy eating. Though she tried to change the subject, after every few sentences I went back to the topic of what foods were healthy. As we sat there I saw a look of growing disgust on her face, along with an eagerness for this awful evening to end. I walked her back to her hotel and felt she was already eager to get rid of me.

Of course she never called me again. I could picture her telling her lady friends about an Israeli man she met on a plane that seemed appealing, how she went all the way to New York to meet him again, and how, over dinner, he turned out to be a total nutcase.

Not long after moving to Los Angeles, I again flew to Israel. And again, a nice, attractive woman sat next to me; this one was Israeli and in her early thirties. She worked in Los Angeles as a fitness trainer. Amazingly, her flight back from Israel was on the exact same day as mine. Even more amazingly, she had scheduled a flight to Eilat, also on the same day that I had. We ended up spending some time together.

But not all my trips were pleasant.

On one of my flights from Los Angeles to Israel via New York, I saw, as I entered the plane, that an ultra-Orthodox Jewish woman was sitting in the window seat assigned to me. Next to her, in the middle seat, sat her husband.

I have a hard time falling asleep on a flight unless I am sitting by the window. I said to the woman in English, in the polite American style, "Excuse me, but I believe the seat you're sitting in is mine." She replied in English with a strong Yiddish accent, "That's impossible; the travel agent booked our tickets and this seat is mine." I summoned the flight attendant and explained the problem to her, and she asked the ultra-Orthodox woman to move to the aisle seat and vacate the seat I had been given by the window.

The woman then turned to her husband and said to him in Hebrew, "Damn him, because of him I dropped the pages on the floor." I said to her in Hebrew, "Excuse me, but why are you cursing me?"

I realized there was no point talking any further with this couple and fell silent. After a few minutes, though, the woman started complaining about me to her husband in Yiddish. I said to her, "Ma'am, don't complain about me in Yiddish. I understand that language too." Only then did she stop.

Meanwhile my business ventures were branching out internationally, as I made connections in Europe and South America. It felt strangest, though, to do business with Egypt. I had fought against its army in the Six-Day War, the War of Attrition, and the Yom Kippur War.

The flight to Egypt from Israel seemed completely ordinary, with a security check, passport checks, and a wait. Superficial thoughts passed through my mind but were quickly forgotten. Should one fly to Cairo with a Hebrew newspaper? And what about my Israeli passport? I boarded an Air Sinai plane with no less than three Israeli newspapers, and we took off. The flight attendant's Arabic instructions grated on my ears, as the Arabic language always has. I recalled how in my childhood, from the fourth floor where we lived, I would throw tomatoes and other vegetables at the café across the street, from which Arab music loudly pulsed and trilled. But now I overcame the aversion with a different thought, reminding myself that I had never felt animosity toward Egypt. In the end they were people like us. Even the Egyptian soldiers I encountered in battles appeared to me as suffering victims, men whose luck had gone badly enough to have to face our heavy guns.

The plane quickly reached Cairo. Another thought passed through my mind: While the distance from Tel Aviv to Cairo is equal to the distance from Los Angeles to Las Vegas, in this case it covers an expanse of war, killing, and suffering. This flight did not at all resemble the first time I returned to my base from being home for leave after the Yom Kippur War. On that occasion I flew to Fayed Airport, west of the Suez Canal. Because we feared Egyptian antiaircraft missiles, the Hercules plane almost brushed the tops of small mounds of sand and trees. Nor did this current flight resemble other flights, after the war, when about a hundred soldiers and officers would sit packed like sardines in a cargo plane so we could go where we longed to be – home for a leave.

The Air Sinai plane crossed the shoreline and flew briskly over Egyptian soil. The last time I had entered Egypt it was from the area we dubbed the Yard, where we forded the Suez Canal. At that time, the air was red from artillery fire and the ground was strewn with wounded and dead.

As the flight attendant announced that we were landing at Cairo International Airport, the suburbs of the city appeared through the clouds. One square city block after another sat in the midst of an endless desert. These undoubtedly were the same sights our pilots had seen as they flew in for the attack during our various wars. I made out old military trucks that reminded me of the forlorn, damaged convoys along the roads in the Six-Day and Yom Kippur wars.

We landed in cloudy Cairo. The airport looked shabby, quite similar to the military airports in Sinai but with service people trying to play their roles. Here the passport checker did not wear the authoritative look of officials in all of the world's airports; he looked like an ordinary clerk.

The passport check reminded me of the joke about the policemen who work in pairs, one reading while the other writes. The passport checker glanced at the passport, handed the form to another clerk, and after the passport was duly checked they handed it to another clerk, who returned it to me. The shoeshine man did not quote a price, just suggested I pay whatever seemed right to me. The coffee server in the snack bar got distracted, and only after three reminders came through with my long-awaited change.

There was no flight display board, and I asked the coffee server about the flight to Alexandria. He told me in garbled English that the passengers were already getting on the bus. I ran to the spot where they told me the flight would take off. Luckily the security official saw I was headed for the wrong flight and directed me to the right one. I was last to arrive for the flight to Alexandria, which was getting ready to leave without me.

The plane passed over the Nile. I saw green cultivated areas, exactly like a mirage I had seen in the War of Attrition as my company took positions along the Suez Canal, twenty-five years earlier.

As the plane descended toward the airport in Alexandria, I fixed my tie; I would be welcomed by Yusri the engineer, a representative of an Egyptian company that belonged to the prestigious Ragab family. They were Egyptian representatives for major companies like Nissan, and they had good connections with the Egyptian authorities.

They were mainly interested in agricultural equipment that was manufactured and purchased on credit in the U.S., which the U.S. government made available to Egypt. They said their previous representative had brought them agricultural equipment manufactured in Yugoslavia instead of the U.S., violating the regulations for U.S. aid. That representative, they told me, had not even bothered to remove the lettering showing the Yugoslav origin.

Yusri, a portly, bespectacled, smiling man, took me to see the company grounds, timber storerooms, agencies for selling cars and replacement parts, and so on. He overflowed with Arab hospitality.

The two of us diligently exchanged pleasantries. We were like the two men in the story who keep politely saying "You first" to each other, until they start shoving.

When the professional tour was finished, we left my suitcases at the hotel and went on a tour of Alexandria. We saw the palaces of King Farouk,[70] the fantastic opulence contrasting starkly with the dire poverty around us. These palatial spaces had been the homes of Farouk, his wives, and his servants. In the plaza beside the women's quarters, Yusri told me, an orchestra would play non-stop, twenty-four hours a day. We went on to see the fortress that defended Alexandria against Napoleon, not with great success, the proof of which can be seen at the Egyptian obelisk in Paris, which was taken as plunder.

Not far from the palace, we went to a wonderful restaurant surrounded by a garden. The food was superb. I took Yusri's advice and ordered a roast pigeon. He dismissed any notion that I would pay; in Alexandria, he said, only he would pay. After the meal, he bought me a tray of baklava cookies and a Burma cake, and then we continued on our way.

While Yusri was eating his daily ice cream, I asked him about Islam in Egypt and extremist Muslims. He said the religion was deeply rooted in every Egyptian. The thief, before he steals, asks Allah for forgiveness. Even the prostitute, before each customer, asks Allah for forgiveness and adds the request that no one should know of her act.

Yusri claimed Egypt was ripe for an Iranian-style popular Islamic revolution and could turn into an Islamic state completely dominated by religion. Indeed, the Islamic takeover that occurred in Egypt almost twenty years after my first visit there did not surprise me – I had always remembered his words. Yusri also told me that Egyptians did not like Anwar Sadat[71] because he began

[70] King of Egypt from 1936 until he was deposed in a coup in 1952. Farouk died in 1965.

[71] An Egyptian president who signed a peace treaty with Israel in 1979 and was

*Me, Geza Kahan (*left*), 1981*

Left to right: *Arik Sharon, Shlomo Nakdimon, Shlomo Lahat, 1981*

Yitzhak Rabin (right) *with Shlomo Lahat* (left) *at the* brit, *1984*

Yitzhak Rabin, the sandak *at the* brit milah *of my son, Barak, with me at the left, 1984*

Miri and me, 1988

Right to left: *my friend Miki Stark, me, and Miki's wife Batya, 1981*

My children; left to right: *Yarriv, Lior, Tali, and Dana, 1987*

A trip to the Sea of Galilee; left to right: *my children Tali, Lior, and Dana, with me, 1988*

Major General Moshe Nativ with Yitzhak Rabin

Arik and Lily Sharon, with Miri in the middle, at a 1990s conference at Latrun of our brigade officers from the Yom Kippur War

A visit with Miri to the pyramids, 1996

A visit to the Egyptian Museum in Cairo, 1996

Yusri and Miri at the Egyptian Museum in Cairo, 1996

Miri in China with women who have very long hair, but show it only for payment, 2003

Miri and me in China, 2003

René   *Miri at the train station in Shanghai, 2011*

Miri and me in Shanghai, 2011

*Miri and me
in Thailand*

Cordoba, Spain, statue of Maimonides, 1992

Mexico, 2000

Lausanne, Switzerland, 2009

Florence, Italy, 2011

Saint Petersburg, 2013

Family trip to Thailand, 2003; left to right: *my son Barak, Miri's daughter Dana, me, Miri, my daughter Dana, Miri's daughter Sharoni, my son Ron*

My son Barak, 2013

Left to right: *my son-in-law Alex, my son Lior, Miri, me, my daughters Tali and Dana, 2006*

My daughter Dana, son-in-law Golan, and grandchildren Uri and Ella, 2013

*Miri's daughter Sharoni, her husband Mark, their son Ethan
and their daughter Maya, 2013*

*Miri's daughter Dana, her husband Lance (whose
photograph of me is on the back page of this book),
and their son Dylan, 2013*

My son Yarriv and granddaughter Yullie, 2013

My son Lior, daughter-in-law Hagar, and grandson Ophir, 2014

My daughter Tali, son-in-law Alex, and grandchildren Yonatan and Emma, 2013

With my grandson, Yonatan, 2014

With my grandchildren Uri and Ella, 2014

behaving like a false god. At the time of his assassination he even remained standing instead of taking cover, shouting at the assassins that they did not know what they were doing. However, the masses had admired Nasser.[72] Yusri also criticized then President Mubarak and said he did not address the problem of governmental corruption.

From there our conversation moved to issues of Arab, American, and Israeli women. Yusri knew about American women because he had spent a year in Texas. In his view, the best woman was a religious Muslim who did not leave the house. We also discussed his wives. His previous wife was a flight attendant for the Jordanian airline who promised she would leave her job, but when she failed to keep her promise he divorced her. His current wife was a religious Muslim who remained at home.

I could not help noticing his hypocrisy. Despite his comments about the ideal Muslim wife, he kept asking me to bring him pornographic films from the U.S. This was an unpleasant task for me. Yusri told me exactly which films to buy, including the names of the actresses starring in them. Back in the U.S., the salesmen in the video shops looked at me in amazement when I insisted on films with particular porn actresses. And when I returned to Egypt with this loot, I wondered what would happen if Egyptian customs caught me with it.

Next we went for some coffee in a café that Yusri told me was especially popular. Later in the evening, he said, one could not get a seat. To me it looked like a depressing low-end café, with old chairs like the ones my Aunt Yaffa and Uncle Luzer used to have forty years ago. Yusri smoked a hookah, and from there we went to the shopping district. We passed through stores selling clothes at ridiculous prices. Yusri suggested I buy clothes of certain colors, and if I had wanted to resemble a parrot or the Egyptian singer Farid al-Atrash, I would have done so. He had very bad taste. As

---

assassinated by Islamists in 1981.

[72] Gamal Abdel Nasser was president of Egypt from 1956 to 1970.

for the famous singer, Yusri told me his father was a good friend of Farid al-Atrash. Both were compulsive gamblers, and together they lost large sums in casinos.

The next day we had business meetings, and afterward we went to a fine fish restaurant. The owner, a pretty woman, seated us at a table. Yusri told me she was once the most famous dancer in Alexandria, but was imprisoned for trafficking young girls, whose ages she lied about, to elderly sheikhs. The Egyptian women are pleasant and friendly. Anyone who is not aware of Arab culture and honor killings could make a fatal mistake.

From Alexandria I flew on to Cairo, where I decided to stay for two days and visit the pyramids and the Egyptian Museum. It was exciting to see the pyramids and learn about the history and ways of the pharaohs. I thought about our ancestors, who according to the Bible, had to build "treasure cities" for Pharaoh.

In Cairo I stayed at the Marriott. To my surprise there was a casino in the hotel, and of course I went there to play blackjack, which I had gotten good at in New York. On my right sat a Saudi who looked a lot like Zaki Yamani, the Saudi energy minister who, during the Yom Kippur War, had embargoed Saudi oil exports to the West, causing a dramatic spike in oil prices. This man had the same pugnacious look and sharp, small beard. "Zaki," however, turned out to be a very poor player who lost constantly. He kept taking wads of hundred-dollar bills from his wallet and losing them at a dizzying pace. I felt sorry for him and asked if I could give him some advice. He said yes, and the pace of extracting the hundred-dollar bills slowed dramatically.

To keep building my business in Egypt, I made another visit there, this time with my wife Miri. This was in 1996, when a Druze Israeli, Azzam Azzam, was imprisoned in Egypt for spying. Although friends warned me that it was dangerous for an Israeli to go there, I decided to go anyway.

Yusri welcomed us at the Cairo Airport and took us to a hotel. As we passed through a square called Ataba, Yusri said, "This is where the whole thing happened." We had no idea what he was talking about. When we asked what happened, he said he was amazed we did not know – the whole country was abuzz over it.

Yusri explained that in broad daylight a woman had gotten off a bus, and a man had pressed his fingers between her legs! That did not sound to us like a sensation, but over the next few days we followed the Egyptian press in English, and each day there was a front-page article on the incident. The country was divided into two camps: The religious side claimed it happened because people had strayed from religion. The nonreligious side said it was because the religion's excessive rigidity drove people to adventures with their fingers. The man was caught and arrested, and two days later his version appeared. He said he was disabled, and when he got off the bus, someone had pushed him so that he fell on the woman. It was incredible to see a whole country preoccupied with such an event, with all sorts of fabrications – reminiscent of *One Thousand and One Nights* – swirling around it.

Yusri took us to a meeting with the Cairo police chief, who wanted to buy American equipment for his force. When we got there, we had to laugh inwardly; supposedly savvy Israelis had warned us that we would be thrown in jail as soon as we set foot in Cairo. The police chief did not know a word of English. He had a serious, stolid mien, a well-trimmed, Saddam Hussein-style moustache. During our meeting, including while Yusri was giving his presentation, the police chief intermittently picked up the receiver of either the red telephone or the green one sitting on his desk and said the word *aywa* (yes). At the entrance to his office, which was the size of a reception hall, sat a long table, upon which a succession of rural visitors had placed, each in his turn, various tributes of eggs and cheese, vegetables and fruits as gifts for the chief.

After the meeting we went to a restaurant. I did not want Yusri to be the one to always pay the bill, and when he went to the restroom, I seized the opportunity and paid. But as we were walking into the parking lot, the waiter came charging out of the restaurant with a mortified expression and handed me back the money I had paid. He told me he had to do this because Yusri insisted on paying. There's nothing like Egyptian hospitality.

The highlight of the visit was a meeting with the director general of the Egyptian Agriculture Ministry. I told Yusri that I had my MA in agricultural economics but knew nothing at all about agriculture. Yet during our meeting with the director general, Yusri said, "Dr. Diskin is the Middle East's leading expert on agriculture." The people Yusri had brought with him also lauded me as the Middle East's number-one authority in the field. I had a knot in my stomach. What if someone actually started talking to me about these matters?

These events and others showed me the dominant role of the imagination in Egypt – reality is not important. Likewise in my conversations with Yusri, an intelligent and educated person, I heard fantasies about Egyptian feats and triumphs in the Yom Kippur War. In general, my visits to the country made clear to me one of the main reasons Egypt lost all its wars: The people live in a world of imagination, and are not at all realistic.

I asked to visit the "Victory Museum" of the Yom Kippur War, but Yusri declined. The Egyptians knew I was an Israeli but did not know that I had fought them on the battlefield. However, a few months later, after Yusri visited my office in Los Angeles, the Egyptians suddenly cut off all ties with me. After a few days I realized what happened. Miri had put a picture in the office that showed me in uniform with my colonel's insignia. When Yusri realized I was an IDF colonel, he must have looked me up in Egyptian records, and I probably appeared on a blacklist as someone who had fought the Egyptian army and caused them casualties. So they were perhaps afraid of me, suspected I was a spy, or simply wanted nothing more to do with me. It was for the best. I did not like the way the Egyptians worked and did not enjoy their mentality, which was detached from reality.

Another country I tried working with was Venezuela. Geza Kahan, a friend of my former father-in-law, Abe, who also became my friend, convinced me to do business there. Geza was a Jew of Hungarian extraction who divided his time between Caracas and New York, and had a plush apartment in both. He loved bridge and played every evening. Geza made his great fortune in the 1950s, and he loaned a large sum to Abe, my ex-father-in-law. Countless times he repeated the same story word for word, "I loaned Abe a million dollars, which he gave me back without interest. Abe made millions from that loan, and I made bupkes." Geza also warned me not to deal in stocks. He had lost $1 million, at that time an enormous sum, playing the stock market in the 1950s. In those days he dealt only in sums of at least $1 million.

Geza had connections with the Venezuelan government, and when I went there for a visit, he made them available to me. Among others, he introduced me to the Pocaterra family. They were close to the president of Venezuela at the time, and one of their sons was the interior minister.

Geza also connected me with the company of two partners who sold equipment to the Venezuelan air force. One partner was a Venezuelan, the other a Yugoslav aristocrat whose family had fled to Venezuela. I reached an agreement with them that they would represent me in dealing with the Venezuelan air force, and we set up a meeting with their lawyer to sign a representation contract. It was I who prepared the contract. Having learned from different lawyers how to word such contracts appropriately, I preferred to write them myself rather than let a lawyer do it. First, it meant saving on expenses, and second, I had learned that lawyers often encumber the contract with irrelevant clauses about things that are unlikely to occur. When the other side sees such a long contract, they get scared and flee.

Back when I launched my business in New York, I sent a contract prepared by a lawyer to a company I wanted to represent. The owner of the company called me and asked, "Why did you send me a contract written by a lawyer from Philadelphia?" (Philadelphia lawyers were known for long-winded philosophizing.) He told me he had no more interest in working with me.

When we met with the Venezuelan lawyer, he took me to a private room and said, "Why should you sign a contract with them? I have better connections with the military. You should sign with me, not with them." It amazed me that this lawyer actually wanted to dupe his customers and leave them out of the deal. I found myself sticking up for them, telling him, "I gave a promise to your customers to represent me in dealing with the Venezuelan air force, and I keep my promises. But if you can prove to me that you have connections with the Venezuelan navy, I'll sign a contract with you that deal with that." I was not simply trying to fend him off with some sort of excuse. I knew that Venezuelan businessmen often made claims about government connections that turn out to be baseless, so I asked for proof.

A few days later I had a meeting and dinner scheduled with the Pocaterra family, including the son who was the interior minister. Coming down from my hotel room, I stopped at the reception desk to hand over my room key. The clerk told me there was an envelope for me. It was from the same lawyer who wanted to represent me. When I opened the envelope, I was aghast. It contained the five-year procurement plan of the Venezuelan navy. At the top of each page was a bold heading, in red: "Top Secret." I was horrified. I thought if I got caught with this, I would go straight to jail. And no one would believe my explanation that the document was given to me by a lawyer as proof of his connections. I immediately hid the envelope in the inside pocket of my suit.

The Pocaterra family was already waiting for me in the lobby, and they did not give me a chance to get rid of the papers. During the dinner I did not even listen to the conversation. I only wanted to get back to my room and burn the document. Finally I got back and burned it in the bathroom, but that set off the smoke alarm. The hotel maintenance called, and I assured them everything was fine.

I tossed the remaining scraps from the fire in the toilet and flushed them. The next day the lawyer called, asking if I had received the document and when we would sign the representation contract. I told him I had a busy schedule but would soon be free. I could not wait to leave Venezuela and be done with this nuisance.

While still in Venezuela, I met with an air force general who asked, in return for approving a deal, that I buy him an apartment in Manhattan. I was astonished at how business is done in Venezuela. When I told the people in the company I was associated with that I had served in the IDF's Armored Corps, they told me about a deal they had made for tank treads they bought in Germany and sold in Venezuela. There was only one problem: When the tank turned, the tread tore. I said, "Then the deal definitely failed."

"No," they replied, "the deal succeeded, we just had to pay an extra $5,000 to the technical sergeant who approved it."

"And what if there's a war?" I asked in amazement.

"Nothing to worry about, there hasn't been a war here for two hundred years, the tanks are only for parades."

At the five-star hotel where I was staying, there were no towels in the rooms. If I gave the maid a one-dollar tip, I got one towel – two dollars, two towels. As I waited in line to take a taxi from the hotel, a businessman suddenly approached the person in charge of the line, gave him five dollars, and went straight to the front. Before I went to the hotel, experienced friends warned me that, even though I had a confirmed reservation, I would not get my room unless I gave the reception clerk a tip of about twenty dollars. So when I got to the hotel, I put a tip of twenty dollars on the counter with my credit card for the reception clerk to see. He immediately found my reservation and even sent me to eat a free breakfast until my room was ready.

While I was chatting with the clerk, I saw an American businessman arguing with the other reception clerk, who was telling him he could not find his reservation, even though the guest had shown him written confirmation. After I finished breakfast and went back to the desk to get my room key, I saw the American was still arguing with the clerk who "could not find his reservation." I pitied him, took him aside, and told him that if he wanted the room he had to put a twenty-dollar bill on the counter. He took my advice, and I heard the reception clerk say, "What's this? You write your name with an H, and I thought it was written with an A." Of course, he immediately got the room.

I found very wealthy people in Venezuela who lived in a veritable ghetto, with round-the-clock protection by security guards, cameras, and high-tech surveillance gadgets. They had private art collections with original works by painters like Salvador Dali, while most of the country's population lived in severe poverty. Despite the wonderful food and pleasant social encounters, I was happy to leave Venezuela. At the airport early in the morning, the clerk weighed my suitcase, told me it was too heavy, and said I had to pay another eighty dollars. I gave him my credit card, and he stared at me in astonishment. I did not even think about, and it was only as I got in my seat on the plane that I realized the clerk thought I was an utter dolt. If I had slipped him twenty dollars, of course I would not have had to pay the fine.

Things are similar in other third world countries. In Mexico City, I drove through one of the markets with a customer named Philippe, a young Jew who owned a chain of stores with his mother. We moved along the packed street at about three miles per hour. Philippe told me that about a week earlier while he was driving on this same street, also at three miles per hour, a woman had suddenly sprung toward the driver's window, screaming that he had run over her foot. Immediately someone else materialized and claimed he had witnessed the event. A few seconds later, a policeman came and told Philippe he had to arrest him for twenty-four hours because of the "accident." He also told him outright that if he paid a hundred dollars right then, to be divided between him, the "injured" woman, and the witness, the policeman would see the matter as settled. Of course, Philippe preferred to part with a hundred dollars than spend twenty-four hours in lockup.

The situation is no better in African countries. A bandage manufacturer with whom I had a business connection told me about his deals in Nigeria. One day he visited the Nigerian Health Ministry and saw an announcement on a bulletin board about a tender for bandages running to over $1 million. The tender, which was opened and published on that day, was also supposed to be closed on that day. He submitted his proposal for the tender and won it. It turned out that a senior official in the Health Ministry had already arranged for a British company to win it. Since the law required the tender to be published, this official had made sure the tender would be opened and closed on the same day, thinking there was no chance another competitor would look at the bulletin board in the Health Ministry on that specific day.

The British firm paid my acquaintance good money to withdraw his proposal for the tender. He said he ended up getting more money than if he had supplied the merchandise. For the British company it was worth it; even after paying him the sum and the official his bribe, it made a good profit.

Having had my fill of unpleasant experiences doing business in countries like Egypt, Venezuela, and others, I decided I would stick to the United States, Israel, and Europe.

Chapter 15
"A GOOD NAME IS BETTER THAN PRECIOUS OINTMENT"
Ecclesiastes 7:1

My business flourished, and I branched out into new ventures. One of these involved the manufacture and supply of rain suits to the IDF. Jackie Ardon, who had served as a lieutenant colonel in the Quartermaster's Division, knew a lot about textile manufacturing. After his discharge, he moved to New Jersey, and set up a military textiles plant in West Virginia.

We became business partners, and I submitted a proposal to the Defense Ministry's New York delegation, wherein Jackie's factory would do the manufacturing for the rain suits. Before I found out that I had been awarded the tender, the buyer for the delegation called and asked if I knew what I was doing (again that same question). He explained that the price I submitted was 30 percent lower than the one proposed by two large American firms that made the same product for the U.S. government. Apparently I did know what I was doing, since we won the tender, supplied the product to the IDF's satisfaction, and made a nice profit. The IDF kept buying tens of thousands of rain suits from us for several years.

In 1991, Brig. Gen. Rami Dotan, who once headed a maintenance squadron in the air force, was sentenced to thirteen years in prison for taking bribes from the U.S. companies from which the air force bought equipment. The U.S. government made the most of this corruption scandal, forcing Israel to make all its U.S.

military aid purchases (amounting to about $2.5 billion annually) through the U.S. administration. In the case of the rain suits, that meant the Israeli government had to pay an additional 30 percent (the higher price that the U.S. government paid for them) plus a fixed commission of about 4 percent.

From Israel's standpoint, the real purchasing power of U.S. military aid declined. From my standpoint, now that the Defense Ministry delegation had to buy the rain suits directly from the U.S. government, it stopped buying them from me. Because I had opened other markets, particularly the American one, my company stayed in good shape and the profits accumulated.

I now ventured into real estate too, acquiring properties that included apartment buildings and warehouses. I put into practice the truism that to succeed in business, one buys when market prices are low and sells when they are high. It worked well for me.

I specialized in converting rental buildings into condominium buildings. Rental units in the U.S. cannot be sold individually, unlike in Israel. However, through a complicated bureaucratic procedure, rental buildings can be turned into condominium buildings, and then the condominiums can be sold separately. The procedure is indeed expensive and tedious, but the potential profit is great because a condominium is worth much more than the same apartment in a rental category. Of course, all this depends on the condition of the U.S. real estate market.

The municipality also profits from the transactions. In one case, I changed a building's designation, and the City of Los Angeles decided to expropriate an area in front of the property so it could use it to widen the street in the future. This area was about thirty feet long and the width of my building's front garden. Having no choice, I agreed to this, thinking that once the project was finished, I would get the decree annulled.

And indeed, at the end of the project I had an idea that was based on the advice of my engineer, Ben Menash. In front of the building stood three tall pine trees, and to make use of this area, the municipality would have to uproot them. So I recruited its forestry department to my side; they did not, heaven forbid, want the trees to be harmed. With their help, I submitted an appeal to the city council. The council went along with me, supported as I was by the forestry department, and opposed the municipality's planning department. So I won back the land in question. This case illustrates the fact that most problems have a solution, and you just have to look until you find it.

The United States is a pleasant and convenient place to do business. Everyone seems to understand the purpose of business is to make a profit, and businessmen usually allow those they do business with enough latitude to also make a profit. Compared with their colleagues in other countries, businessmen in the U.S. are also more decent. Of course, there are American businessmen who are scoundrels, but the chances of encountering that sort are lower than in other countries. Over many years, I came to the conclusion that decency in business pays off in the long run. When businessmen and companies build a reputation of honesty and decency, they themselves stand to benefit. As is written in Ecclesiastes: "A good name is better than precious ointment."

Also, academic studies and degrees are not necessarily what bring success in business; most often what really counts in business is experience, common sense, and in particular, adherence to your goals. Those really are the winning factors, and the common denominators among people who have succeeded in business.

A typical case is that of Harland David "Colonel" Sanders, who founded Kentucky Fried Chicken. Sanders had a "secret recipe" for seasoning chicken. He tried to sell it and was turned down. Instead of giving up, he listened carefully to the criticism he received when pitching it, and each time improved the recipe accordingly. The story goes that he was turned down more than a hundred times but did not give up, finally hitting upon a successful formula.

Kentucky Fried Chicken became one of the leading fast-food chains in the U.S., and Sanders became a multimillionaire. (As for where the nickname "Colonel" came from, Sanders served as a mule driver for the U.S. army in Cuba, at the rank of private. When he was sixty, the governor of Kentucky awarded him the honorary rank of colonel for his great contribution to the state's economy and status.)

I – a real military colonel – worked hard as a businessman and did not give up. At the start of my business career, when I made the deal for the reconditioned tents, there was a point at which I was turned down both by the customer – the IDF – and the supplier – the American Canvas Company. But I did not throw in the towel, and with great effort managed to close the deal. Optimism is important, even critical, in finding the way to success. It is important to believe that the project will succeed and the deal will go through. If one feels pessimistic from the outset, there is a significantly greater chance of what psychologists call a "self-fulfilling prophecy," and the project will fail. I always stayed optimistic, and even in difficult situations believed I would prevail, since in the past I had always found a way out of every predicament.

As I wrote before, I do not regard an academic background as a must for success in business. However, I have to acknowledge that, where appropriate, I applied three insights from my own studies to my business activity, and they helped me succeed.

First, I made sure to increase the chances that the project or deal would succeed. How? For each project or deal, I carefully considered which factors would facilitate success and which would cause failure. Then I did all I could to increase the probability of success, and tried to diminish the probability of failure. By dealing thoroughly with all of the positive and negative factors in each case, I was able to boost the chances that the project or deal would succeed.

For example, in the tent deal with the Defense Ministry, I met separately with each of those who opposed it and tried to soften their opposition. I even met with almost all of those who supported it and tried to strengthen their support. As for the product itself, I highlighted its positive features and glossed over its negative ones. I emphasize, though, that I gave no false impressions or misleading data.

Another concept I took from the academic world and applied to my business deals is that of risk dispersion, which entails branching out into different lines of business. If you avoid putting all your eggs in one basket, you reduce the overall chances of failure. Just as there are general market cycles, with global ups and downs, there are also business cycles in more limited areas.

When I was starting out, and the envelope sales came to an end, I still had the tent market, and it began to develop. Years later, when Israel started getting free tents from the U.S. government and had no more need for mine, I changed course and sold on a large scale to the U.S. market, as well as to others that I had cultivated earlier, so I was not left in the lurch. The business market is dynamic, and if you do not constantly take the initiative and advance, you stay behind and your business suffers.

I applied another concept from academia. This one came mainly from my doctoral work in the field of risk; I called it "overall risk." I only ventured into deals that, even if they failed, would still leave me on my feet with other options.

Even talented, successful businessmen sometimes foul up in this regard. We all have a subjective outlook on future success or failure. But excessive optimism can sometimes lead us to downplay or even ignore the risk of failure. The rule I can offer is the following: A businessman must not get involved in any deal that, should it fail, would ruin him financially.

I have seen what happened to some of the best people when they did not operate on that principle. The Reichmann brothers, experienced Canadian Jewish businessmen, invested billions to set up a new European financial center on the outskirts of London. It was called Canary Wharf and comprised twenty-eight multistory buildings and shopping centers. Unfortunately for them, just when the project was about to end, England fell into a recession, financial groups were not eager to move to the new location, and the subway line to the financial center was never built. The Reichmann brothers did not anticipate any of this in their estimations, which were quite rosy. So the project failed, they ran up a debt of $20 billion, and they had to file for bankruptcy. If the Reichmann brothers had failed at a smaller project, they could have financially withstood the failure, and would not have gone bankrupt.

At the beginning of the 1990s, when I did business with the Defense Ministry, I became aware of some failings that caused large sums of money to be wasted, and had some ideas on how to remedy them.

I set up a meeting with Lt. Gen. Ehud Barak, then chief of staff of the IDF (and later prime minister). Many Israelis know about Barak's military record: He served in the elite Sayeret Matkal (the General Staff Reconnaissance Unit) and commanded it, he commanded a tank battalion in the Yom Kippur War, and afterward he was a brigade commander and a division commander. But few know that throughout 1970, Ehud Barak commanded the same Company B of the 79th Battalion that I had commanded a year and a half earlier in the War of Attrition. Even fewer, if any, know for what, and why, Barak was awarded citations for valor that made him the most decorated soldier in the history of the IDF – his greatest military exploits have been kept secret from the public.

In our meeting, I suggested some ways to improve how the IDF did business. He said they were good suggestions, and that I should meet with the head of the Quartermaster's Division so he could consider and implement them. I do not remember who was head of the Quartermaster's Division at that time, but I did not think he would manage to put my ideas into practice.

I told Barak, "I live abroad and my time is precious, and I don't want to waste it. Nothing will come of this unless you take care of it."

He replied, "I'm the chief of staff, I have to deal with other things, and I can't get involved with this."

In hindsight he was right, but because I did not want to waste my time in fruitless pursuits I dropped the matter.

It is worth a side note to say that I have never understood the fierce resentment some Israelis feel toward Ehud Barak as a politician and a prime minister. He may have made some errors in his political career, and he may not have succeeded in all his efforts, but he has done a great deal for the country. He does not get enough credit for his contributions. Unfortunately, people tend to see others in black-and-white terms instead of shades of gray. To me, it is clear that when we evaluate someone, we should look at the whole picture, the failures as well as the achievements.

Later I also got involved in supplying uniforms and accessories to security companies, police forces, and departments of the State of California and the City of Los Angeles, such as the Department of Water and Power, the Los Angeles Transportation Authority, and the Los Angeles County Sheriff's Department.

I had decided not to sell to, or do business with, non-Western countries after my bad experiences in Egypt and South America, but because manufacturing costs are much cheaper in China, I had no choice but to buy there in order to stay competitive. I did most of my manufacturing in China, a country that is a story in itself.

When Miri and I landed there for the first time, we were received by Haim Oman, then head of the Israeli Defense Ministry delegation in China. I first met Haim when he was deputy head of the Defense Ministry's Acquisition Administration. He was one of those who supported my position on bringing an American boot manufacturer to Israel to compete with the Israeli industry, thereby lowering the prices the ministry paid for boots. That effort succeeded, and we had been friends ever since.

The visit to China was fascinating, and the country's many facets often amazed us. With Haim's guidance we found ourselves, for instance, dancing to the sounds of a cassette tape on a frozen lake in a suburb of Beijing. I myself danced with a pretty and smiling Chinese woman who unluckily, or for lack of funds, did not get orthodontic care as a child.

With the help of private guides, we reached remote and interesting areas. The aim of my trip was to find textile manufacturers, but I did not succeed at that, so we settled for an enjoyable visit.

After the first unsuccessful trip, salvation came from an unexpected source. David Bukai, an Israeli manufacturer who supplied textiles to the Defense Ministry, was one of the heads of the lobby opposing me while I competed against the local Israeli industry in the 1990s. In those days, I won one of the Defense Ministry's tenders for supplying Gore-Tex winter clothing. I did not compete for the next tender, and Bukai won it. Despite his previous resentment, he was grateful for that and introduced me to his friend René, a Moroccan-born Israeli Jew who was living in Hong Kong, spoke Chinese, and had connections with Chinese textile manufacturers.

I got along with René, and he arranged to manufacture uniforms for me in China. René, then in his fifties, sporting a well-trimmed moustache and great powers of persuasion, had a special personality. He was endowed with a peculiar trait: He thought every woman who looked at him fell in love with him immediately.

Each year Miri and I would take a trip to the island of Phuket in southern Thailand, not far from China. On one of these visits René joined us. We rented a boat and sailed to a fish restaurant overlooking a wooden platform, which was owned by Muslim residents of Thailand. A mischievous mood came over me, and I told one of the waitresses, a pretty girl in her twenties, that René was a Muslim and very wealthy. In these poor areas, money is the key. After the meal, I asked the young woman to stand next to René, and I took their picture. After we left René said, "Did you see the sad look on that girl's face as I was walking out? Poor thing, she fell in love with me."

That was one case out of many where René told me about "poor" girls who had fallen in love with him.

We did some deals together, but after Rene's output of uniforms decreased, I replaced him with Laurence, a Chinese man who divided his time between Los Angeles and China. I met him through a Turkish businessman who owned textile plants in Eastern Europe and Turkey that supplied the German and Turkish armies. Laurence became my supplier for a few years until his brother, who lived in China, was arrested and Laurence had to devote his time to helping him.

As Laurence told it, a fierce fight broke out among a group sitting at a restaurant where his brother was eating, and a member of the group killed someone. Laurence claimed his brother had no part in the murder, but the group bribed the local police commander and only his brother was arrested, tried, and given a long prison sentence. Laurence said the Chinese legal system was thoroughly corrupt and bribery was routine.

After our collaboration ended I replaced him with Jason, another Chinese individual. My son-in-law, Golan, husband of my daughter Dana and sales manager of my company, searched the Internet for potential Chinese manufacturers and found three of them. I went to China, visited the three plants, and chose the one where Jason was sales manager.

He was a young fellow of about thirty and an efficient professional. However, he made statements that bore no connection to reality. For example, once when we visited his factory, Miri asked him to take us to a fish restaurant for lunch. We hated restaurants that served frog heads, turtle legs, and the like. Jason took us to a fish restaurant beside a wide river that looked dirty and polluted. Miri told Jason she hoped the fish served at the restaurant had not been caught in that river. Jason replied with certitude that the fish could not be from that river because there were no fish in it.

As we were leaving the restaurant Miri saw someone sitting on the riverbank, a large straw hat on his head and a fishing rod in his hand. She asked Jason, "What is that man doing?"

Jason, who had forgotten his recent assertion that there were no fish in the river, answered, "Fishing."

Miri responded with, "How could that be? You just said there were no fish in the river."

Jason kept his cool and replied, "There can't be any fish in the river. Everyone knows that man is not completely sane. He just imagines that he's catching fish with his rod."

Later we sipped coffee at a cafe where there was a man who looked half black, half Chinese. When Miri remarked to Jason that it was interesting to see such a mix, he answered disdainfully, "That man just spent too much time in the sun."

I learned that in China, the truth is neither at a premium nor overly popular. Another example: At an exhibition in the city of Guangzhou, one of the exhibitors told me his factory was next to Shanghai. Since we were planning to visit Shanghai, I asked him how far it was from there to his factory.

He said, "An hour altogether."

After a bit more thought he added, "To be exact, an hour and a quarter."

Once in Shanghai we asked to visit the plant. We took the fast train, which streaked along at over 125 miles an hour. After two and a half hours, we had only reached the city adjacent to the factory. And that was not the end of the journey. A car awaited us at the station, and it drove us to the factory, a trip that took another hour and a half. Altogether it took four hours instead of the promised hour and a quarter.

As for the food in China, the quality is generally good in the large cities and Western hotels, but in more remote areas, the fare is almost inedible, at least to our Western tastes. On all our trips to China we brought suitcases full of food with us, like strictly kosher religious Jews.

I also learned that the Chinese very much like to show off. Along the highways one sees elegant apartment buildings with impressive lighting systems. But to say that the buildings behind those facades are not at all impressive would be an understatement.

Contact with ordinary inhabitants of China leads me to the conclusion that, even though the population is more than four times larger than America's, the day when China overtakes the U.S. as a superpower is still in the distant future. I say that even though various experts and media outlets offer quite a different view.

China's advantages from a business standpoint are basically cheap manpower and the hard, diligent work ethic of the employees. In Western countries, people work five days a week and take many vacations. In most Chinese factories, people work practically every day, for long hours and extremely low salaries, and their only real vacation is Chinese New Year.

I feel fortunate that I was not born Chinese.

Chapter 16

. . . .

ALL'S WELL THAT ENDS WELL

It was the end of the 1980s when I came to Los Angeles from New York, after Rita moved there with our sons. I was poor and lacking in many things. From that point onward, my business kept growing, and I started to do well. And yet, unlike some people who view money as the most important thing, I always saw it as merely a means to an end, not an end in itself.

I have always thought a man needs enough money for a comfortable life, but he should not enslave himself to the pursuit of wealth. How one defines a comfortable life is of course subjective. One person will settle for a modest apartment, another will not rest until he has an impressive house of his own with a garden and a swimming pool, while another will still need more. The pursuit can be endless.

In the United States, the main and sometimes exclusive criterion for judging someone is the individual's wealth. Some get addicted to money or to a lifestyle they cannot afford, and some feel driven to prove to themselves and to others just how much money they can make. Materialism is everywhere, and it is blatant. Even people who are lacking in funds try to create the impression that they are doing well, by leasing expensive cars and wearing designer clothes.

I realized when I made the transition from modest means to affluence, people began to treat me differently. Once I had money, they showed me more respect, even though I was still the same person.

Of course, treating someone according to his possessions and stature, instead of his character, is nothing new. Society has always treated differently those who climbed higher, whether in finance, academia, the military, or some other area. To balance this approach, our sages said, "Do not look at the jug, rather at what is inside it" (*Avot*, 4:27).

At the same time, one has to give America credit where it is due. If you want to achieve affluence in an honest way, through talent and hard work, and you do not have any strategic connections, your chances are still pretty good in the U.S. But for anyone who is not a U.S. born individual, one should keep in mind that moving to a different country means giving up a lot, and there is no guarantee for success. For every immigrant who moved to the U.S. and succeeded, there are a great many more who did not.

As an American Israeli who managed to make a good life for himself, I would like to offer some tips based on my personal experience. Even in those times when I had little money, I tried to be happy with my lot. I steered clear of envy and did not waste time and energy wondering how much others earned or how they lived. I am grateful to America for letting me get as far as I have, but inwardly, I will always view myself as an Israeli. I maintain close connections with Israel, my country of origin, visiting often, and staying in touch with friends and acquaintances there. Clearly, being that I remain so attached to Israel, it appeals to me when Israeli immigrants remain loyal to Israel and try to contribute as much as they can to it. We all know how much Israel needs the support.

Without overgeneralizing, Americans tend to give one another "space." Personal space can feel good, but the downside is that if someone has a problem, he will often encounter indifference from the people around him. Contrary to this, in Israel, there will be always volunteers that will step forward and help to overcome someone's problem. There is a sense of overcrowding in Israel, both because of its small size and the prevailing inquisitive mentality. People pay more attention to one another. They do not give one another much "space" and may not be very supportive, but in times of need they are usually there to help.

In the U.S. in general, and California in particular, socializing is often superficial and tied to specific activities. People have casual friendships based on small talk and outings to restaurants and movies. And when they meet, the conversations tend to be shallow. Many Israelis who come to the U.S. adapt this style of casual friendship. What has always been missing for me, however, are real friendships that are not based on mere convenience – the kind that I still find in Israel to this day.

The American Jewish community is large; many people are successful, and most live comfortably. Some American Jews speak of the "Babylonia and Jerusalem" model. They see the U.S. as a present-day Babylonia where Jews can live religiously if they choose and enjoy cultural Judaism no less than in Israel. That is one way of looking at it, but one must remember that in the period when Babylonian Jewry flourished, the Jewish people did not have a sovereign state of their own. Nowadays the situation is different; Israel is the independent state of the Jewish people and has no substitute.

I have always seen the Jewish people as one single family that has existed for many generations, with me as one of its offspring. Having visited Jewish communities in different countries, I have felt the deep bond, the common denominator that exists among all Jews, wherever they happen to be. For example, at the Great Synagogue in Rome I watched a film about Italian Jewry during the Holocaust. I had a strong feeling that these were people who were close to me, and I to them.

Quite a few Israelis and quite a few Diaspora Jews take Israel for granted, criticize it incessantly, and forget the wonderful miracle of its rebirth after two thousand years of exile, a unique event in history. Many Jews make light of the anti-Semitism that has spread almost everywhere in the world, and see the Holocaust and the annihilation of six million Jews as a singular occurrence

302 | Yes, It's Possible

that, however horrifying, took place seventy years ago. We tend to focus on the material advantages found elsewhere in the world and forget the cultural and spiritual power embodied by Israel as the state of the Jews. We are a people that has survived persecution for two thousand years, returned to its land, revived its language, and restored its sovereignty. I was a child when the state was established, and I regard Israel as a great miracle, something that has no parallel elsewhere in the world and that is difficult to explain with logic alone.

Once something has existed for a while, people get used to it. They tend to focus on its shortcomings and ignore its merits, which come to be taken for granted. I try to remind myself every day of the positive aspects of things, while setting aside the negative ones. In this way, I think, one can develop a truer perspective on reality.

One of the great sages of Israel, Shammai, the interlocutor of Hillel the Elder, would say, "Receive every man with a friendly countenance." Unfortunately, I have not always applied that maxim to my life. My short fuse has sometimes caused me to lose patience, to be impolite, and even offensive. My drive for perfection, my intense focus on every detail, has indeed helped me succeed, but sometimes also made me irritable. My rigorous military training has also contributed to this bluntness, which I still try to overcome. It would have been better to apply the proverb, "The words of the wise are spoken gently," instead of speaking like a commander giving orders.

I am absolutely certain that we should set our goals and aspirations in life, deciding exactly what they are. As I recounted earlier, once as a child I walked with my mother through the Tel Arza neighborhood in Jerusalem. As we passed a sawmill I told her, "When I grow up I'm going to own a factory like that." Apparently at age eight I was already aiming to be an independent business-man and factory owner, something that came true about forty years later. Naturally, sometimes financial, social, family, health, or other constraints prevent us from fully realizing our goals, but we have to strive for them as much as possible. We all have but one earthly life to live and I think we should live it according to our own inclinations and desires, not according to what family, society, or state dictates to us.

One of the greatest figures in Judaism was Maimonides (Moses Ben Maimon, twelfth century). It is said of him, "from Moses to Moses (Maimonides) there was never anyone like Moses." And it's not only Jews who are aware of his greatness. When Miri and I visited Spain, where Maimonides was born and raised, I was happy to see that he was honored there as well. Among other monuments, a commemorative statue in the city of Cordoba was dedicated to him. I have avidly read Maimonides' books. Not only was he a Torah scholar of the first rank, but he was also an outstanding philosopher and physician. Maimonides' teachings advise us to try and improve our conduct daily. I have tried to adopt this approach – to learn something and achieve some progress each day.

Maimonides suggests dividing one's life into three parts: one-third for Torah study, one-third for family, and one-third for work. Although, in the course of my life I have not put Maimonides' recommendation into practice, I have adopted the principle that we should not concentrate on one area only at the cost of all else. For example, we have to avoid becoming enslaved to work and making money, and pursuing that as our only calling in life. The same goes for one's family. With all the love and well-meaning that we have for our children, our lives are not limited to caring only for them. And this is equally true of attaining pleasure; it should not be the sole focus of one's life. We need to find a balance, and each person needs to find the balance that suits him.

Even when I was working hard, I tried to keep having fun, and in all of my business trips, I set aside time for touring and enjoyment. As for family, I tried to be a good father and give my children as much as I could. These days I have grandchildren as well, and for them too, I try to do as much as I can.

If someone's goal is to show that he is a financial whiz and to prove to everyone, including to himself, that he can earn large sums of money, investing all his time in this endeavor – so be it. If someone is set on reaching the highest plateau of political power and devotes every minute of his life to that – so be it. My own approach at every stage of my life has been to strive for balance and not get addicted to any one pursuit. Presumably, if I had focused my whole life on only one goal, I could have achieved more in that particular area, but would have missed out on others.

To me, as I look back at my life, what was more important than maximizing my achievements was to feel that I did not leave anything out. I took my own path, did what I wanted in life, prioritized my goals and did my best to achieve them. I was with the women who attracted me, and I lived where I desired to live. In my career, I acted in accordance with my own goals. I pursued a military and patriotic career when that appeared to me the right thing to do. I took the academic route when that was called for. When I decided to enter the business world, I did that as well. I am convinced that sticking to my goals enabled me to go far in achieving them.

In my seventh decade, I feel that I have lived the life that I wanted. This is a good feeling, and I wish it for all my friends as well. It should be kept in mind that fulfilling desires means investing a great deal in pursuing them – things do not happen by themselves.

My aim in this book was to tell the story of my life and the lessons I have learned. The story is intertwined with historical events connected to the State of Israel.

I have not always followed a Hebrew maxim that says a person cannot view his own affairs objectively, but I did my best to describe the events in my life accurately, without embellishment. As I have always done in the past, I strove here to get to the real essence of the story, to the heart of the matter. I hope I have succeeded.